总主编 胡壮麟

英语综合教程

修订版

第 4 册

（学生用书）

主　　编　　傅似逸　陈　燕

编　　者　　丁晓君　陈　燕　傅似逸
　　　　　　苏欲晓　张秀明

英文审订　　Dr. Brian Low

北京大学出版社
PEKING UNIVERSITY PRESS

图书在版编目(CIP)数据

英语综合教程(修订版)第4册学生用书/傅似逸,陈燕主编.—2版.—北京:北京大学出版社,2011.8

(21世纪英语专业系列教材)

ISBN 978-7-301-19372-3

Ⅰ.①英… Ⅱ.①傅…②陈… Ⅲ.①英语-高等学校-教材 Ⅳ.①H31

中国版本图书馆CIP数据核字(2011)第164025号

书　　　名：英语综合教程.第4册(学生用书)(修订版)
总　策　划：张　冰
著作责任者：傅似逸　陈　燕　主编
责 任 编 辑：孙　莹
标 准 书 号：ISBN 978-7-301-19372-3/H·2912
出 版 发 行：北京大学出版社
地　　　址：北京市海淀区成府路205号　100871
网　　　址：http://www.pup.cn
电　　　话：邮购部 62752015　发行部 62750672　编辑部 62754382　出版部 62754962
电 子 邮 箱：编辑部 pupwaiwen@pup.cn　　总编室 zpup@pup.cn
印　刷　者：北京虎彩文化传播有限公司
经　销　者：新华书店
　　　　　　787毫米×1092毫米　16开本　15.25印张　415千字
　　　　　　2011年8月第1版　2024年1月第5次印刷
定　　　价：49.00元

未经许可,不得以任何方式复制或抄袭本书之部分或全部内容。
版权所有,侵权必究　举报电话：010-62752024
　　　　　　　　　　电子邮箱：fd@pup.cn

《21世纪英语专业系列教材》编写委员会

（以姓氏笔画排序）

王守仁　王克非　申　丹
刘意青　李　力　胡壮麟
桂诗春　梅德明　程朝翔

《英语综合教程》（修订版）第四册

尊敬的老师：

您好！

为了方便您更好地使用本教材，获得最佳教学效果，我们特向使用本书作为教材的教师赠送本教材配套听力资料。如有需要，请完整填写"教师联系表"并加盖所在单位系（院）公章，免费向出版社索取。

北京大学出版社

教师联系表

教材名称	《英语综合教程》（修订版）第四册			
姓名：	性别：	职务：		职称：
E-mail：		联系电话：		邮政编码：
供职学校：		所在院系：		（章）
学校地址：				
教学科目与年级：		班级人数：		
通信地址：				

填写完毕后，请将此表邮寄给我们，我们将为您免费寄送本教材配套资料，谢谢！

北京市海淀区成府路 205 号
北京大学出版社外语编辑部　孙　莹
邮政编码：100871
电子邮箱：zln120@163.com
　　　　　sunying_najia@hotmail.com

邮购部电话：010-62534449
市场营销部电话：010-62750672
外语编辑部电话：010-62754382

总 序

北京大学出版社自2005年以来已出版《语言与应用语言学知识系列读本》多种，为了配合第十一个五年计划，现又策划陆续出版《21世纪英语专业系列教材》。这个重大举措势必受到英语专业广大教师和学生的欢迎。

作为英语教师，最让人揪心的莫过于听人说英语不是一个专业，只是一个工具。说这些话的领导和教师的用心是好的，为英语专业的毕业生将来找工作着想，因此要为英语专业的学生多多开设诸如新闻、法律、国际商务、经济、旅游等其他专业的课程。但事与愿违，英语专业的教师们很快发现，学生投入英语学习的时间少了，掌握英语专业课程知识甚微，即使对四个技能的掌握也并不比大学英语学生高明多少，而那个所谓的第二专业在有关专家的眼中只是学到些皮毛而已。

英语专业的路在何方？有没有其他路可走？这是需要我们英语专业教师思索的问题。中央领导关于创新是一个民族的灵魂和要培养创新人才等的指示精神，让我们在层层迷雾中找到了航向。显然，培养学生具有自主学习能力和能进行创造性思维是我们更为重要的战略目标，使英语专业的人才更能适应21世纪的需要，迎接21世纪的挑战。

如今，北京大学出版社外语部的领导和编辑同志们，也从教材出版的视角探索英语专业的教材问题，从而为贯彻英语专业教学大纲做些有益的工作，为教师们开设大纲中所规定的必修、选修课程提供各种教材。"21世纪英语专业系列教材"是普通高等教育"十一五"国家级规划教材和国家"十一五"重点出版规划项目《面向新世纪的立体化网络化英语学科建设丛书》的重要组成部分。这套系列教材要体现新世纪英语教学的自主化、协作化、模块化和超文本化，结合外语教材的具体情况，既要解决语言、教学内容、教学方法和教育技术的时代化，也要坚持弘扬以爱国主义为核心的民族精神。因此，今天北京大学出版社在大力提倡专业英语教学改革的基础上，编辑出版各种英语专业技能、英语专业知识和相关专业知识课程的教材，以培养具有创新性思维的和具有实际工作能力的学生，充分体现了时代精神。

北京大学出版社的远见卓识，也反映了英语专业广大师生盼望已久的心愿。由北京大学等全国几十所院校具体组织力量，积极编写相关教材。这就是说，这套教材是由一些高等院校有水平有经验的第一线教师们制定编写大纲，反复讨论，特别是考虑到在不同层次、不同背景学校之间取得平衡，避免了先前的教材或偏难或偏易的弊病。与此同时，一批知名专家教授参与策划和教材审定工作，保证了教材质量。

当然，这套系列教材出版只是初步实现了出版社和编者们的预期目标。为了获得更大效果，希望使用本系列教材的教师和同学不吝指教，及时将意见反馈给我们，使教材更加完善。

航道已经开通，我们有决心乘风破浪，奋勇前进！

胡壮麟
北京大学蓝旗营

修订说明

　　本书是"21世纪英语专业系列教材"之一，2008年4月出版学生用书，同年11月出版教师用书。在全国多所高校使用近3年的情况下，编者根据实际教学需要对本书进行了修订，主要涉及以下方面：

　　一、按课文难易程度调整了单元的顺序，以方便师生循序渐进地学习和讨论；

　　二、根据使用院校对教学内容过多的反映，删除一个单元（第十二单元），与其他三册保持一致；

　　三、修改文字错误，包括标点符号和排版等方面的疏漏或错误；

　　四、修订教师用书的答案部分，添加原来遗漏的少数练习答案。

　　在本书修订的过程中，北京大学胡壮麟教授和北京大学出版社张冰主任提出了具体的指导意见，美国朋友Fran Clawson女士审读了部分练习答案，本书责编孙莹和北京大学出版社外语编辑部的编辑们付出了艰辛的劳动，在此一并致谢。

　　由于编者水平有限，本书可能仍有疏漏，敬请同仁指正。

编者
2010年8月

前 言

《英语综合教程》根据《高等学校英语专业英语教学大纲》编写,旨在培养学生具有扎实的语言基本功、宽广的知识面、一定的相关专业知识、较强的综合能力和较高的人文素质。本套教材是基础英语课程教材,共四册,可供高等学校英语专业一、二年级学生使用。本册为第四册,适用于二年级第二学期。

本册共 14 个单元,每单元包括 TEXT A 与 TEXT B 两篇课文。内容涉及教育、语言、政治、文学等领域。主题包括语言学习、跨文化交际、民族性格、女性意识、社会变迁、人类天性等。体裁包括小说、散文、政论文、传记、演说辞、寓言、神话、科幻故事等。课文的选材力求体现经典性与时代性相结合、知识性与趣味性相结合的原则,同时关注学生的需要、兴趣与语言难易程度。28 篇课文均出自名家之手,稍加改编而成。其中既有思想内涵深刻的经典文章,也有贴近现代生活的轻松读物,体现了比较丰富的人文内涵和审美取向。

本册教材的编排原则与前三册基本一致。各单元包括 8 个部分,体例如下:

Unit Goals —— 教学目标:提出本单元的学习目标

Before Reading —— 读前准备:要求学生在阅读课文前查阅相关资料,培养自主学习和独立思考的能力

A Glimpse into the Text —— 导读:提炼该课的精华,激发学生的兴趣

Text A
- More about the Text
- Check Your Understanding
- Paraphrasing

主课文模块:学生精读作品,了解作者的生平与创作背景,掌握课文的内容要点、难点

Some Information about the English Style —— 文体修辞模块:分析课文的文体特色和相关的修辞要点

Practice —— 练习模块：包括形式多样的词汇、语法、写作、翻译练习，以提高学生综合运用语言的能力

Text B
  ■ Notes
  ■ Comprehension

辅课文模块：提供与主课文主题一致，但风格不同的作品，加深学生的理解，拓展其视野

Further Study —— 延伸性学习：提供进一步学习与研究的资源

本册教材的总体设计具有如下特点：

1. 注重学生的参与，强调让学生动手、动脑，通过查找资料、讨论等形式补充知识，解决问题。
2. 注重启发性教学，引导学生归纳掌握知识。
3. 注重师生互动，课前活动和课后练习的设计注意以学生为主体、以教师为指导。
4. 注重综合技能的训练，各单元练习全面，有助于巩固并拓展所学的知识与技能。
5. 注重培养学生运用语言的得体性，对文化差异的敏感性、宽容性和处理文化差异的灵活性。

本教材配有教师用书，为使用者提供包括教学思路、课堂组织、教学重点与难点、语法修辞等方面的详细指导和参考答案。有助于教师在教学各环节中采用启发式、讨论式、合作式、发现式、归纳式等多种教学方式，开展以任务为中心的互动教学，最大限度地让学生参与学习的全过程。

本册教材由厦门大学主持编写。傅似逸教授和陈燕副教授担任主编，并与张秀明、苏欲晓、丁晓君老师分担全书的选材和编写。在编写过程中，总主编胡壮麟教授给予了精心的指导；加拿大专家 Brian Low 博士审订了全书；英国专家 Mark Hilton 为本册的选材提供了宝贵的意见和帮助，在此我们表示衷心的感谢！本册责任编辑孙莹和北京大学出版社外语编辑部的编辑们为本书的出版付出了艰辛的劳动，在此也一并致谢。

由于编者水平有限，不足与疏漏在所难免，诚望使用本书的教师与学生批评指正。

编者
2008 年元月

Contents

Unit	1	The Power of Rhetoric	1

    Text A   We Force the Spring / 2

    Text B   Ask Not What Your Country Can Do for You / 14

Unit	2	Learning and Teaching	18

    Text A   Miss Sullivan / 18

    Text B   On Being a Scientific Booby / 26

Unit	3	Cross-cultural Communication	33

    Text A   Culture Shock / 34

    Text B   A Canadian Firm's Negotiation in China / 42

Unit	4	Impact of Change	47

    Text A   The Open Road / 47

    Text B   On Going Home / 55

Unit	5	Humor and Irony	60

    Text A   The Night the Ghost Got In / 60

    Text B   The Verger / 68

Unit	6	The Choice of Words	73

    Text A   Politics and the English Language / 74

    Text B   The Choice of Words / 86

Unit	7	Nature and Civilization	93

    Text A   Who Killed King Kong? / 94

    Text B   Yellow Woman and a Beauty of the Spirit / 106

Unit 8 Women's Consciousness 113

Text A   A Room of One's Own   /   113
Text B   Feminist Consciousness after the Women's Movement   /   124

Unit 9 National Character 129

Text A   Paradox and Dream   /   129
Text B   The European's America (23 October 1952)   /   140

Unit 10 The Short Story 148

Text A   Miss Brill   /   148
Text B   The Gift of the Magi   /   157

Unit 11 Education 163

Text A   The School and Social Progress   /   164
Text B   Education by Poetry   /   172

Unit 12 Treasury of Fantasy 178

Text A   Tom Edison's Shaggy Dog   /   178
Text B   Harry Potter and the Philosopher's Stone   /   186

Unit 13 Human Folly 196

Text A   The Folly of Discontent with One's Own Lot   /   196
Text B   The Picture of Dorian Gray   /   206

Unit 14 Human Quest 211

Text A   Yali's Question   /   211
Text B   The Wanderer from *Thus Spoke Zarathustra*   /   220

生词总表   Vocabulary 225

Unit 1

The Power of Rhetoric

Unit Goals

☞ appreciation of Presidential Inaugural Addresses
☞ to learn to use rhetorical devices and figures of speech:
  - Parallelism
  - Metaphor
  - Antithesis
  - Alliteration
☞ development of public speaking skills

Before Reading

1. Listen to the recording of Clinton's Inaugural Address at http://www.bartleby.com/124/pres64.html.
2. Discuss with your partner:
   - What keynote message does Clinton intend to get across to his audience?
   - What impresses you most?

   Share your thoughts with others in the class.
3. Find further information about Bill Clinton and John F. Kennedy, and prepare a Powerpoint presentation to show what you have found out about them. You may focus on their lives, their contributions to American politics, or any other aspects that you are most interested in. You may choose to introduce each of them separately or to do a comparison of the two, but make your presentation less than 10 minutes.

A Glimpse into the Text

William Jefferson Clinton, the 42nd American president, was the first "baby-boomer" to hold that office. His personality—relaxed, confident, and highly sociable—was widely characteristic of his generation, making him a popular figure both at home and abroad. His inaugural speech of 1993, echoing that of John F. Kennedy in 1961, proclaimed a new spring for America. His eight-year presidency produced a relatively peaceful and prosperous America—an era more seasonally symbolic, perhaps, of a summer or early fall in the history of the United States.

Text A

We Force the Spring
The First Inaugural Address of Bill Clinton

My fellow citizens:

Today we celebrate the mystery of American renewal. This ceremony is held in the depth of winter. But, by the words we speak and the faces we show the world, we force the spring, a spring reborn in the world's oldest democracy that brings forth the vision and courage to reinvent America.

When our founders boldly declared America's independence to the world and our purposes to the Almighty[1], they knew that America, to endure, would have to change. Not change for change's sake, but change to preserve America's ideals—life, liberty, the pursuit of happiness[2]. Though we march to the music of our time, our mission is timeless.

Each generation of Americans must define what it means to be an American. On behalf of our nation, I salute my predecessor, President Bush, for his half-century of service to America. And I thank the millions of men and women whose steadfastness and sacrifice triumphed over Depression[3] and fascism.

Today, a generation raised in the shadows of the Cold War[4] assumes new responsibilities in a world warmed by the sunshine of freedom but threatened still by ancient hatreds and new plagues. Raised in unrivaled prosperity, we inherit an economy that is still the world's strongest, but is weakened by business failures, stagnant wages, increasing inequality, and deep divisions among our people.

When George Washington first took the oath I have just sworn to uphold, news traveled slowly across the land by horseback and across the ocean by boat. Now, the sights and sounds of this ceremony are broadcast instantaneously to billions around the world. Communications and commerce are global; investment is mobile; technology is almost magical; and ambition for a better life is now universal. We earn our livelihood in peaceful competition with people all across the earth.

Profound and powerful forces are shaking and remaking our world, and the urgent question of our time is whether we can make change our friend and not our enemy. This new world has already enriched the lives of millions of Americans who are able to compete and win in it. But when most people are working harder for less; when others cannot work at all; when the cost of health care devastates families and threatens to bankrupt many of our enterprises, great and small; when fear of crime robs

---

reinvent /ˌriːɪnˈvent/ *v.*   to present oneself or sth. in a new form or with a new image
steadfastness /ˈstedfɑːstnɪs/ *n.*   from adjective 'steadfast', not changing in attitudes or aims
plague /pleɪɡ/ *n.*   large numbers of an animal or insect that come into an area and cause great damage
unrivaled /ʌnˈraɪvəld/ *adj.*   better or greater than any other
stagnant /ˈstæɡnənt/ *adj.*   not developing, growing or changing
instantaneously /ˌɪnstənˈteɪnɪəsli/ *adv.*   happening immediately
devastate /ˈdevəsteɪt/ *v.*   to make sb. feel very shocked and sad

law-abiding citizens of their freedom; and when millions of poor children cannot even imagine the lives we are calling them to lead—we have not made change our friend.

We know we have to face hard truths and take strong steps. But we have not done so. Instead, we have drifted, and that drifting has eroded our resources, fractured our economy, and shaken our confidence. Though our challenges are fearsome, so are our strengths. And Americans have ever been a restless, questing, hopeful people. We must bring to our task today the vision and will of those who came before us.

From our revolution[5], the Civil War[6], to the Great Depression, to the civil rights movement[7], our people have always mustered the determination to construct from these crises the pillars of our history. Thomas Jefferson[8] believed that to preserve the very foundations of our nation, we would need dramatic change from time to time. Well, my fellow citizens, this is our time. Let us embrace it.

Our democracy must be not only the envy of the world but the engine of our own renewal. There is nothing wrong with America that cannot be cured by what is right with America.

And so today, we pledge an end to the era of deadlock and drift—a new season of American renewal has begun. To renew America, we must be bold. We must do what no generation has had to do before. We must invest more in our own people, in their jobs, in their future, and at the same time cut our massive debt. And we must do so in a world in which we must compete for every opportunity.

It will not be easy; it will require sacrifice. But it can be done, and done fairly, not choosing sacrifice for its own sake, but for our own sake. We must provide for our nation the way a family provides for its children.

Our Founders[9] saw themselves in the light of posterity. We can do no less. Anyone who has ever watched a child's eyes wander into sleep knows what posterity is. Posterity is the world to come—the world for whom we hold our ideals, from whom we have borrowed our planet, and to whom we bear sacred responsibility.

We must do what America does best: offer more opportunity to all and demand responsibility from all. It is time to break the bad habit of expecting something for nothing, from our government or from each other. Let us all take more responsibility, not only for ourselves and our families but for our communities and our country.

To renew America, we must revitalize our democracy. This beautiful capital[10], like every capital since the dawn of civilization, is often a place of intrigue and calculation. Powerful

---

law-abiding /'lɔ:əˌbaɪdɪŋ/ *adj.* obeying and respecting the law

drift /drɪft/ *v.* to do sth. without a particular plan or purpose

erode /ɪ'rəʊd/ *v.* to gradually destroy sth. or make it weaker over a period of time; to be destroyed or make weaker in this way

fracture /'fræktʃə/ *v.* to break, such as a bone; to split a society or organization, etc.

fearsome /'fɪəsəm/ *adj.* making people feel very frightened

muster /'mʌstə/ *v.* to find as much support, courage, etc. as possible

pillar /'pɪlə/ *n.* a basic part or feature of a system, organization, belief, etc.

embrace /ɪm'breɪs/ *v.* to put your arms around sb. as a sign of love or friendship

deadlock /'dedlɒk/ *n.* a complete failure to reach agreement or settle a dispute

posterity /pɒ'sterɪti/ *n.* all the people who will live in the future

revitalize /ˌri:'vaɪtəlaɪz/ *v.* to make sth. stronger, or active or more healthy

intrigue /ɪn'tri:g/ *n.* the activity of making secret plans in order to achieve an aim, often by deceiving people

people maneuver for position and worry endlessly about who is in and who is out, who is up and who is down, forgetting those people whose toil and sweat sends us here and pays our way.

> maneuver /məˈnuːvə/ v. to control or influence a situation in a skilful but sometimes dishonest way
> engulf /ɪnˈɡʌlf/ v. to surround or to cover sb. or sth.
> conscience /ˈkɒnʃəns/ n. a moral sense of right and wrong, esp. as felt by a person and affecting behaviour
> testament /ˈtestəmənt/ n. a thing that shows that something else exists or is true
> engulf /ɪnˈɡʌlf/ v. to surround or to cover sb. or sth.
> conscience /ˈkɒnʃəns/ n. a moral sense of right and wrong, esp. as felt by a person and affecting behaviour
> testament /ˈtestəmənt/ n. a thing that shows that something else exists or is true

Americans deserve better, and in this city today, there are people who want to do better. And so I say to all of us here, let us resolve to reform our politics, so that power and privilege no longer shout down the voice of the people. Let us put aside personal advantage so that we can feel the pain and see the promise of America. Let us resolve to make our government a place for what Franklin Roosevelt called "bold, persistent experimentation," a government for our tomorrows, not our yesterdays. Let us give this capital back to the people to whom it belongs.

To renew America, we must meet challenges abroad as well as at home. There is no longer division between what is foreign and what is domestic—the world economy, the world environment, the world AIDS crisis, the world arms race—they affect us all.

Today, as an old order passes, the new world is more free but less stable. Clearly America must continue to lead the world we did so much to make. While America rebuilds at home, we will not shrink from the challenges, nor fail to seize the opportunities, of this new world. Together with our friends and allies, we will work to shape change, lest it engulf us.

When our vital interests are challenged, or the will and conscience of the international community is defied, we will act—with peaceful diplomacy when ever possible, with force when necessary. The brave Americans serving our nation today in the Persian Gulf, in Somalia, and wherever else they stand are testament to our resolve.

But our greatest strength is the power of our ideas, which are still new in many lands. Across the world, we see them embraced—and we rejoice. Our hopes, our hearts, our hands, are with those on every continent who are building democracy and freedom. Their cause is America's cause.

The American people have summoned the change we celebrate today. You have raised your voices in an unmistakable chorus. You have cast your votes in historic numbers. And you have changed the face of Congress, the presidency and the political process itself. Yes, you, my fellow Americans have forced the spring. Now, we must do the work the season demands.

To that work I now turn, with all the authority of my office. I ask the Congress to join with me. But no president, no Congress, no government, can undertake this mission alone. My fellow Americans, you, too, must play your part in our renewal. I challenge a new generation of young Americans to a season of service—to act on your idealism by helping troubled children, keeping company with those in need, reconnecting our torn communities. There is so much to be done—enough indeed for millions of others who are still young in spirit to give of themselves in service, too.

In serving, we recognize a simple but powerful truth—we need each other. And we must care for one another. Today, we do more than celebrate America; we rededicate ourselves to the very idea of America. An idea born in revolution and renewed through two centuries of challenge. An idea tempered by the knowledge that, but for fate, we—the fortunate and the unfortunate—might have been each other. An idea ennobled by the faith that our nation can summon from its myriad diversity the deepest measure of unity. An idea infused with the conviction that America's long heroic journey must go forever upward.

> myriad /ˈmɪriəd/ *adj.* an extremely large number of sth.
> infuse /ɪnˈfjuːz/ *v.* to make sb. or sth. have a particular quality
> conviction /kənˈvɪkʃən/ *n.* a strong opinion or belief
> scripture /ˈskrɪptʃə/ *n.* the holy books of a particular religion

And so, my fellow Americans, at the edge of the 21st century, let us begin with energy and hope, with faith and discipline, and let us work until our work is done. The scripture says, "And let us not be weary in well-doing, for in due season, we shall reap, if we faint not."

From this joyful mountaintop of celebration, we hear a call to service in the valley. We have heard the trumpets. We have changed the guard. And now, each in our way, and with God's help, we must answer the call.

Thank you and God bless you all.

More about the Text

1. the Almighty

This is an Abrahamic term for God.

2. "life, liberty, the pursuit of happiness"

This is a reference to *The Declaration of Independence*. The whole sentence reads: "We hold these truths to be self-evident, that all men are created equal, that they are endowed by their Creator with certain unalienable Rights, that among these are Life, Liberty and the pursuit of Happiness."

3. Depression

This refers to the Great Depress of 1929, which lasted through most of the 1930s. It centred in North America and Europe, but had devastating effects around the world, particularly in industrialized countries.

4. The Cold War

The Cold War refers to the period of protracted conflict and competition between the United States and the former Soviet Union and their allies from the late 1940s until the late 1980s.

5. our revolution

This refers to the American war for Independence in 1776.

6. the Civil War

This refers to the war between the northern US States (usually known as the Union States) and the Confederate States of the South from 1861 to 1865.

7. the civil rights movement

This refers in part to a set of noted events and reform movements in the US that aimed at abolishing public and private acts of racial discrimination and racism against African Americans between 1954 and 1968, particularly in the southern United States.

8. **Thomas Jefferson**

   Thomas Jefferson was the third President of the United States (1801—1809), the principal author of the *Declaration of Independence.*

9. **our Founders**

   "our founders" refers to those who founded the United States of America, such as George Washington, Thomas Jefferson, etc.

10. **this beautiful capital**

    This refers to Washington, D.C.

Check Your Understanding

1. What meaning do you take from Clinton's expression "We force the spring?"
2. What is meant by "baby boomers?" What do you know about the "baby boom" generation of Americans?
3. Clinton calls the Inaugural Address tradition a celebration of "the mystery of American renewal." In your opinion, what is "the mystery" he is referring to?
4. Clinton refers to the United States as "the world's oldest democracy." Is that true? Can you name any older, existing democracies in the world?
5. How do you understand Clinton's definition of "posterity?" What does it mean to see something "in the light of posterity?"
6. In your own words, explain what Clinton expects his government officials and the American people to do in order to renew America. What does he pledge to do in his tenure of office?
7. What does Clinton challenge the new generation of young Americans to do?
8. What is "the idea" that Clinton elaborates on page 23 (Line 125—130)? How does your understanding of the American ideology compare to Clinton's conception?
9. Can you find an equivalent phrase in Clinton's speech to Kennedy's famous words: "Ask not what your country can do for you—ask what you can do for your country...?" If so, how is it equivalent?
10. Sum up the keynote message(s) that Clinton intends to get across to the American people in his Inaugural Address.

Paraphrasing

1. Though we march to the music of our time, our mission is timeless.
2. Though our challenges are fearsome, so are our strengths. And Americans have ever been a restless, questing, hopeful people. We must bring to our task today the vision and will of those who came before us.
3. Our democracy must be not only the envy of the world but the engine of our own renewal. There is nothing wrong with America that cannot be cured by what is right with America.
4. Let us resolve to make our government a place for what Franklin Roosevelt called "bold, persistent experimentation," a government for our tomorrows, not our yesterdays.
5. The scripture says, "And let us not be weary in well-doing, for in due season, we shall reap,

if we faint not."

Some Information about English Style

Clinton's Inaugural Address demonstrates a skillful use of prominent rhetorical devices and figures of speech, in particular parallelism, metaphor antithesis, alliteration and the periodic sentence.

1. Parallelism

Parallelism is primarily a rhetorical device that writers use to give their sentences force, grace, and rhythm. In its simpler and more elementary form, parallelism is a balancing of noun with noun, an infinitive with another infinitive, a phrase with another phrase, and a clause with another clause. In other words, a parallel structure expresses ideas in the same grammatical and rhetorical pattern.

Look at examples of parallelism in Clinton's Inaugural Address:

- (Paragraph 7)... and that drifting has *eroded* our resources, *fractured* our economy, and *shaken* our confidence. (three verbs in parallel)
- (Paragraph 10) We must *invest more in our own people, in their jobs, in their future* ....(three prepositional phrases in parallel)
- (Paragraph 12) Posterity is the world to come—the world *for whom we hold our ideals, from whom we have borrowed our planet*, and *to whom we bear sacred responsibility*. (three clauses in parallel)

There are other parallel structures in Clinton's speech. Can you find more to add to the list above?

It is worth noting that parallelism is not merely a rhetorical device for orators and professional writers; the knowledge of it is also helpful for student writers. With the knowledge of parallelism, many a deformed or awkward sentence such as the following can be improved.

- The teacher asked us to close our books, to take pen and paper, and that we were to write a short composition. (two infinitives ill-paralleled with a clause)
- Few of us anticipated the intensity of the course or how long it would last. (noun ill-paralleled with a clause)

The two sentences above can be revised as:

- The teacher asked us **to close** our books, **to take** pen and paper, and **to write** a short composition.
- Few of us anticipated **the intensity** or **the duration** of the course.

2. Metaphor

Although all figurative language is usually called metaphorical, some elementary distinctions are useful. A metaphor is a figure that likens one thing to another by saying that one thing *is* another, not literally of course. Typical example:

- Life is but a walking shadow, a poor player.

When the likeness is actually expressed by the use of "as" or "like," the metaphor becomes a simile. Compare:

A. The world is a stage. (metaphor)
B. The world is like a stage. (simile)

A. Thomson was a lion in the fight. (metaphor)
B. Thomson was like a lion in the fight. (simile)

An effective use of metaphor can give your writing greater vividness and clarity. Look at how Clinton uses metaphor in his Inaugural Address:

■ This ceremony is held in the depth of winter. But, by the words we speak and the faces we show the world, we *force the spring*, a spring *reborn* in the world's oldest democracy.... (Paragraph 1)

■ Today, a generation raised *in the shadows of* the Cold War assumes new responsibilities in a world *warmed by the sunshine of freedom* but threatened still by ancient hatreds and *new plagues*. (Paragraph 4)

■ Our democracy must be not only the envy of the world but *the engine of our own renewal*. (Paragraph 9)

■ Yes, you, my fellow Americans **have forced the spring**. Now, we must *do the work the season demands*. (Paragraph 20)

■ "And let us not be weary in well-doing, for *in due season, we shall reap*, if we faint not." (Paragraph 23)

■ From this joyful *mountaintop* of celebration, *we hear a call to service* in the *valley*. We *have heard the trumpets*. We *have changed the guard*. And now, each in our way, and with God's help, we *must answer the call*. (Paragraph 24)

Can you find further examples of metaphor in the Inaugural Address and explain what comparison is involved in each case?

3. Antithesis

In several places of his speech, Clinton uses opposites or expressions of noticeably different meanings to sharpen his ideas. Examples:

■ Though we march to the music of our *time*, our mission is *timeless*.

■ ... in a world *warmed by the sunshine of freedom* but *threatened still by ancient hatreds and new plagues.*

■ ... an economy that is still the world's *strongest*, but is *weakened* by business failures....

■ There is nothing *wrong* with America that cannot be cured by what is *right* with America.

■ We must do what America does best: *offer* more opportunity to all and *demand* responsibility from all.

Such contrast of ideas expressed by parallelism of strongly contrasted words is a rhetorical device called antithesis. It was particularly favoured by the poets of refined and classical style, such as those in England of the 17th—18th century. It is also favoured by public speakers for the purpose of emphasis and rhythm. Arranged in this way, the contrasting ideas provide a sharp and forceful way of measuring difference.

Read the Inaugural Address once again and find further examples of antithesis.

4. Alliteration

Alliteration is a figure of speech in which consonants, especially at the beginning of words, are repeated. In Clinton's speech, there are several examples of alliteration.

■ Now, the *sights* and *sounds* of this ceremony are broadcast instantaneously to billions around the world.

■ ... whose *steadfastness* and *sacrifice* triumphed over....

■ *Profound* and *powerful* forces are shaking and remaking our world....

- ... we pledge an end to the era of *deadlock* and *drift*....
- ... so that *power* and *privilege* no longer shout down the voice of the people.
- ... so that we can feel the *pain* and see the *promise* of America.

Alliteration is a very old device in English verse, and is common in verse generally. It is used occasionally in prose, mainly for the achievement of the special effect. Clinton has employed this device for sound rhyme, musical effect and significant emphasis.

5. The periodic sentence

Read this sentence from Clinton's speech and take note of its structure:

—**when** most people are working harder for less; **when** others cannot work at all; **when** the cost of health care devastates families and threatens to bankrupt many of our enterprises, great and small; **when** fear of crime robs law-abiding citizens of their freedom; and **when** millions of poor children cannot even imagine the lives we are calling them to lead—we have not made change our friend.

The main clause of this sentence "*we have not made change our friend*" is preceded by five dependent clauses introduced by "*when.*" This is a typical example of periodic sentence (圆周句), in which the main idea is held until the end. A periodic sentence is in contrast with a loose sentence, in which the main idea is followed by details and modifiers. Compare:

Loose:
- In recent years many factories were established in the city, especially plants engaged in the manufacture of brass products.

Periodic:
- In recent years many factories, especially plants engaged in the manufacture of brass products, were established in the city.

The effect of a periodic sentence is one of suspense—that is, the reader is asked to wait for the main idea until he has comprehended the details upon which the main idea is based. Not all sentences in English are periodic; a large majority of them are loose. It is precisely for this reason that an occasional periodic sentence is emphatic.

Can you find a further example of periodic sentence in Clinton's speech?

Practice

Developing oratory skills

Read the following loudly and then translate them into Chinese. Make sure that you retain the original oratory style.

(1) Though we march to the music of our time, our mission is timeless.
(2) Today, a generation raised in the shadows of the Cold War assumes new responsibilities in a world warmed by the sunshine of freedom but threatened still by ancient hatreds and new plagues.
(3) Profound and powerful forces are shaking and remaking our world, and the urgent question of our time is whether we can make change our friend and not our enemy.
(4) There is nothing wrong with America that cannot be cured by what is right with America.
(5) We must do what America does best: offer more opportunity to all and demand responsibility from all.

(6) Our hopes, our hearts, our hands, are with those on every continent who are building democracy and freedom. Their cause is America's cause.

(7) You have raised your voices in an unmistakable chorus. You have cast your votes in historic numbers. And you have changed the face of Congress, the presidency and the political process itself. Yes, you, my fellow Americans have forced the spring. Now, we must do the work the season demands.

(8) But no president, no Congress, no government, can undertake this mission alone.

(9) I challenge a new generation of young Americans to a season of service—to act on your idealism by helping troubled children, keeping company with those in need, reconnecting our torn communities.

(10) Today, we do more than celebrate America; we rededicate ourselves to the very idea of America. An idea born in revolution and renewed through two centuries of challenge. An idea tempered by the knowledge that, but for fate, we—the fortunate and the unfortunate—might have been each other. An idea ennobled by the faith that our nation can summon from its myriad diversity the deepest measure of unity. An idea infused with the conviction that America's long heroic journey must go forever upward.

(11) The scripture says, "And let us not be weary in well-doing, for in due season, we shall reap, if we faint not."

(12) From this joyful mountaintop of celebration, we hear a call to service in the valley. We have heard the trumpets. We have changed the guard. And now, each in our way, and with God's help, we must answer the call.

Building word power

1. Fill in each blank with the best answer by choosing A, B, C or D.

(1) Coffee and newspaper are part of my morning _____.
  A. ceremony   B. rite   C. ritual   D. function

(2) The love of my family and friends _____ me through my ordeal.
  A. supported   B. maintained   C. upheld   D. sustained

(3) A combination of _____ and hard work made her the top female athlete in the state.
  A. ambition   B. aspiration   C. pretension   D. emulation

(4) The crops are nearly _____ by the continuous rain.
  A. ravaged   B. devastated   C. laid waste   D. ruined

(5) Good, that's all _____ —you send out the invitations for the party, and I'll organize the food for the party.
  A. decided   B. determined   C. settled   D. resolved

(6) "We are of course a nation of differences. Those differences don't make us weak. They're the source of our _____." (Jimmy Carter)
  A. strength   B. power   C. force   D. might

(7) A good education should not just be a _____ of the rich.
  A. right   B. privilege   C. prerogative   D. birthright

(8) She _____ on a loose paving stone and broke her ankle.
  A. collapsed   B. tumbled   C. caved in   D. tripped

(9) She couldn't overcome her _____ to cucumbers and excused herself when they were

served.

    A. animosity   B. aversion   C. antipathy   D. loathing

(10) Teenagers will _____ against any adult who tries to control them.

    A. disobey   B. defy   C. rebel   D. disregard

(11) It is my personal _____ that all rapists should be locked away for life.

    A. belief   B. conviction   C. faith   D. credit

(12) Steel tends to _____ faster in a salty atmosphere, such as by the sea.

    A. erode   B. corrode   C. disintegrate   D. consume

2. Fill in each blank with an appropriate word by adding to the given word in brackets the necessary prefix or suffix or both as required.

(1) Their success owes a lot to his _____ leadership. (vision)

(2) Life is full of failures, rejection and more than a fair share of _____. (courage)

(3) Ireland is clearly but _____ different to other lands; it has a strange compound of weather, landscape, people and that something extra, the remnants of a pagan and mediaeval past. (define)

(4) By his decease, his sister became the sole _____ of a very large fortune. (inherit)

(5) A _____ advantage is an advantage over competitors gained by offering consumers greater value, either by means of lower prices or by providing greater benefits and service that justifies higher prices. (compete)

(6) Confucius is a philosopher who is widely respected for the _____ of his thinking about politics, education, and spirituality. (profound)

(7) True leaders consider _____ more important than their resources. (resource)

(8) She's in the _____ position of being able to choose who she works for. (envy)

(9) When I was young and _____ I believed it was possible to change the world. (ideal)

(10) The Robert Owen Museum is _____ laid out in a domestic style, which suits the large numbers of pictures on display. (intrigue)

(11) After the earthquake, much of city became a(n) _____ jumble of collapsed buildings and twisted tracks. (recognize)

(12) Continuity of service provides wisdom of experience, but change provides the necessary _____ of new ideas. (infuse)

Grammar and usage

Translate the following sentences into English by using the key words in the brackets.

(1) 失业后,他感到极度绝望。(depth)

(2) 他提出了新的证据。(bring)

(3) 监护人代表那个小孩签了合同。(behalf)

(4) 我错了,我愿为此承担责任。(assume)

(5) 为得到这份工作他与10个人展开竞争。(competition)

(6) 他正试图戒烟。(habit)

(7) 伤残使他再也没有机会对意大利足球产生更深远的影响。(rob)

(8) 政客们最怕面对全球变暖的现实。(face)

(9) 他终于鼓起勇气,请她去看电影。(muster)

(10) 他根据最新进展重新考虑了自己的决定。(light)
(11) 其他董事正设法诱使她辞职。(maneuver)
(12) 这个协议将为两国间持久和平铺平道路。(way)
(13) 经理不得不暂时搁下手头的工作去处理一件紧急事故。(put)
(14) 这项提案招致了很多批评。(call)
(15) 找到这个问题的解决方法是当今科学家所面临的最大挑战之一。(challenge)
(16) 她毕生致力于照顾病人和需要帮助的人。(care)

Improving your writing style

1. Read the following sentences and underline the parts that should be expressed in parallel form. Then rewrite each sentence.

(1) She is a middle-aged woman, short, stocky, blue eyes, and partly gray-haired.
(2) His lectures are witty, interesting and he outlines them very carefully.
(3) He told us that we should read the story and to write a book report on it.
(4) The book is interesting and I can learn from it.
(5) My summer internship proved not only interesting but I have also learned much from it.
(6) A college education is both necessary and many people can afford it.
(7) I wonder whether I should continue with the work or should I return to college.
(8) Wal-Marts prices were lower than the Corner Store.
(9) The manager encouraged the plant employees, and the office employees were motivated by her.
(10) Judy was strong, optimistic, and a woman of courage.
(11) Diana works as a nurse and is volunteering as a firefighter.
(12) The student's paper was brief and clearer.

2. Read the following and comment on the use of figurative language.

(1) The life of the world may move forward into broad, sunlit uplands. (Churchill)
(2) United, there is little we cannot do in a host of co-operative ventures. Divided, there is little we can do.
(3) If a free society cannot help the many who are poor, it cannot save the few who are rich.
(4) Mariners hugged the margins of the continents. (Oscar Handlin)
(5) The water lay gray and wrinkled like an elephant's skin.
(6) Many of us, if we have happy childhoods, are tempted to believe that life is a pony, beribboned and curried, which has been given to us as a present. With the passing of years we, sooner or later, come to learn that, instead of being a pony, life is a mule which unfortunately has more than four legs. To the best of my knowledge, no one who lives long enough fails to be kicked, usually again and again, by that mule. Why this should surprise us or unnerve us, I as an older person have long since ceased to understand.
—John Mason Brown, "Price Day Address," at Groton School for Boys

3. Change each of the following into a periodic sentence.

Example:
- Stop talking if you have nothing more to say.

Periodic:
- If you have nothing more to say, stop talking.

(1) Their performance at once deteriorated when the testing was resumed.

(2) But their ability improved considerably after they had been praised for their improved performance.

(3) For this experiment two control groups were selected who had the same ability to memorize.

(4) It is of course impractical to legislate for those who will behave themselves while completely ignoring those who will not.

Writing task

Choose a topic from the following list and prepare your speech.

(1) The Natural Wonders of China
(2) What Does China Sell to America?
(3) The Moon over China
(4) What Does Education Mean to Me?
(5) The Power of Rhetoric
(6) Growing-up Green (on environmental protection)
(7) Something from the Bottom of My Heart
(8) Making a Dream Come True

When preparing your speech, you may follow the guidance below.

Stage 1: Thinking
- What do I want to say to my listeners?
- What is my major message?
- At what level of formality should I speak?
  (i.e. Who am I going to speak to? How well do I know them?)
- How should I get across to my listeners what I mean?
- What is the best logic to follow?

Stage 2: Writing the script
- Working on vocabulary and sentence patterns for best effect.
- Striving for simple, clear and impressive style.

Stage 3: Rehearsing and improving
- Rehearsing out loud to see whether it sounds right.

Stage 4: Practicing more and taking heed of
- voice (volume, intensity)
- bodily action (eye contacts, gestures, moves)

Stage 5: Presentation

Text B

Ask Not What Your Country Can Do for You
John Fitzgerald Kennedy[1]
(Abridged)

On a frigid winter's day in January 1961, John F. Kennedy took the oath of office as the 35th President of the United States. At age 43, he was the youngest man ever elected to that office. This is an abridged version of the speech he delivered, announcing the dawn of a new era, as young Americans born in the 20th century first assumed leadership of the nation.

My fellow citizens, we observe today not a victory of party, but a celebration of freedom—symbolizing an end, as well as a beginning—signifying renewal, as well as change. For I have sworn before you and Almighty God the same solemn oath our forebears prescribed nearly a century and three quarters ago.

The world is very different now. For man holds in his mortal hands the power to abolish all forms of human poverty and all forms of human life. And yet the same revolutionary beliefs for which our forebears fought are still at issue around the globe—the belief that the rights of man come not from the generosity of the state, but from the hand of God.

We dare not forget today that we are the heirs of that first revolution. Let the word go forth from this time and place, to friend and foe alike, that the torch has been passed to a new generation of Americans—born in this century, tempered by war, disciplined by a hard and bitter peace, proud of our ancient heritage—and unwilling to witness or permit the slow undoing of those human rights to which this Nation has always been committed, and to which we are committed today at home and around the world.

Let every nation know, whether it wishes us well or ill, that we shall pay any price, bear any burden, meet any hardship, support any friend, oppose any foe, in order to assure the survival and the success of liberty.

This much we pledge—and more.

So let us begin anew—remembering on both

---

frigid /ˈfrɪdʒɪd/ *adj.* very cold
deliver /dɪˈlɪvə/ *v.* to give a speech, talk, etc. or other official statement
observe /əbˈzɜːv/ *v.* to celebrate festivals, birthdays, etc.
forebear /ˈfɔːbeə/ *n.* a person who you are descended from, especially one who lived a long time ago
mortal /ˈmɔːtl/ *n.* a human being, especially an ordinary person with little power or influence
abolish /əˈbɒlɪʃ/ *v.* to officially end a law, a system or an institution
generosity /ˌdʒenəˈrɒsɪti/ *n.* the fact of being generous, i.e. willing to give sb. money, gifts, time or kindness freely
heir /eə/ *n.* a person who is thought to continue the work or a tradition started by sb. else
heritage /ˈherɪtɪdʒ/ *n.* the history, traditions and qualities that a country or society has had for many years and that are considered an important part of its character
commit /kəˈmɪt/ *v.* to promise sincerely that you will definitely do sth., keep to an agreement or arrangement, etc.
foe /fəʊ/ *n.* an enemy

sides that civility is not a sign of weakness, and sincerity is always subject to proof. Let us never negotiate out of fear. But let us never fear to negotiate.

Let both sides explore what problems unite us instead of belaboring those problems which divide us. Let both sides, for the first time, formulate serious and precise proposals for the inspection and control of arms—and bring the absolute power to destroy other nations under the absolute control of all nations. Let both sides seek to invoke the wonders of science instead of its terrors. Together let us explore the stars, conquer the deserts, eradicate disease, tap the ocean depths, and encourage the arts and commerce. Let both sides unite to heed in all corners of the earth the command of Isaiah[2]—to "undo the heavy burdens... and to let the oppressed go free." And if a beachhead of cooperation may push back the jungle of suspicion, let both sides join in creating a new endeavor, not a new balance of power, but a new world of law, where the strong are just and the weak secure and the peace preserved.

All this will not be finished in the first 100 days. Nor will it be finished in the first 1,000 days, nor in the life of this Administration, nor even perhaps in our lifetime on this planet. But let us begin. In your hands, my fellow citizens, more than in mine, will rest the final success or failure of our course. Since this country was founded, each generation of Americans has been summoned to give testimony to its national loyalty. The graves of young Americans who answered the call to service surround the globe. Now the trumpet summons us again—not as a call to bear arms, though arms we need; not as a call to battle, though embattled we are—but a call to bear the burden of a long twilight struggle, year in and year out, "rejoicing in hope, patient in tribulation"—a struggle against the common enemies of man: tyranny, poverty, disease, and war itself. The energy, the faith, the devotion which we bring to this endeavor will light our country and all who serve it—and the glow from that fire can truly light the world.

And so, my fellow Americans: ask not what your country can do for you—ask what you can do for your country. My fellow citizens of the world: ask not what America will do for you, but what together we can do for the freedom of man.

Finally, whether you are citizens of America or citizens of the world, ask of us the same high standards of strength and sacrifice which we ask of you. With a good conscience our only sure reward, with history the final judge of our deeds, let us go forth to lead the land we love, asking His blessing and His help, but knowing that here on earth God's work must truly be our own.

---

civility /sɪˈvɪlɪti/ *n.* polite behaviour

belabor /bɪˈleɪbə/ *v.* to repeat an idea, argument, etc. many times to emphasize it, especially when it has already been mentioned or understood

formulate /ˈfɔːmjʊleɪt/ *v.* to create or prepare sth. carefully, giving particular attention to the details

invoke /ɪnˈvəʊk/ *v.* to make sb. have a particular feeling or imagine a particular scene

eradicate /ɪˈrædɪkeɪt/ *v.* to destroy or get rid of sth. completely, especially sth. bad

tap /tæp/ *v.* to make use of a source of energy, knowledge, etc. that already exists

commerce /ˈkɒmɜːs/ *n.* trade, especially between countries; the buying and selling of goods and services

heed /hiːd/ *v.* pay careful attention to sb.'s advice or warning

beachhead /ˈbiːtʃhed/ *n.* a strong position on a beach from which an army that has just landed prepares to go forward and attack

endeavor /ɪnˈdevə/ *n.* an attempt to do sth., especially sth. new or difficult

rest /rest/ *v.* to support sth. by putting it on against sth.; to be supported in this way

summon /ˈsʌmən/ *v.* to order sb. to come to you

testimony /ˈtestɪməni/ *n.* a thing that shows that sth. else exists or is true

embattled /ɪmˈbætld/ *adj.* surrounded by problems and difficulties

twilight /ˈtwaɪlaɪt/ *adj.* used to describe a situation or area of thought that is not clearly defined

rejoicing /rɪˈdʒɔɪsɪŋ/ *n.* the happy celebration of sth.

tribulation /ˌtrɪbjʊˈleɪʃən/ *n.* great trouble or suffering

Notes

1. **John Fitzgerald Kennedy**

John Fitzgerald Kennedy (1917—1963) was the 35th American president, and also the youngest elected president. Of Irish descent, Kennedy was born in Brookline, Massachusetts, on May 29, 1917. He graduated with honours from Harvard University in 1940 and enlisted in the US Navy after graduation to serve his country during Word War II. He was awarded Navy and US Marine Corps medals for heroism in battle. With excellent qualifications both in education and military service, he was elected to Congress from Massachusetts in 1946 by an overwhelming majority. He served three terms as a member of Congress and won the second and third elections by an even greater majority than the first. Kennedy began his campaign for a seat in the US Senate in 1951 and defeated incumbent Henry Cabot Lodge in 1952. Six years later he was re-elected to the Senate by the largest majority in Massachusetts history. His political career reached its peak in 1960 when he narrowly defeated Richard Nixon to become the first Roman Catholic president of the United States. On November 22, 1963, President Kennedy was assassinated in Dallas, Texas.

2. **Isaiah**

Isaiah was a Hebrew major prophet of Judah in the 8th Century BC, teaching the supremacy of the God of Israel and emphasizing the moral demands upon worshippers.

Comprehension

1. Kennedy's Inaugural Address took place in 1961. What do you know of the economic and social conditions in America at that time?
2. Where does Kennedy suggest the "rights of man" come from? Would you agree or disagree with him on this point?
3. What is the torch that Kennedy declares has been passed to a new generation of Americans?
4. Kennedy calls for "both sides" to work together for certain goals. Assuming America composed one side, what nation composed "the other?"
5. Kennedy quotes from Isaiah. Who was Isaiah? How likely was the "other side" to heed Isaiah's words and why?
6. Kennedy calls for both sides to "let the oppressed go free." Who were the oppressed Kennedy was referring to?
7. "Ask not what your country can do for you...." is the most memorable quote from this speech. Is this assertion challengeable? Should citizens not ask what their country can do for them?
8. What determinations about the character of Kennedy can you make based on this speech? Support your contentions with examples from the text.
9. Do the two speeches in this unit reflect a difference in America between Kennedy's presidency and Clinton's? Support your contention with illustrative examples from the two texts.

Further Study

Some more speeches to read

- *"I Have a Dream"* by Martin Luther King, Jr.
- *"To Live or Die amongst You All"* by Queen Elizabeth I of England
- *"Give Me Liberty or Give Me Death!"* by Patrick Henry
- *"The Gettysburg Address"* by Abraham Lincoln
- *"For the Woman I Love"* the Abdication speech of King Edward VIII of England
- *"The Light Has Gone Out of Our Lives"* by Jawaharlal Nehru
- *Houston Ministerial Association Speech* by John Fitzgerald Kennedy
- *Cuban Missile Crisis Address* by John Fitzgerald Kennedy
- Clinton's *Farewell Speech*

Read to discover more about Clinton and Kennedy

- Clinton's Biography *My life*
- Biography of John Fitzgerald Kennedy

Unit 2

Learning and Teaching

Unit Goals

- To learn to be a good teacher and a good learner
- Appreciation of character portrayals of two different teachers
- Appreciation of poetic language for mental revelation
- Use of adjectives or adjective phrases as adverbials

Before Reading

1. Search on the Internet or in the library for information about Helen Keller and her teacher Miss Sullivan.
2. Do you believe that a great teacher is a great artist? Have you ever met a great teacher? Why do you think he (or she) is great?
3. Have you ever met a bad teacher? Why do you think he (or she) is bad?

A Glimpse into the Text

Helen Keller is undoubtedly the most celebrated advocate of all times for the rights of disabled people. She fell ill with a fever as an infant, a condition that left her both deaf and blind and thus unable to learn to talk. A difficult child, often ill-tempered, her relatives advised she should be institutionalized, but her mother instead contacted the famous inventor, Alexander Graham Bell, who recommended a special teacher for the girl, Miss Anne Sullivan, who was herself partially blind. Sullivan changed Keller's life, leading the young girl to a highly renowned career as an author, not merely on the topic of being disabled, but on the larger subject of overall human potential.

Text A

Miss Sullivan
Helen Keller[1]
(Abridged and Edited)

The most important day I remember in all my life is the one on which my teacher, Anne Mansfields Sullivan, came to me. I am filled with wonder when I consider the immeasurable

contrasts between the two lives which it connects. It was the third of March, 1887, three months before I was seven years old.

On the afternoon of that eventful day, I stood on the porch, dumb, expectant. I guessed vaguely from my mother's signs and from the hurrying to and fro in the house that something unusual was about to happen, so I went to the door and waited on the steps.

I felt approaching footsteps. I stretched out my hand as I supposed to my mother. Some one took it, and I was caught up and held close in the arms of her who had come to reveal all things to me, and, more than all things else, to love me.

The morning after my teacher came she led me into her room and gave me a doll. When I had played with it a little while, Miss Sullivan slowly spelled into my hand the word "d-o-l-l." I was at once interested in this finger play and tried to imitate it. When I finally succeeded in making the letters correctly I was flushed with childish pleasure and pride. Running downstairs to my mother I held up my hand and made the letters for doll. I did not know that I was simply making a word or even that words existed; I was simply making my fingers go in monkey-like imitation. In the days that followed I learned to spell in this uncomprehending way a great many words, among them *pin, hat, cup* and a few verbs like *sit, stand* and *walk*. But my teacher had been with me several weeks before I understood that everything has a name.

One day, while I was playing with my new doll, Miss Sullivan put my big rag doll into my lap, also spelled, "d-o-l-l," and tried to make me understand that "d-o-l-l" applied to both. Earlier in the day we had had a tussle over the words "m-u-g" and "w-a-t-e-r." Miss Sullivan had tried to impress upon me that "m-u-g" is mug and that "w-a-t-e-r" is water, but I persisted in confounding the two. In despair she had dropped the subject for the time, only to renew it at the first opportunity. I became impatient at her repeated attempts and, seizing the new doll, I dashed it upon the floor. I was keenly delighted when I felt the fragments of the broken doll at my feet. Neither sorrow nor regret followed my passionate outburst. I had not loved the doll. In the still, dark world in which I lived there was no strong sentiment or tenderness. I felt my teacher sweep the fragments to one side of the hearth, and I had a sense of satisfaction that the cause of my discomfort was removed. She brought me my hat, and I knew I was going out into the warm sunshine. This thought, if a wordless sensation may be called a thought, made me hop and skip with pleasure.

We walked down the path to the wellhouse, attracted by the fragrance of the honeysuckle with which it was covered. Someone was drawing water and my teacher placed my hand under the spout.

lap /læp/ *n.* [C] the top part of your legs that forms a flat surface when you are sitting down
tussle /ˈtʌsəl/ *n.* a short struggle, fight or argument especially in order to get sth.
confound /kənˈfaʊnd/ *v.* (formal) to mix up in one's mind
passionate /ˈpæʃənɪt/ *adj.* having or showing strong feelings of sexual love or of anger, etc.
hearth /hɑːθ/ *n.* the floor at the bottom of a fireplace
fragrance /ˈfreɪɡrəns/ *n.* [C,U] a pleasant smell
honeysuckle /ˈhʌniˌsʌk(ə)l/ *n.* [U,C] a climbing plant with white, yellow or pink flowers with a sweet smell
spout /spaʊt/ *n.* a stream of liquid coming out of somewhere with great force

As the cool stream gushed over one hand she spelled into the other the word *water*, first slowly, then rapidly. I stood still, my whole attention fixed upon the motions of her fingers. Suddenly I felt a misty consciousness as of something forgotten—a thrill of returning thought; and somehow the mystery of language was revealed to me. I knew then that "w-a-t-e-r" meant the wonderful cool something that was flowing over my hand. That living word awakened my soul, gave it light, hope, joy, set it free! There were barriers still, it is true, but barriers that could in time be swept away.

I left the well-house eager to learn. Everything had a name, and each name gave birth to a new thought. As we returned to the house every object which I touched seemed to quiver with life. That was because I saw everything with the strange, new sight that had come to me. On entering the door I remembered the doll I had broken. I felt my way to the hearth and picked up the pieces. I tried vainly to put them together. Then my eyes filled with tears; for I realized what I had done, and for the first time I felt repentance and sorrow.

I learned a great many new words that day. I do not remember what they all were; but I do know that *mother, father, sister, teacher* were among them—words that were to make the world blossom for me. It would have been difficult to find a happier child than I was as I lay in my crib at the close of the eventful day and relived the joys it had brought me, and for the first time longed for a new day to come.

I had now the key to all language, and I was eager to learn to use it. Children who hear acquire language without any particular effort; the words that fall from others' lips they catch on the wing, as it were, delightedly, while the little deaf child must trap them by a slow and often painful process. But whatever the process, the result is wonderful. Gradually from naming an object we advance step by step until we have traversed the vast distance between our first stammered syllable and the sweep of thought in a line of Shakespeare.

At first, when my teacher told me about a new thing I asked very few questions. My ideas were vague, and my vocabulary was inadequate; but as my knowledge of things grew, and I learned more and more words, my field of inquiry broadened, and I would return again and again to the same subject, eager for further information. Sometimes a new word revived an image that some earlier experience had engraved on my brain.

I remember the morning that I first asked the meaning of the word, "love." This was before I knew many words. I had found a few early violets in the garden and brought them to my teacher. She tried to kiss me; but at that time I did not like to have any one kiss me except my mother. Miss Sullivan put her arm gently round me and spelled into my hand, "I love Helen."

"What is love?" I asked

She drew me closer to her and said, "It is here," pointing to my heart, whose beats I was conscious of for the first time. Her words puzzled me very much because I did not then understand anything unless I

---

gush /gʌʃ/ *v.* to flow or pour suddenly and quickly out of a hole in large amounts
reveal /rɪˈviːl/ *v.* to make sth. known to sb.
quiver /ˈkwɪvə/ *v.* to shake slightly; to make a slight movement
repentance /rɪˈpentəns/ *n.* [U] ~ (**for sth.**) the fact of showing that you are sorry for sth. wrong that you have done
crib /krɪb/ *n.* a small bed with high sides for a baby or young child
on the wing (literary) (of a bird, insect, etc.) flying
as it were used when a speaker is giving his or her own impression of a situation or expressing sth. in a particular way
traverse /ˈtrævɜːs/ *v.* (formal or technical) to cross an area of land or water
stammer /ˈstæmə/ *v.* to speak with difficulty, repeating sounds or things and often stopping, before saying things correctly
engrave /ɪnˈɡreɪv/ *v.* [often passive] to cut words or designs on wood, stone, metal, etc.

touched it.

I smelt the violet in her hand and asked, half in words, half in signs, a question which meant, "Is love the sweetness of flowers?"

"No," said my teacher.

Again I thought. The warm sun was shining on us.

"Is this not love?" I asked, pointing in the direction from which the heat came, "Is this not love?"

It seemed to me that there could be nothing more beautiful than the sun, whose warmth makes all things grow. But Miss Sullivan shook her head, and I was greatly puzzled and disappointed. I thought it strange that my teacher could not show me love.

A day or two afterward I was stringing beads of different sizes in symmetrical groups—two large beads, three small ones, and so on. I had made many mistakes, and Miss Sullivan had pointed them out again and again with patience. Finally I noticed a very obvious error in the sequence and for an instant I concentrated my attention on the lesson and tried to think how I should have arranged the beads. Miss Sullivan touched my forehead and spelled with decided emphasis, "Think."

In a flash I knew that the word was the name of the process that was going on in my head. This was my first conscious perception of an abstract idea.

For a long time I was still—I was not thinking of the beads in my lap, but trying to find a meaning for "love" in the light of this new idea. The sun had been under a cloud all day, and there had been brief showers, but suddenly the sun broke forth in all its southern splendor.

Again I asked my teacher, "Is this not love?"

"Love is something like the clouds that were in the sky before the sun came out," she replied. Then in simpler words than these, which at that time I could not have understood, she explained: "You cannot touch the clouds, you know; but you feel the rain and know how glad the flowers and the thirsty earth are to have it after a hot day. You cannot touch love either; but you feel the sweetness that it pours into everything. Without love you would not be happy or want to play."

The beautiful truth burst upon my mind—I felt that there were invisible lines stretched between my spirit and the spirits of others.

From the beginning of my education Miss Sullivan made it a practice to speak to me as she would speak to any hearing child; the only difference was that she spelled the sentences into my hand instead of speaking them.

It was the genius of my teacher, her sympathy, her love which made my first years of education so beautiful. All the best of me belongs to her. Everything I am today was awakened by her loving touch.

> symmetrical /sɪˈmetrɪkəl/ adj. (of a body, a design, an object, etc.) having two halves, parts or sides that are the same in size and shape
>
> perception /pəˈsepʃən/ n. [U] (formal or technical) the way you notice things, especially with the senses

More about the Text

1. Helen Keller

Helen Keller was born on June 27, 1880, in Tuscumbia, Alabama. At nineteen months old an acute illness nearly took her life and left her deaf and blind. At the recommendation of Alexander Graham Bell, her parents contacted the Perkins Institute for the Blind in Boston, and Anne Sullivan was sent to tutor Helen. The story of their early years together, and of Helen's remarkable psychological and intellectual growth, is told in *The Story of My Life*, which first appeared in installments in *Ladies' Home Journal* in 1902. With Anne Sullivan, the "Teacher," at her side, Helen Keller graduated from Radcliffe College in 1904, an extraordinary accomplishment for any woman of her time. Helen was dedicated to helping the blind and handicapped, raising funds for the American Foundation for the Blind and lobbying for commissions for the blind in thirty states. A women's-rights activist, a Swedenborgian, a socialist, and a world-famous celebrity, Helen Keller received the Presidential Medal of Freedom and many honorary degrees. Her other books include *The World I Live In* (1908), *Midstream: My Later Life* (1929), *Helen Keller's Journal* (1938), and *Let Us Have Faith* (1940). She died in 1968, and was buried in the National Cathedral in Washington, D.C.

2. *The present text*

The present text is selected from *The Story of My Life*, which contains three parts. The first is Helen Keller's autobiographical account of her life from childhood to the beginning of her studies at Radcliffe. This chronicle describes the transformation of Helen's life brought about by the arrival of Anne Sullivan, her teacher and mentor, when she succeeded in conveying to Helen the "mystery of language." Part II contains Helen's letters to her family and friends, arranged in chronological sequence, and documents her growth in thought and expression through her writing. The third part, a supplementary section, contains an account of Helen Keller's life and education written by John Macy, based for the most part on the records and observations of Anne Sullivan.

The Story of My Life has become an enduring classic of American literature. It has been the most popular of Helen Keller's works, with numerous editions published throughout the years. Today, the book is available in more than 50 languages, including most European languages, Swedish, Russian, and Japanese, as well as African languages.

Check Your Understanding

1. How did Helen's family react to Miss Sullivan's coming to teach Helen? Why do you think so?
2. How did Helen begin to understand that everything has a name? What is the significance of the understanding?
3. What made Helen feel repentance and sorrow for the first time? Why?
4. What metaphor did Helen use to compare the process of learning a language for a hearing child and a deaf and dumb one?
5. How did Helen acquire her first conscious perception of an abstract idea?
6. Find instances demonstrating Miss Sullivan's love towards her student.
7. What are Miss Sullivan's teaching methods that appeal to you most?
8. Find some instances that show that Helen Keller is an eager learner.

Paraphrasing

1. Suddenly I felt a misty consciousness as of something forgotten—a thrill of returning thought; and somehow the mystery of language was revealed to me.
2. Children who hear acquire language without any particular effort; the words that fall from others' lips they catch on the wing, as it were, delightedly, while the little deaf child must trap them by a slow and often painful process.
3. Gradually from naming an object we advance step by step until we have traversed the vast distance between our first stammered syllable and the sweep of thought in a line of Shakespeare.
4. Sometimes a new word revived an image that some earlier experience had engraved on my brain.
5. The beautiful truth burst upon my mind—I felt that there were invisible lines stretched between my spirit and the spirits of others.

Some Information about English Style

1. Poetic language for mental revelation

As Helen tells us, it is her teacher, Miss Sullivan, that has made the otherwise painful process of learning one of enlightenment and ecstasy. Look at how Helen describes such delightful moments of mental revelation:

- I stood still, my whole attention fixed upon the motions of her fingers. Suddenly I felt a misty consciousness as of something forgotten—a thrill of returning thought; and somehow the mystery of language was revealed to me. I knew then that "w-a-t-e-r" meant the wonderful cool something that was flowing over my hand. That living word awakened my soul, gave it light, hope, joy, set it free! There were barriers still, it is true, but barriers that could in time be swept away.
- In a flash I knew that the word ("think") was the name of the process that was going on in my head. This was my first conscious perception of an abstract idea.
- The beautiful truth burst upon my mind—I felt that there were invisible lines stretched between my spirit and the spirits of others.

Expressions such as "suddenly," "thrill," "mystery," "in a flash," "burst upon" all contribute to the effect of epiphany.

Can you recall any such delightful moment of mental revelation of your own? Share your experience with your classmates.

2. The use of "before"

Read the following two sentences taken from the present text. Do you see any difference in the use of "before"?

(1) It was the third of March, 1887, three months **before** I was seven years old.
(2) But my teacher had been with me several weeks **before** I understood that everything has a name.

In the first sentence, "before" means "earlier than the time when"; while in the second sentence it is used for saying how much time has passed until something happens.

Can you tell the meaning of **before** in each of the following sentences and then translate it into Chinese?

(1) It was three days before he came back.
(2) Did she leave a message before she went?
(3) Do it before you forget.
(4) It may be many years before the situation improves.

3. The use of adjectives or adjective phrases as adverbials

Adjectives or adjective phrases may be used as adverbials in written English. Here are some examples of such usage in the present text:

(1) On the afternoon of that eventful day, I stood on the porch, dumb, expectant.
(2) I left the well-house eager to learn.
(3) ... and I would return again and again to the same subject, eager for further information.

Further examples of the same usage:

- Unhappy, she returned to work.
- Anxious for a quick decision, the chairman called for a vote.
- Ripe, these apples are sweet.
- Long and untidy, his hair played in the breeze.

Can you give more examples?

Practice

Building word power

1. Fill in each blank with the proper form of the right word from each set of the words below.

A. skip   bound   hop   leap   spring

(1) His dog came _____ to meet him.
(2) The frog _____ along the shore of the pond.
(3) The monkeys _____ from tree to tree.
(4) He _____ on his enemy with a knife in his hand.
(5) The screen door _____ shut after the children rushed out to play.
(6) The little girl _____ along at her mother's side.
(7) Boys like to _____ flat stones across the pond.
(8) The ball _____ from the wall.

B. shake   quiver   shiver   shudder   tremble

(1) The dog came out of the water and _____ itself.
(2) The leaves _____ in the faint breeze.
(3) Her whole body _____ with delight.
(4) She began to _____ as the intense cold pervaded the room.
(5) She _____ inwardly at the thought of having to explain to her mother why she had stayed out so late.

24

(6) Her hands _____ with eagerness as she opened the letter.
(7) She _____ at the sight of a snake.
(8) He _____ at the memory of what happened the night before.
(9) The branches _____ in the wind.

C. flow   gush   pour   run   stream

(1) The water _____ forth from a hole in the tank.
(2) This morning I saw a man run down by a car and blood _____ from his head.
(3) We watched the river as it _____ on under the bridge.
(4) When it is quiet we can hear the river _____.
(5) In which direction does the river _____?
(6) From this tall building people can see cars _____ over the bridge.
(7) We can see water _____ over the dam.
(8) The cast iron was melted and _____ into sand moulds.

2. **Fill in each blank with an appropriate word by adding to the given word in brackets the necessary prefix or suffix or both as required.**
   (1) The _____ (appear) of the secret documents created a scandal.
   (2) Izzy Archibald merely shook his head _____ (approve).
   (3) I do hope that Natalie hasn't done anything _____ (grace) in London.
   (4) He was annoyed by a fly's _____ (persist) in landing on his nose.
   (5) He was raw and _____ (adequate) trained.
   (6) Perhaps, _____ (conscious), I've done something to offend her.
   (7) The novel is full of historical _____ (accurate).
   (8) The question is interesting but _____ (relevance) to the problem.
   (9) On this hot day the ice cream is _____ (resist).
   (10) She was a(n) _____ (response) mother to leave her young children alone in the house.
   (11) The teacher must make an effort to maintain a classroom atmosphere charged with _____ (friend) and acceptance.
   (12) We need _____ (adapt) workers who are willing to learn new skills.
   (13) As a Christian, his personal morality was _____ (separate) from his religious beliefs.
   (14) This bus will stop briefly in Houston just to _____ (fuel).

3. **Translate the following sentences into English by using the key words in the brackets.**
   (1) 曼德拉可以说变成了国父。(as it were)
   (2) 那件事一瞬间就过去了。(in a flash)
   (3) 被告对其所犯的罪行感到真心的悔恨，这点我们必须考虑在内。(repentance)
   (4) 那动人的景色突然出现在我面前。(burst upon)
   (5) 他的好恶爱憎非常强烈。(passionate)
   (6) 他谈到了中国革命走过的道路。(traverse)
   (7) 问他为什么迟到，他结结巴巴地说了个理由。(stammer)
   (8) 他们期待在最后解决中东问题上取得进展。(expectant)
   (9) 几年之后我才意识到戴维对我撒了谎。(before)

(10) 我要趁还没忘记先把这件事办了。(before)
(11) 你走以前不再喝一杯吗？(before)
(12) 还要过一些时间我们才能知道事情的全部结果。(before)

Grammar and Usage

Translate the following sentences by using adjectives or adjective phrases as adverbials.

(1) 她笑得甜甜的,急于要讨好。
(2) 无论是健康还是有病,是镇定还是忧愁,她总是克制自己,不露声色。
(3) 她认真热情,把说的话一字不漏地记了下来。
(4) 由于好奇,我们向四周看看还有什么客人。
(5) 城里活不下去了,他们只好搬到乡下去。
(6) 我发现他四仰八叉地躺在床上,睡得死死的。
(7) 她容易满足,笑逐颜开地接过那小礼品：一条不值钱的围巾。
(8) 他文质彬彬,和蔼可亲,结果却是个伪君子。
(9) 汤姆继续看书,似乎没有觉察到我在场。
(10) 周总理是那样谦逊、随和、易于接近,大家很快都不紧张了。
(11) 她满脸通红,气喘嘘嘘,从大门口跑了进来。
(12) 热心的时候他们是很合作的。

Writing task

Describe an experience of significant mental revelation of your own.

Text B

On Being a Scientific Booby[1]

Nancy Mairs[2]
(Abridged)

An unwritten rule in the world of academic science decrees that scientific writing must be concise and to the point—devoid of literary devices such as narrative, metaphor, or elaborate description—or it risks losing its credibility. The rule stems from a centuries-old separation in Western civilization of the sciences from the humanities—a separation of the head from the heart, metaphorically speaking. In this article, the author argues that enforcing this old rule among young scientists and young writers unnecessarily limits the potential of each to develop a talent in both fields—and conversely, if the head and heart could remain connected, it might well be to the benefit of both.

> **booby** /ˈbuːbi/ *n.* a person regarded as stupid
> **decree** /dɪˈkriː/ *v.* to decide, judge or order sth. officially
> **devoid** /dɪˈvɔɪd/ *adj.* ~ **of sth.** (written) completely lacking in something
> **dissect** /dɪˈsekt/ *v.* to cut up a dead person, animal or plant in order to study it

My daughter is dissecting a chicken. Her first. If she wants dinner (and she does),

she will make this pale, chubby chicken into eight
15 pieces I can fit into the fry pan. To encourage her, I
tell her that her great-great-grandfather was a butcher.
This is true, not something I have made up to con her
into doing a nasty job.

Now that she's gotten going, she is having a
20 wonderful time. She has made the chicken crow and
flap and dance all over the cutting board, and now it
lies quiet under her short, strong fingers as she slices
the length of its breastbone. She pries back the ribs and
peers into the cavity. "Oh, look at its mesenteries[3]!"
25 she cries. She pokes at some filmy white webs. Mesenteries, she informs me, are the membranes
that hold the chicken's organs in place. She turns the chicken over and begins to cut along its
spine. As her fingers search out joints and the knife severs wing from breast, leg from thigh,
she gives me a lesson in the comparative anatomy of this chicken and the frog she and her
friend Emily have recently dissected at school.

30   I am charmed by her enthusiasm and self-assurance. During her junior year in high school,
she is taking a college-level introductory course in biology. I took much the same course
when I was a freshman in college. But if I entered that course with Anne's self-confidence, I
certainly had none of it by the time I wrote the last word of my final examination. As the result
of Miss White and her quadrat report, I am daunted to the point of dysfunction by the notion
35 of thinking or writing "scientifically."

That woman—damn that woman!—turned me into a scientific cripple, and did so in the
name of science at a prestigious women's college that promised to school me that I might
"have life and have it abundantly." And really, I have had it abundantly, so I suppose I oughtn't
to complain if it's been a little short in *Paramecia*[4] and *Amanita phalloides* and *Drosophila*
40 *melanogaster*, whose eyes I have never seen.

Still, Miss White should not have been allowed to teach freshman biology because she
had a fatal idiosyncrasy (fatal, that is, to the courage of students, not to herself, though I believe
she is dead now of some unrelated cause): She could not bear a well-written report. One could
be either a writer or a scientist but not both, she told me one afternoon, her fingers flicking the
45 sheets of my latest lab write-up. She was
washing her hands of me, I could tell by the
weariness of her tone. She didn't even try
to make me a scientist. She simply wrinkled
her nose at the odor of my writing, handed
50 me the sheets, and sent me away. We never
had another conference. At the end of the
semester, I wrote my quadrat report, and Miss
White failed it.

All the same, I liked my quadrat, which
55 was a twenty-by-twenty plot in the college
woods behind the library. Mine was dull
compared to some others: Pam Weprin's, I
remember, had a brook running through it, in

---

chubby /'tʃʌbi/ *adj.* slightly fat in a way that people usually find attractive

con /kɔn/ *v.* ~ **sb.** (into doing sth./out of sth.)(informal) to trick sb., especially in order to get money from them or persuade them to do sth. for you

cavity /'kævɪti/ *n.* a hole or empty space inside sth. solid

sever /'sevə/ *v.* (formal) ~ **sth.** (from sth.) to cut sth. into two pieces; to cut sth. off sth.

anatomy /ə'nætəmi/ *n.* the structure of an animal or a plant

dysfunction /dɪs'fʌŋkʃən/ *n.* abnormal or impaired functioning, especially of a bodily system or organ

idiosyncrasy /ˌɪdɪə'sɪŋkrəsi/ *n.* a person's particular way of behaving, thinking, etc., especially when it is unusual; an unusual feature

which she discovered goldfish. It turned out that her magical discovery had a drab explanation: In a heavy rain the water from Peacock Pond backed up and spilled its resident carp into the brook. Even so, her quadrat briefly held an excitement mine never did. Mine was, in fact, as familiar as a living room. The lichen grew on the north side of the trees. In the rain the humus turned black and rank. A fallen log would sprout ears of tough, pale fungus.

Each freshman biology student received a quadrat. I visited mine to observe its progress through the seasons and wrote up my observations—and then discovered that I had somehow seen and spoken wrong. I wish now that I had kept the report. I wonder exactly what I said. Probably something about ears of fungus. Good God.

With a D+ for the first semester I continued, perversely, to like biology, but I also feared it more and more. I pinned and opened a long earthworm, marveling at the delicately-colored organs. I dissected a beef heart. For weeks I explored the interior of a rat, which I had opened neatly, like the shutters over a window. At the end of each lab, I would reluctantly close the shutters, wrap my rat in his plastic bag, and slip him back into the preserving jar.

Biology itself held more fascination and delight than fear. But with each report I grew more terrified of my own insidious poetic nature, which Miss White sniffed out in the simplest statement about amoeba[5] or ventricles. Years later, when I became a technical editor and made my living translating the garbled outbursts of scientists, I learned that I had done nothing much wrong. My understanding was limited, to be sure, but Miss White would have forgiven me my ignorance, even stupidity I think, if I had sufficiently muddled the language. As it was, I finished biology with a C-. I have always thought that the biology department awarded me a passing grade simply so that they wouldn't have to deal with me another year.

And they didn't. Nor did anyone else. I never took another science course, although I surprised myself afterward by becoming a competent amateur herpetologist[6]. My husband arrived home one afternoon with a shoebox containing a young bull snake, which he had bought for a quarter from some of his students at a school for emotionally disturbed boys so that they wouldn't try to find out how long a snake keeps wriggling without its head. This was Ferdinand, who was followed by two more bull snakes, Squeeze and Beowulf, and by a checkered garter snake[7] named Winslow J. Tweed, a black racer[8] named Jesse Owens, a Yuma king snake[9] named Hrothgar, and numerous nameless and short-lived blind snakes, tiny and semi-transparent, brought to us by our cats Freya, Burton Rustle, and Vanessa Bell. I grew so knowledgeable that when my baby boa constrictor[10], Crictor, contracted a respiratory ailment, I found that I was more capable of caring for him than were any of the veterinarians in the city. In fact, I learned, veterinarians do not do snakes; I could find only one to give Crictor the shot of a broad-spectrum antibiotic he needed.

But I do do snakes. I have read scientific treatises on them. I know that the Latin name for the timber rattlesnake is *Crotalus horridus horridus*. I know that Australia has more varieties of venomous snakes than any other

---

perverse /pəˈvɜːs/ *adj.* showing deliberate determination to behave in a way that most people think is wrong, unacceptable or unreasonable

insidious /ɪnˈsɪdɪəs/ *adj.* (formal, disapproving) spreading gradually or without being noticed, but causing serious harm

garbled /ˈɡɑːbəld/ *adj.* (of a message or story) told in a way that confuses the person listening, usually by sb. who is shocked or in a hurry

muddle /ˈmʌdl/ *v.* ~ **sth. (up)** to put things in the wrong order or mix them up

wriggle /ˈrɪɡəl/ *v.* to twist and turn your body or part of it with quick short movements

treatise /ˈtriːtɪs/ *n.* ~ **(on sth.)** a long and serious piece of writing on a particular subject

venomous /ˈvenəməs/ *adj.* (of a snake, etc.) producing venom

continent, among them the lethal sea snakes and the willfully aggressive tiger snake. I know how long one is likely to live after being bitten by a mamba[11] (not long). I read the treatises; but I don't, of course, write them. Although as a technical editor I grew proficient at unraveling snarls in the writing of scientists, I have never, since Miss White, attempted scientific experimentation or utterance.

Aside from my venture into herpetology, I remain a scientific booby. I mind my stupidity. I feel diminished by it. And I know now that it is unnecessary, the consequence of whatever quirk of fate brought me into Miss White's laboratory. Twenty years later, I am now cynical enough to write a quadrat report badly enough to pass her scrutiny, whereas when I had just turned seventeen I didn't even know that cynicism was an option—knowledge that comes, I suppose, from "having life abundantly." I've learned, too, that Miss White's bias, though unusually strong, was not peculiar to herself but arose from a cultural rift between the humanities and the sciences, resulting in the assumption that scientists will naturally write badly, that they are, in fact, rhetorical boobies. Today I teach technical writing. My students come to me terrified of the word-world from which they feel debarred, and I teach them to breach the boundaries in a few places, to step with boldness at least a little way inside. Linguistic courage is the gift I can give them.

In return, they give me gifts that I delight in—explanations of vortex centrifuges, evaluations of copper-smelting processes, plans for extracting gums from paloverde beans[12]. These help me compensate for my deficiencies, as do the works of the popularizers of science. Carl Sagan[13], Loren Eiseley[14], Lewis Thomas[15] and his insightful reflections subtitled *Notes of a Biology Watcher*. I watch television too. *Nova. Odyssey*[16]. *The Undersea World of Jacques Cousteau*.[17] But always I am aware that I am having translated for me the concepts of worlds I will never now explore for myself. I stand with my toes on the boundaries, peering, listening.

Anne has done a valiant job with the chicken. She's had a little trouble keeping its pajamas on, and one of the thighs has a peculiar shape, but she's reduced it to a workable condition. I brown it in butter and olive oil. I press in several cloves of garlic and then splash in some white wine. As I work, I think of the worlds Anne is going to explore. Some of them are listed in the college catalogues she's begun to collect: "Genetics, Energetics, and Evolution;" "Histology of Animals;" "Vertebrate Endocrinology;" "Electron Microscopy;" "Organic Synthesis;" "Animal Morphogenesis."

Anne can write. No one has yet told her that she can be a scientist or a writer but not both, and I trust that no one ever will. The complicated world can ill afford such lies to its children. As she plunges from my view into the thickets of calculus, embryology, and chemical thermodynamics, I will wait here for her to send me back messages. I love messages.

---

willful /ˈwɪlfəl/ *adj.* (disapproving) [usually before noun] of a bad or harmful action done deliberately, although the person doing it knows that it is wrong **willfully** *adv.*

unravel /ʌnˈrævəl/ *v.* if you unravel threads that are twisted, woven or knitted, or if they unravel, they become separated into loose treads

snarl /snɑːl/ *n.* (formal) something that has become twisted in an untidy way

quirk /kwɜːk/ *n.* a strange thing that happens, especially accidentally

rift /rɪft/ *n.* a serious disagreement between people that stops their relationship from continuing

debar /dɪˈbɑː/ *v.* [usually passive] ~ **sb. (from sth./ from doing sth.)** (formal) to prevent sb. from doing sth., joining sth., etc.

valiant /ˈvæliənt/ *adj.* (especially literary) very brave or determined

Notes

1. On Being a Scientific Booby

This essay comes from *Plaintext* (1986), Nancy Mairs' first collection of essays and also her dissertation. The book earned her a reputation as a "brilliant" American essayist.

2. Nancy Mairs

Nancy Mairs (1943—   ), born in Long Beach, California, grew up in the north of Boston. In 1964, she received the A.B. from Wheaton College (Norton, Massachusetts), which made her a Doctor of Humane Letters thirty years later. She did editorial work at the Smithsonian Astrophysical Observatory and the Harvard Law School before moving to Tucson, Arizona, where she earned the M.F.A. in creative writing (poetry) in 1975 and the Ph.D. in English literature (with a minor in English education) in 1984 from the University of Arizona. She has taught writing and literature at Salpointe Catholic High School, the University of Arizona, and the University of California at Los Angeles.

A poet and an essayist, Nancy Mairs was awarded the 1984 Western States Book Award in poetry and a National Endowment for the Arts Fellowship in 1991. She and her husband, George, a retired high-school English teacher, continue to live in Tucson, though they make public appearances throughout the country. A Research Associate with the Southwest Institute for Research on Women, she also serves on the boards of ARTability, the Sonora Fund, Korc Press, and the Coalition of Arizonans to Abolish the Death Penalty.

3. mesentery

Any of several folds of the peritoneum that connect the intestines to the dorsal abdominal wall, especially such a fold that envelops the jejunum and ileum. 肠系膜：任一种将小肠和腹腔后壁联结起来的腹膜，尤指包被着空肠及回肠的这种腹膜

4. Paramecia

Any of various freshwater ciliate protozoans of the genus Paramecium, usually oval and having an oral groove for feeding. 草履虫：一种有纤毛的淡水草虫履属原生动物，通常呈卵形且有摄食用的口沟

5. amoeba

A protozoan of the genus Amoeba or related genera, occurring in water and soil and as a parasite in other animals. An amoeba has no definite form and consists essentially of a mass of protoplasm containing one nucleus or more surrounded by a delicate, flexible outer membrane. It moves by means of pseudopods. 变形虫

6. herpetologist

A zoologist who studies reptiles and amphibians. 爬虫学者

7. checkered garter snake

Checkered Garter Snakes are brown or olive colored snake with a distinctive black checker board pattern along their bodies and cream or white stripes along their top and sides. Their underbodies are white, occasionally tinted with green, yellow or gray. They grow to between 13—42 inches in length, but are more typically in the range of 28 inches. 白化丝带蛇

8. black racer

Black Racers are slender black snakes of adult size from 30 to 60 inches in length. They are called "racers" because they are active, fast moving snakes. Adult Black Racers are satiny or shiny black above and gray or bluish-gray of the belly. They have a white on the chin and throat. (美洲产的)游蛇属黑蛇

9. Yuma king snake

A subspecies of the Common Kingsnake. The Common Kingsnake is a non-venomous member of the "harmlesss" Colubridae Family, which includes gopher snakes, garter snakes and whip snakes. Mature adults are 30 to 85 inches long and come in a variety of colors and patterns, usually chocolate brown to black. 王蛇

10. baby boa constrictor

The boa constrictor is a non-poisonous tropical snake belonging to a specialized group of reptiles—the first vertebrate class completely independent of water. It is found in Central and South America and often reaches lengths of up to 4 m (13 ft.). 小蟒蛇

11. mamba

Any of several venomous arboreal snakes of the genus Dendroaspis of tropical Africa, especially D. angusticeps, a green or black tree snake having an often fatal bite. 树眼睛蛇, 曼巴(非洲有毒树蛇)

12. paloverde beans

The fruit of mall spiny leguminous trees or shrubs (genus Cercidium) that have greenish branches and are found chiefly in dry regions of the southwestern U.S. and Mexico. 假紫荆属树木的果实

13. Carl Sagan

Founder and First President of The Planetary Society.

14. Loren Eiseley

(1907—1977): American Anthropologist.

15. Lewis Thomas

(1913—1993): Twentieth-century American Nature Writer.

16. Odyssey

Composed around 700 BC, The Odyssey is one of the earliest epics still in existence and, in many ways, sets the pattern for the genre, neatly fitting the definition of a primary epic (that is, one that grows out of oral tradition). The hero is long-suffering Odysseus, king of Ithaca and surrounding islands and hero of the Trojan War. He has been gone 20 years from his homeland, his wife, Penelope, and his son, Telemachus. Odysseus embodies many of the virtues of ancient Greek civilization and in some ways defines them. 《奥德赛》(古希腊史诗)

17. The Undersea World of Jacques Cousteau

This early TV series, produced aboard the marine research vessel "Calypso", catalogues what is more or less Jacques-Yves Cousteau in Wonderland. 电视节目"雅克·库斯托的海底世界"

Comprehension

1. What was the main fault of Miss White as a teacher? What is her "fatal idiosyncrasy"?

2. Can you determine, based on the context clues, the meaning of "quadrat"?
3. What was the author's attitude toward biology before she took Miss White's class? What was her attitude while she was attending the class? What is her attitude now?
4. What is the author's present job?
5. Based on the article, what is a "scientific booby"? Do you believe that the author is a "scientific booby"? What is your evidence? Whom does the author blame for her condition?
6. What is the "word-world" from which the author's students, or students of sciences in general, often feel debarred? What advice does the author give to her students to solve the problem?
7. What do you think is the conflict between a "scientist" and a "writer"? Do you agree with the author that one can be both a good scientist and a good writer? Explain your reasoning.
8. How do the shifts in tense contribute to our understanding of this article?
9. What is the main point of this essay? As teachers, what are the major differences between Miss Sullivan and Miss White?

Further Study

Some more articles to read

- "On Becoming a Better Student" by Donna Farhi Schuster
- "My Teacher, My Hero" by Bill Macwithey
- "A Lesson in Living" by Maya Angelou
- "A Teacher to Remember" by John T. Moore
- "My Father's Lessons" by Cathy Downs

Read to discover more about Helen Keller

- "The Story of My Life" by Helen Keller
- "The World I Live In" by Helen Keller
- "Out of the Dark" by Helen Keller

Unit 3

Cross-cultural Communication

Unit Goals

☞ To cultivate cultural awareness for cross-cultural communication
☞ To use analogy as a means of exposition
☞ To write a problem-solution essay

Before Reading

1. Investigate the meaning of "culture." Obtain as many definitions as possible, and then come to your own understanding.
2. In medical terms, "shock" is a medical condition caused by severe injury, pain, loss of blood or fear which slows down the flow of blood through the body. What do you think a "cultural shock" might be?
3. Have you heard the term "reverse culture shock?" It means that people who have lived abroad often find the adjustment to returning home is as difficult as their adjustment to the foreign culture. Interview a Chinese-born person who has just returned home after living abroad for some years to find out how difficult it was for them to adjust to their home country. Prepare an oral report to present to the class.

A Glimpse into the Text

   Citizens who never live outside their own country commonly imagine that living abroad must be a thrilling adventure. Reciprocally, they often anticipate that foreigners will find their own nation delightfully different than the one they left behind. In both cases, they are most often right—but, at some point in either circumstance, a shift in attitude commonly occurs, the adventure sours, and a psychological problem begins to manifest itself in the mind and behaviour of the foreign visitor: "culture shock." In this article, the author describes this phenomenon in detail and suggests some ways of coping with it.

Text A

Culture Shock[1]

Kalervo Oberg[2]
(Abridged and edited)

Culture shock might be called an occupational disease of people who have been suddenly transplanted abroad. Like most ailments it has its own etiology, symptoms, and cure.

Culture shock is precipitated by the anxiety that results from losing all our familiar signs and symbols of social intercourse. These signs or cues include the thousand and one ways in which we orient ourselves to the situations of daily life: when to shake hands and what to say when we meet people, when and how to give tips, how to give orders to servants, how to make purchases, when to accept and when to refuse invitations, when to take statements seriously and when not. Now these cues which may be words, gestures, facial expressions, customs, or norms are acquired by all of us in the course of growing up and are as much a part of our culture as the language we speak or the beliefs we accept. All of us depend for our peace of mind and our efficiency on hundreds of these cues, most of which we do not carry on the level of conscious awareness.

Now when an individual enters a strange culture, all or most of these familiar cues are removed. He or she is like a fish out of water. No matter how broad-minded or full of good will you may be, a series of props have been knocked from under you, followed by a feeling of frustration and anxiety. People react to the frustration in much the same way. First they reject the environment which causes the discomfort: "the ways of the host country are bad because they make us feel bad." When Americans or other foreigners in a strange land get together to grouse about the host country and its people—you can be sure they are suffering from culture shock. Another phase of culture shock is regression. The home environment suddenly assumes a tremendous importance. To an American everything American becomes irrationally glorified. All the difficulties and problems are forgotten and only the good things back home are remembered. It usually takes a trip home to bring one back to reality.

Some of the symptoms of culture shock are: excessive washing of the hands; excessive concern over drinking water, food, dishes, and bedding; fear of physical contact with attendants or servants; the absentminded, far-away stare (sometimes called the tropical stare); a feeling of helplessness and a desire for dependence on long-term residents of one's own nationality; fits of anger over delays and other minor frustrations; delay and outright refusal to learn the language of the host country; excessive fear of being cheated, robbed, or injured; great concern over minor pains and eruptions of the skin;

---

etiology /ˌiːtiˈɒlədʒi/ *n.* (AmE)=aetiology [U] the scientific study of the causes of disease

precipitate /prɪˈsɪpɪteɪt/ *v.* (formal) to make sth., especially sth. bad, happen suddenly or sooner than it should; ~ **sb./sth. into sth.** to suddenly force sb./sth. into a particular state or condition

orient /ˈɔːrient/ *v.* [usually passive] ~ **sb./sth. (to/towards sb./sth.)** to direct sb./sth. towards sth.; to make or adapt sb./sth. for a particular purpose

prop /prɒp/ *n.* a person or thing that gives help or support to sb./sth. that is weak

grouse /ɡraʊs/ *v.* ~ **(about sb./sth.)** (informal) to complain about sb./sth. in a way that other people find annoying

regression /rɪˈɡreʃən/ *n.* [U, C] ~ **(to sth.)** the process of going back to an earlier or less advanced form or state

outright /ˈaʊtraɪt/ *adj.* [only before n.] complete and total; open and direct

erupt /ɪˈrʌpt/ *v.* (of spots, etc.) to suddenly appear on the skin

and finally, that terrible longing to be back home.

Individuals differ greatly in the degree in which culture shock affects them. Although not common, there are individuals who cannot live in foreign countries. Those who have seen people go through culture shock and on to a satisfactory adjustment can discern steps in the process. During the first few weeks most individuals are fascinated by the new. They stay in hotels and associate with nationals who speak their language and are polite and gracious to foreigners. This honeymoon stage may last from a few days or weeks to six months, depending on circumstances. If one is a very important person he or she will be shown the show places[3], will be pampered and petted, and in a press interview will speak glowingly about progress, goodwill, and international amity.

But this mentality does not normally last if the foreign visitor remains abroad and has seriously to cope with real conditions of life. It is then that the second stage begins, characterized by a hostile and aggressive attitude towards the host country. This hostility evidently grows out of the genuine difficulty which the visitor experiences in the process of adjustment. There is maid trouble, school trouble, language trouble, house trouble, transportation trouble, shopping trouble, and the fact that people in the host country are largely indifferent to all these troubles. They help but they just don't understand your great concern over these difficulties. Therefore, they must be insensible and unsympathetic to you and your worries. The result, "I just don't like them." You become aggressive; you band together with your fellow countrymen and criticize the host country, its ways, and its people. But this criticism is not an objective appraisal but a derogatory one. Instead of trying to account for conditions as they are through an honest analysis of the actual conditions and the historical circumstances which have created them, you talk as if the difficulties you experience are more or less created by the people of the host country for your special discomfort.

You take refuge in the colony of your countrymen and its cocktail circuit which often becomes the fountainhead of emotionally charged labels known as stereotypes[4]. This is a peculiar kind of invidious shorthand which caricatures the host country and its people in a negative manner. The "dollar grasping American" and the "indolent Latin American" are samples of mild forms of stereotypes. This second stage of culture shock is in a sense a crisis in the disease. If you overcome it you stay, if not, you leave before you reach the stage of a nervous breakdown.

If the visitor succeeds in getting some knowledge of the language and begins to get around by himself, he is beginning to open the way into the new cultural environment. The visitor still has difficulties but he takes a "this is my cross[5] and I have to bear it" attitude. Usually in this stage the visitor takes a superior attitude to people of the host country. His sense of humor begins to exert itself. Instead of criticizing, he jokes about the people and even cracks jokes about his or her own difficulties. He or she is now on the way to

---

pamper /'pæmpə/ *v.* (sometimes disapproving) to take care of sb. very well and make them feel as comfortable as possible

aggressive /ə'gresɪv/ *adj.* angry, and behaving in a threatening way; ready to attack

appraisal /ə'preɪzəl/ *n.* [C, U] a judgement of the value, performance or nature of sb./sth.

colony /'kɒləni/ *n.* [C+sing./pl. v.] a group of people from the same place or with the same work or interests who live in a particular city or country or who live together

stereotype /'steriətaɪp/ *n.* a fixed idea or image that many people have of a particular type of person or thing, but which is often not true in reality

invidious /ɪn'vɪdɪəs/ *adj.* (formal) unpleasant and unfair; likely to offend sb. or make them jealous

indolent /'ɪndələnt/ *adj.* (formal) lazy; not wanting to work

recovery.

In the fourth stage your adjustment is about as complete as it can be. The visitor now accepts the customs of the country as just another way of living. You operate within the new milieu without a feeling of anxiety although there are moments of strain. Only with a complete grasp of all the cues of social intercourse will this strain disappear. For a long time the individual will understand what the national is saying but he is not always sure what the national means. With a complete adjustment you not only accept the foods, drinks, habits, and customs but actually begin to enjoy them. When you go on home leave you may even take things back with you and if you leave for good you generally miss the country and the people to whom you have become accustomed.

In an effort to get over culture shock, there is some value in knowing something about the nature of culture and its relationship to the individual. In addition to living in a physical environment, an individual lives in a cultural environment consisting of man-made physical objects, social institutions, and ideas and beliefs. An individual is not born with culture but only with the capacity to learn it and use it. The culture of any people is the product of history and is built up over time largely through processes which are, as far as the individual is concerned, beyond his awareness. It is by means of culture that the young learn to adapt themselves to the physical environment and to the people with whom they associate. And as we know, children and adolescents often experience difficulties in this process of learning and adjustment. But once learned, culture becomes a way of life, the sure, familiar, largely automatic way of getting what you want from your environment and as such it also becomes a value. People have a way of accepting their culture as both the best and the only way of doing things; they identify themselves with their own group and its ways to the extent that any critical comment is taken as an affront to the individual as well as to the group. If you criticize my country you are criticizing me; if you criticize me you are criticizing my country.

Now any modern nation is a complex society with corresponding variations in culture. In composition it is made up of different ethnic groups, it is stratified into classes, it is differentiated into regions, it is separated into rural and urban settlements, each having its distinctive cultural characteristics. Yet superimposed upon these differences are the common elements of official language, institutions, and customs which knit it together to form a nation. These facts indicate that it is not a simple matter to acquaint oneself with the culture of a nation. An objective treatment of your cultural background and that of your new environment is important for understanding culture shock. There is a great difference in knowing what is the cause of your disturbance and not knowing. Once you realize that your trouble is due to your own lack of understanding of other people's cultural background and your own lack of the means of communication rather than the hostility of an alien environment, you also realize that you yourself can gain this understanding and these means of communication. And the sooner you do this, the sooner culture shock will disappear.

---

milieu /ˈmiːljɜː/ *n.* [C, usually sing.] (pl. **milieux** or **milieus**) (from French, formal) the social environment that you live or work in

affront /əˈfrʌnt/ *n.* [usually sing.] ~ (**to sb./sth.**) a remark or an action that insults or offends sb./sth.

stratify /ˈstrætɪfaɪ/ *v.* [usually passive] (formal or technical) to arrange sth. in layers or strata

superimpose /ˌsuːpərɪmˈpəʊz/ *v.* [T] to put especially a picture, words, etc. on top of something else, especially another picture, words, etc., so that what is in the lower position can still be seen, heard, etc.

More about the Text

1. Culture Shock

The present selection is an adaptation from a talk that Oberg gave to the Women's Club of Rio de Janeiro on August 3, 1954. Bobbs-Merrill published this talk later in 1954 and it was then republished in *Practical Anthropology* (7:177-182) in 1960.

2. Kalervo Oberg

Kalervo Oberg (1901—1973) was born to Finnish parents in British Columbia, Canada, and became a US citizen in 1944. He was a world-renowned applied anthropologist. He received a bachelor's degree in economics from the University of British Columbia, and a Master's degree in economics from the University of Pittsburg. He did extensive fieldwork on three distinctly different continents and wrote about the experiences.

3. show places

A show place is an impressive place that tourists often visit.

4. stereotype

Often a stereotype is a negative caricature or inversion of some positive characteristics possessed by members of a group.

5. cross

In this context, "cross" means "burden." If you describe something as a cross that someone has to bear, you mean it is a problem or disadvantage which they have to deal with or bear.

Check Your Understanding

1. What precipitates culture shock?
2. What are the signs of culture shock?
3. Why does Oberg call the first stage of culture shock the "honeymoon stage"?
4. What are the symptoms of the second stage of culture shock? Why is this stage a crisis in a sense?
5. What attitude does a visitor usually take toward people of the host country in the third stage of culture shock?
6. How does a sufferer of "culture shock" usually feel in the fourth stage?
7. What advice does Oberg give to those who suffer from culture shock to help them get over the problem?
8. What is the nature of culture and its relationship to the individual?
9. Why is it important to know you own cultural background and your new environment?
10. Is Oberg's explanation of "culture shock" clear or not? What expository means does he resort to in order to make his ideas clear? Illustrate with details from the text.

Paraphrasing

1. All of us depend for our peace of mind and our efficiency on hundreds of these cues, most of which we do not carry on the level of conscious awareness.
2. No matter how broad-minded or full of good will you may be, a series of props have been

knocked from under you, followed by a feeling of frustration and anxiety.
3. You take refuge in the colony of your countrymen and its cocktail circuit which often becomes the fountainhead of emotionally charged labels known as stereotypes.
4. But once learned, culture becomes a way of life, the sure, familiar, largely automatic way of getting what you want from your environment and as such it also becomes a value.
5. Now any modern nation is a complex society with corresponding variations in culture. In composition it is made up of different ethnic groups, it is stratified into classes, it is differentiated into regions, it is separated into rural and urban settlements, each having its distinctive cultural characteristics.

Some Information about English Style

1. Analogy

In this essay, Kalervo Oberg tells us that culture shock is a "disease" or an "ailment" which has its own "symptoms" and "cure." By saying so, he is using an analogy to explain what culture shock is. He is using words to mean something other than what they normally mean. In his comparison of culture shock to a disease, expressions such as "symptoms," "cure," "discomfort," and "crisis in the disease" are all figurative. They build up associations in the reader's mind, thus making the concept of culture shock easier to understand.

What is an analogy?

An analogy is a a form of comparison, either brief or extended. A brief analogy can be a metaphor or simile, such as

- New York is a sucked orange. (R.W. Emerson)   (metaphor)
- An orange is like a smile: both are sweet.   (simile)

An extended analogy provides a more thorough comparison and can be a means of organizing a paragraph, or even a whole essay. For instance, Oberg's comparison of culture shock to an occupational disease (the first paragraph) and his explanation of the different stages of culture shock using a medical metaphor throughout the essay can be regarded as an extended analogy.

In analogy, writers use something familiar to explain something unfamiliar. For example, a geologist often describes the structure of the earth's crust by comparing the strata to the layers of an onion. Sometimes writers use analogy in an attempt to persuade.

An analogy can be developed through as many parallel similarities as the writer can think of, to convince the reader that since the two things are similar in so many ways, a conclusion drawn from one suggests a similar conclusion from the other.

What is a formal analogy?

Analogies may take the form of well-developed comparisons that reveal particular similarities between members of the same or different classes. Writers, inventors, scientists, and mathematicians make regular use of analogies in their work to create unexpected comparisons between items from very different classes. Analogies help people notice details in appearance, function, location, and so on. Formal analogies are in this general form:

a:b::c:d

This is read as: "*a* is to *b* as *c* is to *d*." It means that the relationship between "a" and "b" is similar somehow to the relationship between "c" and "d." Take "*Shells were to ancient cultures as dollar bills are to modern culture.*" as an example. It simply means shells functioned in some ancient cultures as printed money functions in our culture today. More common forms of analogy may read something like this: "*An orange is like a smile: both are sweet,*" for which we may say "both are pleasant." In other words, analogies tend to suggest that existing similarities imply further similarities.

What are the limitations of analogies?

Although analogies are helpful in pointing out relationships that may not at first be visible, they have their limitations. An analogy may break down, which means that it is only suggestive and does not follow in every detail. They break down or don't hold except in narrow ways. Analogies are most useful in helping people see similarities not otherwise apparent; they set out to persuade or to explain, but do not necessarily set out to prove.

2. The Problem-Solution Essay

In the present selection, Oberg first points out a problem that many experience when they are in a strange culture: they feel anxious for having lost their familiar signs and symbols of social intercourse. To prove this is a real problem, Oberg lists several symptoms, and outlines four steps in adjusting to the new culture. Finally, he offers some suggestions as to how to cope with this ailment, which he calls "culture shock." This essay, in which Oberg convinces the reader of the existence of a problem and comes up with potential solutions to it, falls into the category of the problem-solution essay.

The problem-solution essay is, as the name implies, an essay that has as its focus the solution to a problem. Such an essay offers insights into a problem and the possible solution(s). In some essays, the problem, because of its enormity, receives more emphasis while the solution may be hardly touched upon because the writer is not sure of the solution. In other essays, the solution may be emphasized more. The writer may offer one or more possible solutions to a problem that is well known. Sometimes, the problem and solution are given equal treatment. The topic helps to determine whether more emphasis is laid upon the problem or the solution or both equally.

Practice

Building word power

1. Fill in each blank with the best answer for each of the following sentences.

(1) Bill is suffering from a rare nerve _____ that can cause paralysis of the arms.
 A. disease   B. disorder   C. ailment   D. syndrome

(2) It was a _____ of his unfamiliarity with Hollywood that he didn't understand that an agent was paid out of his client's share.
 A. sign   B. mark   C. token   D. symptom

(3) The local council _____ him planning permission to build an extra bedroom.
 A. declined   B. refused   C. rejected   D. turned down

(4) Pattie shot Tom in a _____ of jealous rage.
 A. fit   B. attack   C. access   D. spasm

(5) Could you _____ which of them was telling the truth?
 A. see   B. observe   C. perceive   D. discern

(6) He was there and saw what happened, so his is the only _____ account.
   A. authentic   B. genuine   C. veritable   D. bona fide
(7) We should make _____ use of the resources available to us.
   A. sensible   B. practical   C. judicious   D. sensitive
(8) When visiting a foreign country, we must respect the country's _____.
   A. habits   B. practices   C. usages   D. customs
(9) With the new machines we finally have the _____ to do the job properly.
   A. ability   B. capacity   C. capability   D. genius
(10) She gave a long _____ explanation that no one could follow.
   A. complex   B. complicated C. intricate   D. involved
(11) Making some simple _____ in your diet will make you feel fitter.
   A. changes   B. alterations C. variations   D. modifications
(12) It is hard to _____ her from her twin sister.
   A. distinguish   B. differentiate C. discriminate D. ascertain

2. The following is a list of idioms and phrasal verbs taken from the reading selection. Fill in each blank with the appropriate form of one of them. (Each expression may be used only once.)

> a thousand and one   be like a fish out of water   cope with
> grow out of   result from   get around
> exert oneself   on the/one's way to
> for good (and all)   build up

(1) Ballroom dancing could be _____ becoming an Olympic sport.
(2) Among so many well-dressed and cultured people, the country girl felt _____.
(3) I can't stand around chatting—I've got _____ things to do this morning.
(4) Spain last week and Germany this week—He _____, doesn't he?
(5) It must be very difficult to _____ three children and a job.
(6) The idea for the story _____ a strange experience I had last year.
(7) They gave him soup to _____ his strength.
(8) The accident _____ a defective brake.
(9) Once he has made up his mind it is made up _____.
(10) I was too tired to _____.

Grammar and Usage

1. Translate the following sentences into English by using the key words given in the brackets.
   (1) 边境事件使两国突然陷入战争。(precipitate)
   (2) 这门课程非常注重语法。(orient)
   (3) 他因滥用职权被免职。(remove)
   (4) 对这种直截了当的质问,他感到既惊愕又难以置信。(react)
   (5) 林依轮在中央一台主持一档烹饪节目。(host)
   (6) 被告装出一副无辜的样子。(assume)
   (7) 那部电影美化战争和暴力,因此遭禁播。(glorify)

(8) 双方在工资协议的条款上仍然存在分歧。(differ)
(9) 没有父母愿意孩子与吸毒者和酒徒交往。(associate)
(10) 绝不能让陌生人进入。(account)
(11) 让我们把杯子斟满,为他的健康干杯。(charge)
(12) 他善于行使自己的权力。(exert)
(13) 他自称是这家人的老朋友。(identify)
(14) 公司没有足够的钱投资新产品。(lack)

2. Cloze

The stories each culture (1) _____ their people, whether in the (2) _____ of folk tales, legends, or myths, are all intended to transmit the culture from person to person and from generation to generation. Whether it (3) _____ Pinocchio's nose growing larger because of his lies, Columbus being glorified because he was daring, Abraham Lincoln learning to read by drawing letters on a shovel by the fireside, or the Power Ranges defending democracy and fighting for (4) _____ is "right," folklore constantly reinforces our fundamental values. A case in (5) _____ is the popular folk tale "Cinderella." Although nearly every culture has its own (6) _____ of this story, the emphasis varies. In the American version, Cinderella's attractiveness is crucial; she is also rather passive and weak. In the Algonquin Indian tale, the virtues of truthfulness and honesty are the basis of Cinderella's character. The Japanese story accentuates intellectual ability and gentleness. In one Japanese version, there are only two sisters and they wish to go to a Kabuki play. In place of the famous slipper test is the challenge of having to (7) _____ a song extemporaneously. One sister manages only a simple, unimaginative song, which she sings in "a loud harsh voice." But Cinderella composes a song that has both meter and metaphor, and she sings it in "sweet gentle tones." Traits that are important to the specific culture are reflected in each version of the tale.

Every culture has thousands of tales, each stressing a fundamental value. Americans revere the tough, independent, fast-shooting cowboy of the Old West; the English admiration of good manners, courtly behavior, and dignity is reflected in *The Canterbury Tales*; the Japanese learn about the importance of duty, obligation, and loyalty in the ancient story of *The Tale of the Forty-Seven Ronin*; and the Sioux Indians use the legend of *Pushing Up the Sky* to teach what people can accomplish if they work together.

Legends, folk tales, and myths (8) _____ more than accent cultural values: "they confront cosmic questions about the world as a whole." In addition, they can tell us about specific details of life that might be important to a group of people. Myths are useful tools for teaching culture because they cover a wide (9) _____ of cultural concerns. Perhaps their most significant contribution is that they deal with the ideas that matter most to a culture—ideas about life, death, relationships, nature, and the like. Campbell tells us, "Myths are stories of our search (10) _____ the ages for truth, for meaning, for significance. We all need to tell our story and to understand our story." Because myths offer clues into culture, Campbell urges us not only to understand our story, but to "read other people's myths." We strongly concur with Campbell—when you study the myths of a culture, you are studying the heart of that culture.

Improving your writing style

1. Part of the statement in an analogy is based on identifying similar function or other relationship. Try to complete the following analogies by identifying the similarities. Then compare your answers with those of your partner.

(1) A clock is to time as a scale is to _____.
(2) Shoe is to foot as tire is to _____.
(3) Followers are to a leader as planets are to a _____.
(4) Up is to down as in is to _____.

2. Use your imagination and draw analogies for the following.

(1) The world is like _____.
(2) Life is like _____.
(3) Love is like _____.
(4) Friendship is like _____.
(5) The brain is like _____.

Text B

A Canadian Firm's Negotiation in China

Iris Varner and Linda Beamer[1]

Any foreigner who has lived in China for sometime knows the basic taboos of the culture, such as never give a clock or an umbrella as a gift, but some more subtle social rules often elude even long-time foreign residents in the country. Acquiring these depends on having grown up with the culture or having studied Chinese etiquette
5   conscientiously. Social expectations concerning relationships, priorities, the use of time, and decorum may lead an unwary foreigner to unconsciously leave a negative impression with his or her Chinese hosts. Such was the case for two Canadian businessmen, as is documented below.

10   A Canadian team of two men representing Canwall, a wallpaper printing equipment manufacturer, were on their way to a town north of Shanghai in the province of Jiangsu, China, to negotiate a sale to a new wallpaper production company. Charlie Burton, president of Canwall, was traveling with his marketing director, Phil Raines. The company had never before sold its equipment outside Canada, and the two Canadians were about to be delighted with the
15   warm reception they would receive in China.

This wasn't to be the first meeting between the Canadian company and the Chinese wallpaper factory. The manager of the Chinese company, Mr. Li, had been a member of a
20   delegation to Canada. He had met with one of Canwall's senior salespersons and the director of

> **taboo** /təˈbuː/ *n.* an action or word avoided for religious or social reasons
> **elude** /ɪˈluːd/ *v.* to escape the understanding or grasp of
> **decorum** /dɪˈkɔːrəm/ *n.* behaviour that is controlled, calm and polite
> **unwary** /ˌʌnˈweəri/ *adj.* not aware of or careful about possible risks and dangers

manufacturing. Subsequently a trade representative from Canada had been in China representing Canwall's interests to the Chinese manager. After these meetings and numerous letters and faxes, Canwall's top people were now ready to negotiate the sale.

The day they arrived they were met at the airport in Shanghai by Manager Li himself and transported in a chauffeur-driven car 90 miles to the town. Their accommodations were in a newly built hotel, which while not luxurious, was certainly comfortable. A few hours after their arrival they were treated to a 12-course banquet given by their host, with several high-level municipal officials present. This red-carpet treatment[2] made them feel optimistic about the sale.

The next day they were taken to see the sights nearby: a large, new port for container ships and several factories that indicated the prosperity of the region. They were eager to begin discussing the sale, but after lunch they were given time to rest. In the late afternoon one of the manager's English-speaking employees came by with the news that they would be taken to see a local dance company's performance that night.

The third day they finally sat down to meetings. Progress seemed very slow with each side presenting generalizations about itself that seemed unrelated to the sale. The Canadians used an interpreter supplied by the Chinese, who was eager to please them, so the Canadians felt comfortable with her, but translation slowed down communication. After listening to various apparently unrelated points, the Canadians thought, "So what?"

The Chinese also spent a lot of time talking and asking about the Canadian trade agent who had been in their town earlier. Burton wasn't able to tell them much about that person, since he had never met him.

When the Canadians at last were able to make the sales presentation they had prepared, they were surprised at the number of people who showed up. There were 10 Chinese facing them across the table. Still, the Chinese frequently nodded, smiled, and said yes. Burton and Raines had carefully prepared sales data and were able to show, effectively they thought, that within five years the factory could double its present production. At the end of the day, the jubilant Canadians returned to their hotel rooms confident they had sold the equipment.

The next day they were asked to explain once again things they thought had been covered already, to a Chinese team with four new faces in it. They were confused about who their negotiating counterparts really were. Their jubilation began to evaporate. They were asked to explain the technology in minute detail. Neither Burton nor Raines had been involved in the engineering of the high-tech component that was the heart of the equipment. After doing the best they could, they returned to the hotel exhausted.

Their interpreter also seemed to be unfamiliar with technological terms, since she and the interpreter for the factory spent some time discussing things between themselves. Because the Canadian side's interpreter was a woman, the Canadians had to meet her in the hotel lobby to discuss their plan for the next day. The two tired men would have preferred to sit in their room while they talked with her, rather than in

chauffeur /'ʃəʊfə/ n. (AmE) a person whose job is to drive a car, especially for sb. rich or important
generalization /ˌdʒenərəlaɪ'zeɪʃən/ n. [C,U] a general statement that is based on only a few facts or examples; the act of making such statements
jubilant /'dʒuːbɪlənt/ adj. (written) feeling or showing great happiness because of a success
cover /'kʌvə/ v. to include sth.; to deal with sth.
jubilation /ˌdʒuːbɪ'leɪʃən/ n. a feeling of great happiness because of a success
evaporate /ɪ'væpəreɪt/ v. to disappear, especially by gradually becoming less and less

the noisy lobby where they were the object of curiosity, but she requested they remain in a public place because as a woman she could not meet with them in their room.

The next day they were asked again about the technological details. This time one member of the first-day team pointed out discrepancies between what they had said and what the manufacturing director, an engineer, had told them in Canada. Burton and Raines were chagrined. The Chinese were reproachful about the discrepancies, as if the Canadians had been caught in a shameful act. At lunch the two Canadians quickly faxed Canada for specifications and explanations. The afternoon session was uncomfortable, although everyone was polite. Burton and Raines were a bit unsettled when a middle-aged woman suddenly burst into the negotiating room and whispered into the ear of one of the key Chinese speakers who immediately got up and left the room. The Canadians expected some explanation for the emergency but none ever came.

Not until the next day, because of the time difference, did the Canadians receive some of the documentation they needed by fax. Discussions resumed with the same questions being asked yet again. It all went very slowly. The Chinese appreciated the high quality of the Canadian product but worried they wouldn't be able to fix the equipment if it broke down. They suggested—delicately, so as not to imply they *expected* breakdowns—that perhaps the Canadians could give them some help with maintenance training. The Canadians pointed out the expense and difficulty of keeping someone in their city for several weeks or months and expressed confidence there wouldn't be any problems the manual didn't cover. The Chinese would be able to look after the equipment just fine.

Finally, the technical discussions gave way to the issue central to most negotiations in most countries: price. This proved to be the most difficult of all. The Chinese began by asking for a 20 percent price discount. The Canadians thought this was an outrageous negotiating ploy; they stuck to their price, which they knew to be fair, and offered a three percent discount on the printing cylinders.

Although Burton and Raines had heard that negotiations took time in China, they had thought a week would be ample. Now time was running out, and they were due in Beijing in two days. They already had learned that getting plane tickets wasn't easy, so they were anxious to be on the plane as previously arranged. The Canadians began to ask pointed questions about what the Chinese were unhappy with and where they needed to go over issues again. During the last two sessions, the Canadians tried to get the Chinese to focus on the unresolved points, but the Chinese seemed reluctant to do so.

A number of issues remained unresolved when the farewell banquet was held the following noon. The question of price seemed near solution, but not the method of payment. That was the final,

---

discrepancy /dɪˈskrepənsɪ/ *n.* a difference between two or more things that should be the same

chagrined /ˈʃæɡrɪnd/ *adj.* (formal) disappointed or annoyed, especially when caused by a failure or mistake

reproachful /rɪˈprəʊtʃfəl/ *adj.* expressing blame or criticism

specification /ˌspesɪfɪˈkeɪʃən/ *n.* [C, U] a detailed description of how sth. is, or should be, designed or made

documentation /ˌdɒkjʊmənˈteɪʃən/ *n.* the documents that are required for sth., or that give evidence or proof of sth.

delicate /ˈdelɪkɪt/ *adj.* needing to be done carefully

outrageous /aʊtˈreɪdʒəs/ *adj.* very unusual and slightly shocking

ploy /plɔɪ/ *n.* sth. that is done or said in order to get an advantage, often dishonestly

ample /ˈæmpəl/ *adj.* enough or more than enough

pointed /ˈpɔɪntɪd/ *adj.* aimed in a clear and often critical way against a particular person or their behavior

apparently insurmountable, hurdle since the Chinese couldn't guarantee the payment schedule; it seemed tied to deadlines and requirements of the municipal officials. Nevertheless, Manager Li smiled and spoke of mutual cooperation for the future, and past Chinese-Canadian relations, and the great amount he and his factory could learn from the Canadians. They signed an expanded version of the letter of intent that had been signed nine months earlier in Canada. The Canadians left with expressions on both sides of willingness to continue to discuss the sale through mail and fax.

The Canadians were stunned to learn two weeks later that the factory had decided to buy from a Japanese equipment manufacturer. They knew their product was good and their price was fair. What had happened to derail their sale?

> insurmountable /ˌɪnsəˈmaʊntəbəl/ adj. (formal) (of difficulties; problems, etc.) that cannot be dealt with successfully
> hurdle /ˈhɜːdl/ n. a problem or difficulty
> derail /ˌdiːˈreɪl/ v. (fig.) to prevent a plan or process from succeeding

Notes

1. Iris Varner and Linda Beamer

Iris Varner and Linda Beamer are co-authors of *Intercultural Communication in the Global Workplace* (Irwin/McGraw-Hill: 1995; McGraw-Hill, 2005), a book used worldwide, and a book from which the present selection is taken. Both have been university teachers, giving lectures in many countries, and receiving many honours. The present selection, according to Dr. Varner, is "based on a true story mixed with elements from other events."

2. red-carpet treatment

In Western culture, a red carpet is always rolled out for dignitaries and celebrities to walk on. The phrase "red carpet treatment" is used to mean "special V.I.P. treatment, or special treatment with great fanfare."

Comprehension

1. With whom had the Chinese wallpaper production company formed a relationship before they met Burton and Raines?
2. Did the two Canadians expect to spend so much time eating, resting, and sightseeing? What had they expected to do while in China?

3. Why did the Chinese spend a long time discussing the technical specifications of the equipment?
4. Why was maintenance training difficult for the Canadians to provide? How did their refusal to provide help strike the Chinese?
5. How did the Canadians respond to the price concessions the Chinese had asked for?
6. Why was the payment schedule a thorny problem for the Chinese?
7. What were the goals of the Chinese in the negotiations?
8. What changes occurred in the mood of the Canadians during the negotiations?
9. What might the factors be that determined the deal?
10. What role did culture play in framing the priorities of the negotiators?

Further Study

Search on the Internet and try to answer the questions below:
- What is culture?
- What situations can culture shock be applied to?

Unit 4

Impact of Change

Unit Goals

- ☞ To arouse students' awareness of the impact of change
- ☞ To read children's classics for enjoyment
- ☞ To discover stylistic features of children's classics
- ☞ To learn to use nominative absolute constructions

Before Reading

1. Search on the Internet or in the library for information about children's literature. Get some idea of children's classics and the stylistic features of this genre.
2. Recall what children's literature you have read and share your experience with others in the class. Tell why (or why not) you enjoyed reading them.
3. Find information about Kenneth Grahame[1], author of *The Wind in the Willows*[2], and the main idea of the book.

📖 A Glimpse into the Test

The Wind in the Willows (1908) is one of the most beloved of all children's novels in British literature. As well as being endearing, it has also been most enduring—having remained a popular bedtime read for English children for almost a century, and sharing a distinction with Winnie the Pooh of having been popularized in America as an animated movie by Walt Disney. However, there is more to The Wind in the Willows than mere childhood fiction. Its theme relates to the end of a romantic, agricultural period in Britain and to the impact of new technology on social relations of that period—in this case, the advent of the automobile and its impact on the social lives of the animals of River Bank.

Text A

The Open Road

Kenneth Grahame

They were strolling along the high road easily, the Mole by the horse's head, talking to him, since the horse had complained that he was being frightfully left

> frightfully /ˈfraɪtfəli/ *adv.* (old-fashioned, especially BrE) very, extremely

out of it, and nobody considered him in the least; the Toad and the Water Rat walking behind the cart talking together—at least Toad was talking, and Rat was saying at intervals, "Yes, precisely; and what did *you* say to *him*?"—and thinking all the time of something very different, when far behind them they heard a faint warning hum, like a drone of a distant bee. Glancing back, they saw a small cloud of dust, with a dark centre of energy, advancing on them at incredible speed, while from out the dust a faint "Poop-poop!" wailed like an uneasy animal in pain. Hardly regarding it, they turned to resume their conversation, when in an instant (as it seemed) the peaceful scene was changed, and with a blast of wind and a whirl of sound that made them jump for the nearest ditch, it was on them! The "Poop-poop" rang with a brazen shout in their ears, they had a moment's glimpse of an interior of glittering plate-glass and rich morocco, and the magnificent motor-car, immense, breath-snatching, passionate, with its pilot tense and hugging his wheel, possessed all earth and air for the fraction of a second, flung an enveloping cloud of dust that blinded and enwrapped them utterly, and then dwindled to a speck in the far distance, changed back into a droning bee once more.

  The old grey horse, dreaming, as he plodded along, of his quiet paddock, in a new raw situation such as this simply abandoned himself to his natural emotions. Rearing, plunging, backing steadily, in spite of all the Mole's efforts at his head, and all the Mole's lively language directed at his better feelings, he drove the cart backwards towards the deep ditch at the side of the road. It wavered an instant—then there was a heart-rending crash—and the canary-coloured cart, their pride and their joy, lay on its side in the ditch, an irredeemable wreck.

  The Rat danced up and down in the road, simply transported with passion. "You villains!" he shouted, shaking both fists. "You scoundrels, you highwaymen, you—you—road-hogs!—I'll have the law on you! I'll report you! I'll take you through all the Courts!" His home-sickness had quite slipped away from him, and for the moment he was the skipper of the canary-coloured vessel driven on a shoal by the reckless jockeying of rival mariners, and he was trying to recollect all the fine and biting things he used to say to masters of steam-launches when their wash, as they drove too near the bank, used to flood his

---

drone /drəʊn/ *n.* a continuous low noise

brazen /ˈbreɪzən/ *adj.* sounding harsh and loud like struck brass

morocco /məˈrɒkəʊ/ *n.* [U] fine soft leather made from the skin of a goat, used especially for making shoes and covering books

speck /spek/ *n.* a very small spot; a small piece of dirt, etc.

plod /plɒd/ *v.* to walk slowly with heavy steps, especially when tired

paddock /ˈpædək/ *n.* a small field in which horses are kept

heart-rending /ˈhɑːtˌrendɪŋ/ *adj.* (usually before noun) causing feelings of great sadness

canary-colored /kəˈneəriˌkʌləd/ *adj.* greenish to moderate yellow

irredeemable /ˌɪrɪˈdiːməb/ *adj.* (formal) too bad to be corrected, improved or saved

transport /trænsˈpɔːt/ *v.* to carry away with strong and often intensely pleasant emotion

road-hog /ˈrəʊdhɒɡ/ *n.* (informal, disapproving) a person who drives in a dangerous way without thinking about the safety of other road users

skipper /ˈskɪpə/ *n.* the captain of a small ship or fishing boat

shoal /ʃəʊl/ *n.* a small hill of sand just below the surface of the sea

reckless /ˈrekləs/ *adj.* showing a lack of care about danger and the possible results of your actions

jockey /ˈdʒɒki/ *v.* ~ **(for sth.)** to try all possible ways of gaining an advantage over other people

mariner /ˈmærɪnə/ *n.* (old-fashioned or literary) a sailor

parlour carpet at home.

Toad sat straight down in the middle of the dusty road, his legs stretched out before him, and stared fixedly in the direction of the disappearing motor-car. He breathed short, his face wore a placid, satisfied expression, and at intervals he faintly murmured "Poop-poop!"

The Mole was busy trying to quiet the horse, which he succeeded in doing after a time. Then he went to look at the cart, on its side in the ditch. It was indeed a sorry sight. Panels and windows smashed, axles hopelessly bent, one wheel off, sardine-tins scattered over the wide world, and the bird in the bird-cage sobbing pitifully and calling to be let out.

The Rat came to help him, but their united efforts were not sufficient to right the cart. "Hi, Toad!" they cried. "Come and bear a hand, can't you!"

The Toad never answered a word, or budged from his seat in the road; so they went to see what was the matter with him. They found him in a sort of trance, a happy smile on his face, his eyes still fixed on the dusty wake of their destroyer. At intervals he was still heard to murmur "Poop-poop!"

The Rat shook him by the shoulder. "Are you coming to help us, Toad?" he demanded sternly.

"Glorious, stirring sight!" murmured Toad, never offering to move. "The poetry of motion! The *real* way to travel! The *only* way to travel! Here to-day—in next week tomorrow! Villages skipped, towns and cities jumped—always somebody else's horizon! O bliss! O poop-poop! O my! O my!"

"O stop being an ass, Toad!" cried the Mole despairingly.

"And to think I never *knew*!" went on the Toad in a dreamy monotone. "All those wasted years that lie behind me, I never knew, never even *dreamt*! But now—but now that I know, now that I fully realize! O what a flowery track lies spread before me, henceforth! What dust-clouds shall spring up behind me as I speed on my reckless way! What carts I shall fling carelessly into the ditch in the wake of my magnificent onset! Horrid little carts—common carts—canary-coloured carts!"

"What are we to do with him?" asked the Mole of the Water Rat.

"Nothing at all," replied the Rat firmly. "Because there is really nothing to be done. You see, I know him from old. He is now possessed. He has got a new craze, and it always takes him that way, in its first stage. He'll continue like that for days now, like an animal walking in a happy dream, quite useless for all practical purposes. Never mind him. Let's go and see what there is to be done about the cart."

A careful inspection showed them that, even if they succeeded in righting it by themselves, the cart would travel no longer. The axles were in a hopeless state, and the missing wheel was shattered into pieces.

The Rat knotted the horse's reins over his back and took him by the head, carrying the bird-cage and its hysterical occupant in the other hand. "Come on!" he said grimly to the Mole. "It's five or six miles to the

---

parlour /ˈpɑːlə/ *adj.* used or suitable for a parlor

sardine /sɑːˈdiːn/ *n.* a small young sea fish (for example, a young pilchard) that is either eaten fresh or preserved in tins/cans

budge /bʌdʒ/ *v.* (usually in negative sentences) to move slightly; to make sth./sb. move slightly

trance /trɑːns/ *n.* a state in which you are thinking so much about sth. that you do not notice what is happening around you

despairing /dɪsˈpeərɪŋ/ *adj.* showing or feeling the loss of all hope

onset /ˈɒnset/ *n.* the beginning of sth., especially sth. unpleasant

knot /nɒt/ *n.* a joint made by tying together two pieces or ends of string, rope, etc. *v.* to fasten sth. with a knot or knots

nearest town, and we shall just have to walk it. The sooner we make a start the better."

"But what about Toad?" asked the Mole anxiously, as they set off together. "We can't leave him here, sitting in the middle of the road by himself, in the distracted state he's in! It's not safe. Supposing another Thing were to come along?"

"O, *bother* Toad," said the Rat savagely; "I've done with him!"

They had not proceeded very far on their way, however, when there was a pattering of feet behind them, and Toad caught them up and thrust a paw inside the elbow of each of them, still breathing short and staring into vacancy.

"Now, look here, Toad!" said the Rat sharply, "as soon as we get to the town, you'll have to go straight to the police-station, and see if they know anything about that motor-car and who it belongs to, and lodge a complaint against it. And then you'll have to go to a blacksmith's or a wheelwright's and arrange for the cart to be fetched and mended and put to rights. It'll take time, but it's not quite a hopeless smash. Meanwhile, the Mole and I will go to an inn and find comfortable rooms where we can stay till the cart's ready, and till your nerves have recovered their shock."

"Police-station! Complaint!" murmured Toad dreamily. "Me *complain* of that beautiful, that heavenly vision that has been vouchsafed me! *Mend* the *cart*! I've done with carts for ever. I never want to see the cart, or to hear of it, again. O, Ratty! You can't think how obliged I am to you for consenting to come on this trip! I wouldn't have gone without you, and then I might never have seen that—that swan, that sunbeam, that thunderbolt! I might never have heard that entrancing sound, or smelt that bewitching smell! I owe it all to you, my best of friends!"

The Rat turned from him in despair. "You see what it is?" he said to the Mole, addressing him across Toad's head. "He's quite hopeless. I give it up—when we get to the town we'll go to the railway station, and with luck we may pick up a train there that'll get us back to River Bank tonight. And if ever you catch me going a-pleasuring with this provoking animal again!" He snorted, and during the rest of that weary trudge addressed his remarks exclusively to Mole.

On reaching the town they went straight to the station and deposited Toad in the second-class waiting-room, giving a porter two-pence to keep a strict eye on him. They then left the horse at an inn stable, and gave what directions they could about the cart and its contents. Eventually, a slow train having landed them at a station not very far from Toad Hall, they escorted the spell-bound, sleep-walking Toad to his door, put him inside it, and instructed his housekeeper to feed him, undress him, and put him to bed. Then they got out their boat from the boat-house, sculled down the river home, and at a very late hour sat down to supper in their own cozy riverside parlour, to the Rat's great joy and contentment.

The following evening the Mole, who had risen late and taken things very easy all day, was sitting on the bank fishing, when the Rat, who had been looking up his friends and gossiping, came strolling along to find him. "Heard the news?" he said. "There's nothing else being talked about, all along the river bank. Toad went up to

---

vouchsafe /vaʊtʃˈseɪf/ *v.* ~ **sth. (to sb.)** (old-fashioned or formal) to give, offer or tell sth. to sb., especially as a privilege

entrancing /enˈtrɑːnsɪŋ/ *adj.* someone or something that is entrancing is so beautiful or impressive that you give them all your attention

bewitching /bɪˈwɪtʃɪŋ/ *adj.* (written) so beautiful or interesting that you cannot think about anything else

scull /skʌl/ *n.* one of a pair of small oars used by a single person rowing a boat, one in each hand
v. to row a boat using sculls

Town by an early train this morning. And he has ordered a large and very expensive motor-car."

More about the Text

1. Kenneth Grahame

Kenneth Grahame (1859—1932) was born in Edinburgh, and after school in Oxford entered the Bank of England, where he became Secretary in 1898. As a young man he contributed to "The Yellow Book" and was encouraged by Editor W. E. Hensley, who published many of the essays which later appeared in *Pagan Papers* in 1893. He later published *The Golden Age* (1895) and its continuation, *Dream Days* (1898). The sharp, authentic visions of childhood, and the shrewd observation of the child narrator, were widely praised.

2. The Wind in the Willows

The Wind in the Willows, based largely on bedtime stories and letters to his son, was never intended by Grahame to become published. The manuscript was given reluctantly to an importunate American publisher, who then rejected it. Published in England in 1908, its reception was muted, and it was not for some years that the story of the Rat, Mole, Badger, and Toad, and their life by the river, became established as a children's classic. The book was dramatized in 1929, and has been performed widely since.

Check Your Understanding

1. What is the "poop-poop" sound that the characters hear?
2. How do you understand the sentence "…for the moment he was the skipper of the canary-coloured vessel driven on a shoal by the reckless jockeying of rival mariners, and he was trying to recollect all the fine and biting things he used to say to masters of steam-launches when their wash, as they drove too near the bank, used to flood his parlour carpet at home."?
3. Paraphrase the exclamation "The poetry of motion!".
4. How do you understand the statement by Toad: "Here to-day—in next week tomorrow! Villages skipped, towns and cities jumped—always somebody else's horizon!"?
5. "And to think I never knew," says Toad in a dreamy monotone. What is it that Toad never knew?
6. Why do you suppose that Rat and Mole deposited Toad in the "second-class waiting-room," not in first-class?
7. What do you think will happen next?
8. What literary genre would you classify the present story? How is this different from fables, fairy tales or fantasy fiction?
9. Did you enjoy reading the story? What do you like the best about it?
10. Is there a theme in the story?

Paraphrasing

1. ...and the magnificent motor-car, immense, breath-snatching, passionate, with its pilot tense and hugging his wheel, possessed all earth and air for the fraction of a second....
2. The old grey horse, dreaming, as he plodded along, of his quiet paddock, in a new raw situation such as this simply abandoned himself to his natural emotions.
3. Here to-day—in next week tomorrow! Villages skipped, towns and cities jumped—always somebody else's horizon! "O bliss! O poop-poop! O my! O my!"
4. "O, bother Toad," said the Rat savagely; "I've done with him!"

Some Information about English Style

1. Animal characters in children's literature

Employing animal characters is a major feature of children's literature. In ***The Wind in the Willows***, Grahame presents a wonderful constellation of animal characters, with the Toad in the centre.

The episode of the sudden appearance of the motor-car, as described in the above selection, is a sketch of fascinating personalities. Look at how the animal characters react to this single incident:

- *The Rat danced up and down in the road, simply transported with passion. "You villains!" he shouted, shaking both fists. "You scoundrels, you highwaymen, you—you—road-hogs!—I'll have the law on you! I'll report you! I'll take you through all the Courts!"*
- *Toad sat straight down in the middle of the dusty road, his legs stretched out before him, and stared fixedly in the direction of the disappearing motor-car. He breathed short, his face wore a placid, satisfied expression, and at intervals he faintly murmured "Poop-poop!"*
- *The Mole was busy trying to quiet the horse, which he succeeded in doing after a time. Then he went to look at the cart, on its side in the ditch.*
- *The Rat came to help him, but their united efforts were not sufficient to right the cart. "Hi, Toad!" they cried. "Come and bear a hand, can't you!"*

Instead of using evaluative adjectives such as "dreamy" for Toad, or "stern" for Rat, or "mild and considerate" for Mole, the author simply dramatizes the characters.

Read the story carefully and summarize each character's personality.

2. Use of verbal nominative absolute constructions

Look at these two sentences from the text:

- It was indeed a sorry sight. *Panels and windows smashed, axles hopelessly bent, one wheel off, sardine-tins scattered over the wide world, and the bird in the bird-cage sobbing pitifully and calling to be let out.*
- They found him in a sort of trance, *a happy smile on his face, his eyes still fixed on the dusty wake of their destroyer.*

The italicized parts illustrate the usage of verbal nominative absolute constructions, which is a feature of written English, often employed in formal descriptions.

Do you see any rules in such constructions? What comments can you make on the stylistic effect of such grammatical structures?

Practice

Building word power

Fill in each blank with the proper form of the correct word from each set of the words below.

A. **gaze glance glare peer stare**
   (1) On the bus I always manage to _____ at the headlines in the newspaper.
   (2) Children should be taught not to _____ at handicapped people.
   (3) Near-sighted people often _____ at you when they are not wearing their glasses.
   (4) He _____ surreptitiously into his wallet to see if he had enough money to pay the bill.
   (5) The people stood _____ at the beautiful picture.
   (6) He _____ at her, fascinated.
   (7) He _____ at the envelope and recognized his uncle's handwriting.
   (8) The men who were fighting _____ at each other.
   (9) The angry father _____ at his son.
   (10) The high-school boys gather on the corner to _____ at the passing girls.

B. **weep cry sob wail**
   (1) She _____ copiously over the death of her dog.
   (2) Charles _____ for his mother to stay with him.
   (3) The child _____ himself to sleep.
   (4) The play ends with the heroine _____ desperately as her lover resolutely walks away.
   (5) The child was _____ loudly that she had hurt her foot.
   (6) "She's taken my apple, mummy," he _____ mournfully.

C. **charming bewitching enchanting entrancing fascinating**
   (1) Against his will, he found himself caught up again and again in the life of this most _____ of people.
   (2) For her all simplicity, he considered the girl next door _____.
   (3) Jim has developed a _____ personality.
   (4) The young man stared back at every _____ smile she gave him.
   (5) I have long thought of it as the most _____ village in England.
   (6) The book is so _____ that I can't put it down.
   (7) Yesterday evening the famous dancer gave a _____ performance.

D. **remember recollect recall memorize**
   (1) He caught himself _____ how his first wife would have cooked the same meal.
   (2) He _____ his last evening with his fiancée whenever he felt depressed.
   (3) He settled back with great relish and began to _____ those battles in the war that he had witnessed at first hand.
   (4) Those famous actors were good at quickly _____ their parts.
   (5) If you _____ a poem, you can say it without looking at a book.
   (6) In his closing speech to the jury, the Crown prosecutor _____ the mass of

incriminating evidence he had developed during the trial.
(7) I can still _____ every detail in my old dormitory room at school.
(8) I am trying to _____ a forgotten address.

Grammar and Usage

1. Fill in each blank with a suitable preposition. Do not look at the text until you have finished the exercise.

They were strolling ___(1)___ the high road easily, the Mole ___(2)___ the horse's head, talking to him, since the horse had complained that he was being frightfully left ___(3)___ ___(4)___ it, and nobody considered him ___(5)___ the least; the Toad and the Water Rat walking behind the cart talking together— ___(6)___ least Toad was talking, and Rat was saying ___(7)___ intervals, when far ___(8)___ them they heard a faint warning hum, like a drone of a distant bee. Glancing back, they saw a small cloud of dust, with a dark centre of energy, advancing on them ___(9)___ incredible speed, while ___(10)___ ___(11)___ the dust a faint "Poop-poop!" wailed like an uneasy animal ___(12)___ pain. Hardly regarding it, they turned to resume their conversation, when ___(13)___ an instant (as it seemed) the peaceful scene was changed, and with a blast of wind and a whirl of sound that made them jump ___(14)___ the nearest ditch, it was ___(15)___ them!

2. Translate the following sentences by using the given words or expressions from the text.

(1) 迷途的孩子陷入了绝望。(abandon oneself)
(2) 听到这一消息他怒不可遏。(be transported with)
(3) 锁匙转了一下,门却一动也不动。(budge)
(4) 一个疯狂的念头缠住了他。(possess)
(5) 工人们向总经理提出额外增加工资的要求。(lodge)
(6) 那单调的声音总是停一阵子,然后又响起。(at intervals)
(7) "你的意思是说他把钱据为己有了?""对极了。"(precisely)
(8) 如蒙惠许,不胜荣幸。(vouchsafe)

Improving your writing style

1. Rewrite the following sentences by using verbal nominative absolute constructions.

(1) The room was in chaos. Empty soda bottles and beer cans were everywhere. Soiled clothes were strewn on the floor and cosmetics were scattered over the dresser.
(2) Mrs. Kennedy walked by the coffin. Her hand was on it. Her head was down. Her hat was gone, and her dress and stockings were spattered. (Tom Wicker "The Assassination")
(3) He sat in the front row. His mouth was half open. His head was thrust forward so as not to miss any word.
(4) The fall came early that year. The trees turned bare overnight. Their yellow leaves were scattered by the winds.

2. **Translate the following sentences by using verbal nominative absolute constructions**

(1) 他脸朝天头枕着手躺着。
(2) 汤姆走了进来,眼睛微微有些肿,耳朵都冻红了。
(3) 老头坐了下来,由于痛苦脸色发白,两颊上还带有泪痕。
(4) 他骑着马向前驰去,他的狗叫着跟在后面跑。
(5) 她不声不响地坐着,两眼盯着地板。
(6) 她转身走了,我们像往常一样,跟在后面。

Writing task

Describe an experience of coping with a personal or social change, either successfully or unsuccessfully.

Text B

On Going Home
Joan Didion[1]

Joan Didion has been appropriately described as the quintessential Californian essayist. Her family background, prosperously rooted in the pioneering history of that state, has provided her easy access to
5 all subjects Californian—from politicians to rock stars, from freeways to waterways—all of which she writes about with distinctive prose that seems to spring from California itself. In this essay, she opens a door onto her own family, thereby revealing her mixed feelings
10 for home.

I am home for my daughter's first birthday. By "home" I do not mean the house in Los Angeles where my husband and I and the baby live, but the place where my family is, in the Central Valley of California. It is a vital although troublesome distinction. My husband
15 likes my family but is uneasy in their house, because once there I fall into their ways, which are difficult, oblique, deliberately inarticulate, not my husband's ways. We live in dusty houses ("D-U-S-T,", he once wrote with his finger on surfaces all over the house, but no one noticed it) filled with mementos quite without value to him (what could the Canton dessert plates[2] mean
20 to him? How could he have known about the assay scales,[3] why should he care if he did know?), and we appear to talk exclusively about people we know who have been committed to mental hospitals, about people we know who have been
25 booked on drunk-driving charges, and about

oblique /əˈbliːk/ *adj.* not preserved or done in a direct way
inarticulate /ˌɑːrˈtɪkjʊlɪt/ *adj.* (of speech) not using clear words; not expressed clearly
memento /mɪˈmentəʊ/ *n.* (pl. -os) a thing that you keep or give to sb. to remind you or them of a person or place
book /bʊk/ *v.* to enter charges against in a police register

property, particularly about property, land, price per acre and C-2 zoning[4] and assessments and freeway access. My brother does not understand my husband's inability to perceive the advantage in the rather common real-estate transaction known as "sale-leaseback,"[5] and my husband in turn does not understand that when we talk about sale-leasebacks and right-of-way condemnations we are talking in code about things we like best, the yellow fields and the cottonwoods and the rivers rising and falling and the mountain roads closing when the heavy snow comes in. We miss each other's points, have another drink and regard the fire. My brother refers to my husband, in his presence, as "Joan's husband." Marriage is the classic betrayal.

Or perhaps it is not any more. Sometimes I think that those of us who are now in our thirties were born into the last generation to carry the burden of "home," to find in family life the source of all tension and drama. I had by all objective accounts a "normal" and a "happy" family situation, and yet I was almost thirty years old before I could talk to my family on the telephone without crying after I had hung up. We did not fight, nothing was wrong, and yet some nameless anxiety colored the emotional charges between me and the place that I came from. The question of whether or not you could go home again[6] was a very real part of the sentimental and largely literary baggage with which we left home in the fifties; I suspect that it is irrelevant to the children born of the fragmentation after World War II. A few weeks ago in a San Francisco bar I saw a pretty young girl on crystal[7] take off her clothes and dance for the cash prize in an "amateur-topless" contest. There was no particular sense of moment about this, none of the effect of romantic degradation, of "dark journey," for which my generation strived so assiduously. What sense could that girl possibly make of, say, Long Day's Journey into Night?[8] Who is beside the point?

That I am trapped in this particular irrelevancy is never more apparent to me than when I am home. Paralyzed by the neurotic lassitude engendered by meeting one's past at every turn, around every corner, inside every cupboard, I go aimlessly from room to room. I decide to meet it head-on and clean out a drawer, and I spread the contents on the bed. A bathing unit I wore the summer I was seventeen. A letter of rejection from *The Nation*.[9] An aerial photograph of the site for a shopping center my father did not build in 1954. Three teacups hand-painted with cabbage roses[10] and signed "E.M.," my grandmother's initials. There is no final solution for letters of rejection from the Nation and teacups hand-painted in 1900. Nor is there any answer to snapshots of one's grandfather as a young man on skis, surveying around Donner Pass[11] in the year 1910. I smooth out the snapshot and look into his face, and do and do not see my own. I close the drawer and have another cup of coffee with my mother. We get along very well, veterans of guerrilla war we never understood.

Days pass. I see no one. I come to dread my husband's evening call, not only because he is full of news of what by now seems to me our remote life in Los Angeles, people he has seen, letters which require attention,

by all accounts according to what other people say
topless /ˈtɒplɪs/ adj. wearing no clothing on the upper body
assiduous /əˈsɪdjuəs/ adj. (formal) working very hard and taking great care that everything is done as well as it can be
assiduously /əˈsɪdjuəsli/ adv.
lassitude /ˈlæsɪtjuːd/ n. [U] (formal) a state of feeling very tired in mind or body; lack of energy
engender /ɪnˈdʒendə/ v. (formal) to make a feeling or situation exist
ski /skiː/ n. (pl. **skis**) one of a pair of long narrow pieces of wood, metal or plastic that you attach to boots so that you can move smoothly over snow
veteran /ˈvetərən/ n. a person who has a lot of experience in a particular area or activity

but because he asks what I have been doing, suggests uneasily that I get out, drive to San Francisco or Berkeley. Instead I drive across the river to a family graveyard. It has been vandalized since my last visit and the monuments are broken, overturned in the dry grass. Because I once saw a rattlesnake in the grass I stay in the car and listen to a Country-and-Western station. Later I drive with my father to a ranch he has in the foothills. The man who runs his cattle on it asks us to the round-up, a week from Sunday, and although I know that I will be in Los Angeles I say in the oblique way my family talks, that I will come. Once home I mention the broken monuments in the graveyard. My mother shrugs.

> **vandalize** /'vændəlaɪz/ v. [usually passive] to damage sth., especially public property, deliberately and for no good reason
> **round-up** /'raʊnd-ʌp/ n. an act of bringing people or animals together in one place for a particular purpose
> **mote** /məʊt/ n. (old-fashioned) a very small piece of dust
> **shaft** /ʃɑːft/ n. (literary) a narrow beam of light
> **slat** /slæt/ n. one of series of thin flat pieces of wood, metal or plastic, used in furniture, fences, etc.
> **ambush** /'æmbʊʃ/ n. [C,U] the act of hiding and waiting for sb. and then making a surprise attack on them

I go to visit my great-aunts. A few of them think now that I am my cousin, or their daughter who died young. We recall an anecdote about a relative last seen in 1948, and they ask if I still like living in New York City. I have lived in Los Angeles for three years, but I say that I do. The baby is offered a horehound[12] drop, and I am slipped a dollar bill "to buy a treat." Questions trail off, answers are abandoned, the baby plays with the dust motes in a shaft of afternoon sun.

It is time for the baby's birthday party: a white cake, strawberry-marshmallow ice cream, a bottle of champagne saved from another party. In the evening, after she has gone to sleep, I kneel beside the crib and touch her face, where it is pressed against the slats with mine. She is an open and trusting child, unprepared for and unaccustomed to the ambushes of family life, and perhaps it is just as well that I can offer her little of that life. I would like to give her more. I would like to promise her that she will grow up with a sense of her cousins and of rivers and of her great-grandmother's teacups, would like to pledge her a picnic on a river with fried chicken and her hair uncombed, would like to give her *home* for her birthday, but we live differently now and I can promise her nothing like that. I give her a xylophone[13] and a sundress from Madeira and promise to tell her a funny story.

Notes

1. Joan Didion

Joan Didion (1934—) was born in Sacramento and raised in the great central plain of California, an area she often describes nostalgically in her work. As an undergraduate English major at the University of California, Berkeley, she won an essay prize sponsored by *Vogue* magazine. As a result, *Vogue* hired her, and for eight years she lived in New York City, while she rose to associate features editor. She published her first novel, *Run River*, in 1963 and in the same year, married the writer John Gregory Dunne. In 1964 the couple returned to California, where they

remained for twenty-five years.

Although Didion wrote four more novels, her reputation rests on her essays collected as *Slouching toward Bethlehem* (1968) and *The White Album* (1979). In addition to her work as a columnist, essayist, and fiction writer, she has collaborated with her husband on a number of screenplays. She has focused her trenchant powers of observation in two documentary, book-length studies: *Salvador* (1983) and *Miami* (1987). Her most recent book is her memoir *The Year of Magical Thinking*, which is about grieving for her husband who died suddenly at the end of 2003.

2. Canton dessert plates

Canton dessert plates refer to ceramic ware exported from China especially during the 18th and 19th centuries by way of Canton.

3. assay scale

It is a device bearing ordered wacks at fixed intervals for the analysis of a substance subject to conditions not imposed on similarly zoned land.

4. C-2 zoning

C-2 zoning refers to conditional zoning for neighborhood business such as small markets and other shops.

5. sale-leaseback

It refers to the leasing of property by the new owner back to the previous owner.

6. whether or not you could go home again

Make reference to a novel by Thomas Wolfe (1900—1938) entitled *You Can't Go Home Again*.

You Can't Go Home Again was the last novel Thomas Wolfe finished before his untimely death at age 37. George Webber, the protagonist, has written a successful novel about corruption, petty politics and racism in his hometown in North Carolina. When he returns to that town he is shaken by the force of the outrage and hatred that greets him. Family and friends feel naked and exposed by the truths they have seen in his book, and their fury drives him from his home. He begins a search for his own identity that takes him to New York and a hectic social whirl; to Paris with an uninhibited group of expatriates; to Berlin, lying cold and sinister under Hitler's shadow. Finally Webber returns to America. The book ends with an open letter to his best friend, where the protagonist pours his heart, a kin to a suicide note.

7. crystal

It is an illegal methamphetamine.

8. Long Day's Journey into Night

It is the autobiographical play by Eugene O'Neil about the conflicts and loves within his family.

9. The Nation

American weekly journal of opinion, the oldest such continuously published periodical still extant. It is generally considered the leading liberal magazine of its king. It was founded in 1865 by Edwin L. Godkin at the urging of Frederick Law Olmsted.

10. cabbage rose

This is a prickly shrub, having large, fragrant, double-petaled pink flowers.

11. Donner Pass

It is a pass, 2,162.1 m (7,089 ft) high, in the Sierra Nevada of eastern California near Lake Tahoe. It is named after the Donner Party of westward migrants whose survivors supposedly practiced cannibalism after being trapped in a snowstorm near here in October 1846. The reason why Didion's grandfather surveyed around Donner Pass is probably that Didion's great-great-grandmother had been one of the original eighty-seven members of the Donner party that had set out from Illinois for California in 1846.

12. horehound

This is an aromalic plant, also called hoar hound.

13. xylophone

Xylophone is a musical instrument made of two rows of wooden bars of different lengths that you hit with two small sticks.

Comprehension

1. How does the author's extended family differ in character from her nuclear family? Why do you suppose this is so?
2. In the first paragraph which sentence do you think is the most important? Why?
3. What does the word "it" in the first sentence of the second paragraph refer to?
4. What is Didion's evidence for thinking, sometimes at least, that her generation is the last "to find in family life the source of all tension and drama?"
5. From the context of the article, how would you define the expression "romantic degradation?" Do you think that opportunities to see oneself as mired in "romantic degradation" no longer exist for the young?
6. What does the last sentence of the second paragraph mean?
7. What does the author mean by the description of her and her mother as "veterans of a guerilla war?" Where else does she pick up that figure of speech?
8. Explain the symbolism of the baby playing with dust motes in Paragraph Five.
9. How do the details in the last line, describing what she gives her daughter for her birthday, underline the differences between her original home and her present one?
10. What does the original home mean to the author?

Further Study

Some more Books to Read

- *Alice's Adventures in Wonderland* by Lewis Carroll
- *Gulliver's Travels* by Jonathan Swift
- *The Adventures of Huckleberry Finn* by Mark Twain

Some More Ariticles to Read

- "Technology's Impact" by Richard J. Coley
- "The Internet Transforms Modern Life" by Steve Almasy
- "The 50 Biggest Changes in the Last 50 Years" by John Steele Gordon

Unit 5

Humor and Irony

Unit Goals

- To read humorous fiction for experience and literary appreciation
- To discuss how irony leads to humor
- To describe scenes and actions in vivid specific language

Before Reading

1. Search on the Internet or in the library for brief biographical information about James Thurber, his style and his most famous works.
2. Have you ever heard of or read about any ghost stories? What do you think of their authenticity? How do you comprehend such supernatural events, which seem to go beyond one's logical comprehension?

A Glimpse into the Text

"The Night the Ghost Got In" is a prime example of the storytelling technique of James Thurber, who is widely considered one of the greatest humor writers that America has ever produced. It was published in his 1933 book, *My Life and Hard Times*, a fictionalized account of his childhood in Columbus, Ohio. Like most of Thurber's best works, the story combines events that are plausible with comic exaggeration, and adds responses that range from hyperbole to deadpan. The characters' inappropriate understanding of their world serves the dual purposes of amusing us while revealing the uneven balances of the human mind.

Text A

The Night the Ghost Got In

James Thurber[1]
(Abridged and Edited)

The ghost that got into our house on the night of November 17, 1915 raised such a hullabaloo of misunderstandings that I am sorry I didn't just let it

> hullabaloo /ˌhʌləbəˈluː/ n. [sing.] a lot of loud noise, especially made by people who are annoyed or excited about sth.

keep on walking, and go to bed. Its advent caused my mother to throw a shoe through a window of the house next door and ended up with my grandfather shooting a patrolman. I am sorry, therefore, as I have said, that I ever paid any attention to the footsteps.

They began about a quarter past one o'clock in the morning, a rhythmic, quick-cadenced walking around the dining-room table. My mother was asleep in one room upstairs, my brother Herman in another; and grandfather in the attic. I had just stepped out of the bathtub and was rubbing myself with a towel when I heard the steps. They were walking rapidly around the dining-room table downstairs. I supposed at first it was my father or my brother Roy, who had gone to Indianapolis but were expected home at any time. I suspected next it was a burglar. It did not enter my mind until later that it was a ghost.

After the walking had gone on for perhaps three minutes, I tiptoed to Herman's room. "Psst!" I hissed, shaking him. "Awp," he said, in the low, hopeless tone of a despondent beagle. "There's something downstairs!" I said. He got up and followed me to the head of the staircase. We listened together. There was no sound. The steps had ceased. Herman looked at me in some alarm: I had only the bath towel around my waist. He wanted me to go back to bed, but I gripped his arm. "There's something down there!" I said. Instantly the steps began again, circling the dining-room table and then started up the stairs toward us, heavily, two at a time. We saw nothing coming; we only heard the steps. Herman rushed to his room and slammed the door. I slammed shut the door at the stairs top and held my knee against it. After a long minute, I slowly opened it again. There was nothing there. There was no sound. None of us ever heard the ghost again.

The slamming of the doors aroused mother: she peered out of her room. "What on earth are you boys doing?" she demanded. Herman ventured out of his room. "Nothing," he said, gruffly, but he was a light green in color. "What was all that running around downstairs?" said mother. So she had heard the steps too! We just looked at her. "Burglars!" she shouted intuitively. I tried to quiet her by starting lightly downstairs.

"Come on, Herman," I said.

"I'll stay with mother," he said. "She's all excited."

"Don't either of you go a step," said mother. "We'll call the police." Since the phone was downstairs, I didn't see how we were going to call the police, but mother made one of her quick, incomparable decisions. She flung up her bedroom window, which faced the bedroom window of a neighbor, picked up a shoe, and whammed it through a pane of glass

patrolman /pəˈtrəʊlmən/ n. (in the US) a police officer who walks or drives around an area to make sure that there is no trouble or crime

cadence /ˈkeɪdəns/ n. (formal) the rise and fall of the voice in speaking

hiss /hɪs/ v. to say sth. in a quiet angry voice

beagle /ˈbiːɡl/ n. a small dog with short legs, used in hunting

venture /ˈventʃə/ v. [V+adv./prep.] to go somewhere even though you know that it might be dangerous or unpleasant

gruff /ɡrʌf/ adj. (of a voice) deep and harsh, and often sounding unfriendly

fling /flɪŋ/ v. (flung, flung) [VN+adv./prep.] to throw sb./sth. somewhere with force, especially because you are angry

wham /wæm/ v. (informal) strike (sth./sb.) violently; move (sth.) quickly, noisily or forcefully

n. (informal) exclamation used to represent the sound of a sudden, loud hit

across the narrow space separating the two houses. Glass tinkled into the bedroom occupied by a retired engraver named Bodwell.

It was now about two o'clock of a moonless night. Bodwell was at the window in a minute, shouting, frothing a little, shaking his fist. "Burglars!" mother shouted at Bodwell. "Burglars in the house!" Herman and I hadn't dared tell her that it was not burglars but ghosts, for she was even more afraid of ghosts than of burglars. Bodwell first thought she meant there were burglars in his house, but finally quieted down and called the police for us over an extension phone by his bed. After he had disappeared from the window, mother suddenly made as if to throw another shoe, not because there was further need of it but, as she later explained, because the thrill of heaving a shoe through a window glass had enormously taken her fancy[2]. I prevented her.

The police were on hand in a commendably short time: a Ford sedan full of them, two on motorcycles, a patrol wagon with about eight in it and a few reporters. They began banging at our front door. "Open up!" cried a hoarse voice. "We're men from Headquarters!" I wanted to go down and let them in, but mother wouldn't hear of it[3]. Finally the cops put their shoulders to our big heavy front door with its thick beveled glass and broke it in: I could hear a rending of wood and a splash of glass on the floor of the hall. Their flashlights played[4] all over the living room, stabbed into hallways, shot up the front stairs, and finally up the back. They caught me standing in my towel at the top. A heavy policeman bounded up[5] the steps. "Who are you?" he demanded. "I live here," I said. "Well, whattsa matta, ya hot?"[6] he asked. It was, as a matter of fact, cold; I went to my room and pulled on some trousers. On my way out, a cop stuck a gun into my ribs. "Whatta you doin' here?" he demanded. "I live here," I said.

The officer in charge reported to mother. "No sign of nobody, lady," he said. "Musta got away—whatt'd he look like?"[7] "There were two or three of them," mother said, "whooping and carrying on and slamming doors."

Downstairs, we could hear the tramping of the other police. Police were all over the place. A half-dozen policemen emerged out of the darkness of the hallway upstairs. They began to ransack the floor: pulled beds away from walls, tore clothes off hooks in the closets, pulled suitcases and boxes off shelves. One of them found an old zither[8] that Roy had won in a pool tournament. "Looky here, Joe," he said, strumming it with a big paw. The cop named Joe took it and turned it over. "What is it?" he asked me. "It's an old zither our guinea pig[9] used to sleep on," I said. It was true that a pet guinea pig we once had would never sleep anywhere except on the zither, but I should never have said so. Joe and the other cop looked at me a long time. They put the zither back on a shelf.

---

froth /frɒθ/ v. to produce a lot of saliva (=liquid in your mouth); (figurative) very angry

heave /hiːv/ v. [+adv./prep.] to lift, pull or throw sb./sth. very heavy with one great effort

beveled /ˈbevəld/ adj. [usually before noun] having a sloping edge or surface whoop /huːp/ v. to shout loudly because you are happy or excited

tramp /træmp/ v. (also AmE informal tromp) to walk with heavy or noisy steps, especially for a long time

ransack /ˈrænsæk/ v. ~sth. (for sth.) to search a place, making it untidy and causing damage, usually because you are looking for sth.

pool /puːl/ n. a game for two people played with 16 coloured balls on a table, often in pubs and bars. Players use CUES (=long sticks) to try to hit the balls into pockets at the edge of the table

tournament /ˈtʊənəmənt/ n. a sports competition involving a number of teams or players who take part in different games and must leave the competition if they lose, only the winner left

strum /strʌm/ v. (–mm–) ~ (on) sth. to play a guitar or similar instrument by moving your fingers up and down across the strings

paw /pɔː/ n. (informal) a person's hand

"No sign o' nuthin'¹⁰," said the cop who had first spoken to mother. "This guy," he explained to the others, jerking a thumb at me "was nekked.¹¹ The lady seems historical.¹²" They all nodded, but said nothing; just looked at me. In the small silence we heard a creaking in the attic. Grandfather was turning over in bed. "What's 'at?"¹³ snapped Joe. Five or six cops sprang for the attic before I could intervene or explain. I realized that it would be bad if they burst in on grandfather unannounced, or even announced. He was going through a phase in which he believed that General Meade's men, under steady hammering by Stonewall Jackson, were beginning to retreat and even desert.

When I got to the attic, things were pretty confused. Grandfather had evidently jumped to the conclusion that the police were deserters from Meade's army, trying to hide in his attic. He bounded out of bed wearing a long flannel nightgown over long woolen underwear. The cops must have realized at once that the indignant white-haired old man belonged in the house, but they had no chance to say so. "Back, ye cowardly dogs!" roared grandfather. "Back t' the lines,¹⁴ ye goddam lily-livered cattle!" With that, he fetched the officer who found the zither a flat-handed smack alongside his head that sent him sprawling. The others beat a retreat, but not fast enough; grandfather grabbed Zither's gun from its holster and let fly. The report seemed to crack the rafters; smoke filled the attic. A cop cursed and shot his hand to his shoulder. Somehow, we all finally got downstairs again and locked the door against the old gentleman. He fired once or twice more in the darkness, then went back to bed. "That was grandfather," I explained to Joe, out of breath. "He thinks you're deserters." "I'll say he does," said Joe.

The cops were reluctant to leave without getting their hands on somebody besides grandfather; the night had been distinctly a defeat for them. A reporter, a thin-faced, wispy man, came up to me. I had put on one of mother's blouses, not being able to find anything else. The reporter looked at me with mingled suspicion and interest. "Just what the hell is the real lowdown here, Bud?" he asked. He gazed at me a long time as if I were a slot machine into which he had, without results, dropped a nickel. Then he walked away. The cops followed him, the one grandfather shot holding his now-bandaged arm, cursing and blaspheming. "I'm gonna get my gun back from that old bird," he said. "Yeh," said Joe. "You—and who else?" I told them I would bring it to the station house the next day.

"What was the matter with that policeman?" mother asked, after they had gone. "Grandfather shot him," I said. "What for?" she demanded. I told her he was a deserter. "Of all things!" said mother. "He was such a nice-looking young man."

Grandfather was fresh as a daisy and full of jokes at breakfast next morning. We thought at first he had forgotten all about what had happened, but he hadn't. Over his third cup of coffee, he glared at Herman and me. "What was the idee¹⁵ of all them cops tarryhootin' round the house last night?" he demanded. He had us there.

---

snap /snæp/ *v.* (**–pp–**) ~ (**at sb.**) to speak or say sth. in an impatient, usually angry, voice

lily-livered /ˈlɪliˌlɪvəd/ *adj.* (dated) cowardly

fetch sb. a blow/ clip (BrE informal) to hit someone

sprawl /sprɔːl/ *v.* to sit or lie with your arms and legs spread out in a relaxed or awkward way

beat a (hasty) retreat to go away or back quickly, especially to avoid sth. unpleasant

holster /ˈhəʊlstə/ *n.* a leather case worn on a belt or on a strap under the arm, used for carrying a small gun

rafter /ˈrɑːftə/ *n.* one of the sloping pieces of wood that support a roof

wispy /ˈwɪspɪ/ *adj.* consisting of small, thin pieces; not thick: a wispy beard

lowdown /ˈləʊdaʊn/ *n.* [*sing.*] ~ **on (sb./sth.)** (informal) the true facts about sb./sth., especially those considered most important to know

fresh as a daisy full of energy

More about the Text

1. James Thurber

James Grover, Thurber (1894—1961), born on December 8, 1894, in Columbus, Ohio, was American cartoonist and author. His writings, which range from gentle whimsy to irony, gained him a place as one of America's greatest 20th-century humorists. Thurber's cartoons, often depicting melancholy-looking animals or oversized wives bedeviling undersized husbands, are also much admired.

"The Night the Ghost Got In" was published in Thurber's 1933 book *My Life and Hard Times*, a fictionalized account of his childhood in Columbus, Ohio. According to Thurber's own account, the story is highly autobiographical. It is based on the night of Thurber's ghostly encounter which was exactly 47 years after the Ohio Lunatic Asylum was burned down (Note: The asylum fire was on November 17, 1868, and the setting of Thurber's ghost story is November 17, 1915). The Asylum covered several blocks of downtown Columbus, including the area where Thurber House now stands. Seven people died in the fire, and their spirits are said to be many of the ghosts around the area.

2. take / catch one's fancy

to attract or please sb.

3. not hear of sth.

(*Spoken*) to refuse to let sb. do sth., especially because you want to help them.

4. play

(of light /smile)(written) to move or appear quickly and lightly, often changing direction or shape

5. bound up / towards / across

to run with a lot of energy, because you are happy, excited, or frightened

6. "... whattsa matta, ya hot?"

"...what's the matter, are you hot?"

7. "No sign of nobody, lady," he said. "Musta got away—whatt'd he look like?"

To put it grammatically: "No sign of anybody, lady," he said. "Must have got away—what did he look like?"

8. zither

A musical instrument with a lot of metal strings stretched over a flat wooden box, an instrument played with fingers or a plectrum/pick.

9. guinea pig

A small animal with short ears and no tail, often kept as a pet.

10. nuthin

Nothing.

11. nekked

Naked.

12. historical

Hysterical. The policeman seems to have committed a malapropism in his confusion and disappointment with their fruitless search.

13. "'at"

"That".

14. "Back t' the lines ..."

"Back to the lines ..." Grandfather seemed to be delusional and took the policemen as deserters in the Civil War battlefield and in his indignation ordered them back to the front lines to continue the battle.

15. idee

Idea.

16. tarryhootin

Tearing about and hollering.

Check Your Understanding

1. What does the author mean by a "hullabaloo of misunderstandings?"
2. What can you surmise about the American family in 1915 considering that the author's grandfather slept in the attic of their house?
3. Who (or what) do you suppose was really running around the dining-room table of the house? Why do you think so?
4. Why did the author's mother want to throw a second shoe through the window?
5. What do you think of the mother in the story?
6. Estimate the total number of policemen who entered the house in response to the call that a burglary was in progress.
7. The police and one of the reporters made various references to the way the narrator was dressed during the hullabaloo. Why do you suppose that is?
8. Why would the grandfather be going through a phase in which he believed that "General Meade's men, under steady hammering by Stonewall Jackson, were beginning to retreat and even desert?"
9. What does the simile "as if I were a slot machine into which he had, without results, dropped a nickel" indicate?
10. What does the last sentence of the story "He had us there" mean? What does it suggest?

Paraphrasing

1. After he had disappeared from the window, mother suddenly made as if to throw another shoe... because the thrill of heaving a shoe through a window glass had enormously taken her fancy.
2. The police were on hand in a commendably short time.
3. Their flashlights played all over the living room.
4. He (grandfather) fetched the officer who found the zither a flat-handed smack alongside his head that sent him sprawling.

5. He (the reporter) gazed at me a long time as if I were a slot machine into which he had, without results, dropped a nickel.
6. Over his third cup of coffee, he glared at Herman and me. "What was the idee of all them cops tarryhootin' round the house last night?" he demanded. He had us there.

Some Information about English Style

1. Irony

Irony, in literature and drama, refers to a statement or action whose apparent meaning is underlain by a contrary meaning. It may be found either in language usage or in the working out of the action of a story. Surprise endings always depend on some sort of irony, often crude.

There are different types of irony: verbal / rhetorical irony and structural / situational irony.

Verbal /rhetorical irony is to say the opposite of what is meant. For instance, "Tiny" is used as a nickname for a gigantic person. In William Shakespeare's play *Julius Caesar*, Mark Antony bitterly describes the men who have murdered Caesar as "honorable." In the present story, the policeman saw the narrator wearing only a towel around his waist in the cold November night, and asked him: "Well, whattsa matta, ya hot?" This is another example of verbal irony. In all these cases, the word or the remarks are used or said to mean the opposite. This kind of irony is close to understatement. Verbal irony lends itself to humor.

Structural irony, or sometimes called "**irony of situation,**" typically takes the form of a discrepancy between appearance and reality, or between what is expected and what is actually revealed. The dominant irony of situation in the present text lies in the discrepancy between what people think they know about the reality and what the reality turns out to be. For instance, the family's knowledge of the mysterious footsteps downstairs, and the senile grandpa's perception of the "retreaters" turn out to be either unbelievable to a logical mind or totally wrong. In the same manner, the policemen's knowledge of the event and the family turns out to be a total confusion, which leads to the opposite of what they are supposed to accomplish: instead of finding the burglar and safeguarding civilians' life and property, they take the family members as suspects and destroy the furniture in the house in their desperate and futile searching and end up with one of them being shot by Grandpa.

Both verbal and structural ironies share the suggestion of a concealed truth conflicting with surface appearances.

Apart from verbal and structural ironies which are the most noticeable features in the two texts of this unit, there are tragic or dramatic irony, Socratic irony and cosmic irony or irony of fate, which have all found their exquisite expressions in such masterpieces as Shakespeare's plays, Plato's dialogues and Thomas Hardy's novels.

2. Vivid descriptions of scenes and actions

The story abounds in vivid descriptions of scenes and actions, which contribute a great deal to the total effect of humour. Look at how Thurber describes the police in action:

(1) Their *flashlights played* all over the living room, *stabbed* into hallways, *shot* up the front stairs, and finally up the back.
(2) Police *were all over the place*. A half-dozen policemen *emerged out of the darkness* of the hallway upstairs. They began to *ransack the floor:* pulled beds away from walls, tore clothes off hooks in the closets, pulled suitcases and boxes off shelves....

Do you appreciate how Thurber describes Mother's response to the crisis? And Grandfather's? What specific language is used in each case?

Practice

Building word power

The following verbs are used in the text to indicate nervous or energetic actions. Can you use them in other contexts, such as the following? (Take note of the correct form of each word when you are filling in the blank.)

spring   froth   wham   bound   heave   grab   jerk   sprawl   snap   fling

(1) The man _____ his fist against the wall in utter despair.
(2) The door was suddenly _____ open when I was still lying in bed with a book in hand.
(3) The dog was _____ at the mouth and little boy was scared.
(4) I was tempted to _____ back angrily at him when he made those unfair remarks.
(5) Something hit her and sent her _____ to the ground.
(6) Suddenly a huge dog came _____ towards me before I realized what was happening.
(7) Though she looked thin and frail, she still managed to _____ the heavy trunk down the stairs.
(8) The moment she picked up the receiver, her mother _____ the phone away from her.
(9) She _____ at the branch, missed and fell.
(10) Everybody _____ to their feet when the principal walked in.

Grammar and Usage

Translate the following sentences with the words and expressions used in the text.

(1) 她仔细查看旅馆广告,终于有一家中了她的意。(fancy)
(2) 西蒙帮我修车,我说要付他钱,他坚决不同意。(hear)
(3) 她看着阳光在水面上闪烁。(play)
(4) 这是这家公司首次涉足电影制作。(venture)
(5) 我还要钱时他气得七窍生烟。(froth)
(6) 把你的脏手从我身上拿开!(paw)
(7) 他伸开手脚坐在电视机前的一张扶手椅上。(sprawl)
(8) 我总算在飞机上睡了觉,到达时精神焕发。(fresh as a daisy)
(9) 她一直在大街上四处奔走寻找工作。(tramp)
(10) 她翻箱倒柜找家人的老相片。(ransack)
(11) 他那天夜里整夜未归,我的心情越来越紧张。(alarm)
(12) John 在家庭生活、社会关系上都很失意,只得遁入幻想世界,把自己想象为一个英雄人物。(retreat)

Improving your writing style

1. Cite examples of irony used by the author and identify their types. How does the author's use of irony contribute to the text?
2. Find examples to illustrate the humor of the story.

Writing task

If there is a ghost in the house that Thurber describes, it does not talk. Write a short story to function as a sequel to this one, explaining who the ghost is and why it is haunting this house.

Text B

The Verger

Somerset Maugham[1]
(Abridged and Edited)

When Albert Edward Foreman, the verger[2] of St. Peter's, Neville Square, with his usual politeness closed the church door behind the vicar and two churchwardens, he could not sustain the air of unruffled dignity with which he had borne the blow
5 inflicted upon him and his lips quivered.

There had been a christening that afternoon, and Albert Edward Foreman still wore his verger's gown. After
10 the christening, as he was quietly replacing the painted wooden cover on the marble font, the new vicar had approached him, still wearing his cassock.
15 The new vicar had been but recently appointed, a red-faced energetic man in his early forties, and Albert Edward still regretted the departure of his predecessor, a clergyman of the old school who preached leisurely sermons in a
20 silvery voice. When the new vicar had come near enough to address the verger without raising his voice he stopped.

"Foreman, will you come into the vestry for a minute. I have something to say to you."
25 "Very good, sir."

---

verger /ˈvɜːdʒə/ *n.* (especially BrE) a Church of England official whose job is to look after the inside of a church and to perform some simple duties during church services
vicar /ˈvɪkə/ *n.* (especially BrE) an Anglican priest who is in charge of a church and the area around it
churchwarden /ˌtʃɜːtʃˈwɔːdn/ *n.* (in the Anglican Church) a person who is chosen by the members of a church to take care of church property and money
unruffled /ʌnˈrʌfəld/ *adj.* (of a person) calm
dignity /ˈdɪɡnɪti/ *n.* a calm and serious manner that deserves respect
christening /ˈkrɪsənɪŋ/ *n.* a Christian ceremony in which a baby is officially named and welcomed into the Christian church
font /fɒnt/ *n.* a large stone bowl in a church that holds water for the ceremony of baptism
cassock /ˈkæsək/ *n.* a long piece of clothing, usually black or red, worn by some Christian priests and other people with specially duties in a church
vestry /ˈvestri/ *n.* a room in a church where a priest prepares for a service by putting on special clothes and where various objects used in worship are kept

The vicar preceded Albert Edward into the vestry. Albert Edward was a trifle surprised to find two churchwardens there as well. He had not seen them come in. They gave him pleasant nods.

"Good afternoon, my lord. Good afternoon, sir," he said to one after the other.

The vicar began briskly.

"Foreman, we've got something rather unpleasant to say to you. You've been here sixteen years and I think we all agree that you've fulfilled the duties of your office to the satisfaction of everybody concerned."

The two churchwardens nodded.

"But a most extraordinary circumstance came to my knowledge the other day and I felt it my duty to impart it to the churchwardens. I discovered to my astonishment that you could neither read nor write."

The verger's face betrayed no sign of embarrassment.

"The last vicar knew that, sir," he replied. "He said it didn't make no difference. He always said there was a great deal too much education in the world for'is taste."

"It's the most amazing thing I ever heard," cried one of the churchwardens.

"Do you mean to say that you've been verger of this church for sixteen years and never learned to read or write?" said the other.

"I went into service when I was twelve, sir. The cook in the first place tried to teach me once, but I didn't seem to 'ave the knack for it, and then what with one thing and another I never seemed to 'ave the time."

The churchwardens gave the vicar a troubled glance and then looked down at the table.

"Well, Foreman," said the vicar, "We've talked this matter over and quite agree the situation is impossible. At a church like St. Peter's, Neville Square, we cannot have a verger who can neither read nor write."

Albert Edward's thin, sallow face reddened and he moved uneasily on his feet, but he made no reply.

"Understand me, Foreman, I have no complaint to make against you. You do your work quite satisfactorily, and we don't want to be harsh with you. But I'm afraid you'll have to go."

Albert Edward had never liked the new vicar; now he straightened himself a little. He knew his value and he wasn't going to allow himself to be put upon[3].

"Yes, sir, I quite understand. I shall be 'appy to 'and in my resignation as soon as you've found somebody to take my place."

Closing the door politely, Albert walked slowly away from the vestry to hang his verger's gown up on its proper peg. He sighed as he thought of all the grand funerals and smart weddings it had seen. He tidied everything up, put on his coat, and hat in hand walked down the aisle. He locked the church door behind him. He strolled across the square, but deep in his sad thoughts he did not take the street that led him home, where a nice strong cup of tea awaited him; he took the wrong turning. He walked slowly along. His heart was heavy. He did not know what he should do with himself. He had saved a small sum, but not enough to live on

---

trifle /ˈtraɪfəl/ *n.* (a trifle) (formal) slightly

brisk /brɪsk/ *adj.* (of a person, their voice or manner) practical and confident; showing a desire to get things done quickly

sallow /ˈsæləʊ/ *adj.* (of a person's skin or face) having a slightly yellow color that does not look healthy

without doing something, and life seemed to cost more every year. He had never thought to be troubled with such questions. The vergers of St. Peter's, like the popes of Rome, were there for life. He had often thought of the pleasant reference the vicar would make in his sermon at evensong[4] the first Sunday after his death to the long and faithful service, and the exemplary character of their late verger, Albert Edward Foreman. He sighed deeply.

Albert Edward was a non-smoker and a total abstainer, but with a certain latitude; that is to say he liked a glass of beer with his dinner and when he was tired he enjoyed a cigarette. It occurred to him now that one would comfort him and since he did not carry them he looked about him for a shop where he could buy a packet of Gold Flakes[5]. He did not at once see one and walked on a little. It was a long street with all sorts of shops in it, but there was not a single one where you could buy cigarettes.

"That's strange," said Albert Edward.

To make sure he walked right up the street again. No, there was no doubt about it. He stopped and looked reflectively up and down.

"I can't be the only man as walks along this street and wants a fag," he said. "I shouldn't wonder but what a fellow might do very well with a little shop here. Tobacco and sweets, you know."

He gave a sudden start.

"That's an idea," he said. "Strange 'ow things come to you when you least expect it."

He turned, walked home, and had his tea.

"You're very silent this afternoon, Albert," his wife remarked.

"I'm thinkin'," he said.

He considered the matter from every point of view and next day he went along the street and by good luck found a little shop to let that looked as though it would exactly suit him. Twenty-four hours later he had taken it and when a month after that he left St. Peter's, Neville Square for ever, Albert Edward Foreman set up in business as a tobacconist and newsagent. Albert Edward did very well. He did so well that in a year or so it struck him that he might take a second shop and put a manager in. He looked for another long street that hadn't got a tobacconist on it and when he found it and a shop to let, took it and stocked it. This was a success too. Then it occurred to him that if he could run two he could run half a dozen, so he began walking about London, and whenever he found a long street that had no tobacconist and a shop to let he took it. In the course of ten years he acquired no less than ten shops and he was making money hand over fist. He went round to all of them himself every Monday, collected the week's takings and took them to the bank.

One morning when he was there paying in a bundle of notes and a heavy bag of silver the cashier told him that the manager would like to see him. He was shown into an office and the manager shook hands with him.

"Mr. Foreman, I wanted to have a talk to you about the money you've got on deposit with us. D'you know exactly how much it is?"

"Not within a pound or two, sir; but I've got a pretty rough idea."

"Apart from what you paid in this morning it's a little over thirty thousand pounds. That's a very large sum to have on

abstainer /əb'steɪnə/ n. a person who never drinks alcohol
latitude /'lætɪtjuːd/ n. (formal) freedom to choose what you do or the way that you do it
fag /fæg/ n. (BrE, informal)=CIGARETTE

deposit and I should have thought you'd do better to invest it."

> transfer /træns'fɜː/ *n.* also **transferal law** a conveyance of title or property from one person to another
> disarming /dɪs'ɑːmɪŋ/ *adj.* make people feel less angry or suspicious than they were before

"I wouldn't want to take no risk, sir. I know it's safe in the bank."

"You needn't have the least anxiety. We'll make you out a list of absolutely gilt-edged securities. They'll bring you in a better rate of interest than we can possibly afford to give you."

A troubled look settled on Mr. Foreman's distinguished face. "I've never 'ad anything to do with stocks and shares and I'd 'ave to leave it all in your 'ands," he said.

The manager smiled. "We'll do everything. All you'll have to do next time you come in is just to sign the transfers."

"I could do that all right," said Albert uncertainly, "but 'ow should I know what I was signin'?"

"I suppose you can read," said the manager a trifle sharply.

Mr. Foreman gave him a disarming smile.

"Well, sir, that's just it. I can't. I know it sounds funny-like but there it is, I can't read or write, only me name, an' I only learnt to do that when I went into business."

The manager was so surprised that he jumped up from his chair.

"That's the most extraordinary thing I ever heard."

"You see, it's like this, sir, I never 'ad the opportunity until it was too late and then some 'ow I wouldn't. I got obstinate-like."

The manager stared at him as though he were a prehistoric monster.

"Do you mean to say that you've built up this important business and amassed a fortune of thirty thousand pounds without being able to read or write? Good God, man, what would you be now if you had been able to?"

"I can tell you that, sir," said Mr. Foreman, a little smile on his features. "I'd be verger of St. Peter's, Neville Square."

Notes

1. W. Somerset Maugham (1874—1965)

A British novelist, playwright, and short story writer, one of the most widely-known Western authors of the 1930s and reportedly the highest paid. He was born in Paris and learned French as his native tongue. He earned a reputation for cynicism and simplicity of style with his 1915 masterpiece *Of Human Bondage*. The semi-autobiographical book chronicles a young medical student's struggle toward maturity. Among his other well-known works are *The Moon and the Six Pence* (1919), a novel about a Gauginesque artist who neglects duty for art, and "Rain", a short story about the conflict between an American prostitute and a Scottish missionary.

2. a verger

A verger (or *virger*, so called after the staff of the office) is a person, usually a layperson, who assists in the ordering of religious services, particularly in Anglican churches. During the service itself, a verger's main duty is to ceremonially precede the religious participants as they move about the church. Maugham's story highlights the irony that when a lowly verger is fired because of his illiteracy, it turns out to be his lucky day.

3. **put upon**
   To take unfair advantage of; impose upon.
4. **Evensong**
   Evening Prayer (Anglican), the Anglican liturgy of Evening Prayer, especially (but not exclusively) so called when it is sung.
5. **Gold Flake**
   This is a widely-sold cigarette brand in India and Pakistan. It is sold in various varieties, including Goldflake Kings (84mm), Goldflake Lights (Filter tipped), Goldflake Small (Filter tipped) and Goldflake Small (filterless). It is a well-positioned brand in India and is the market leader in its segment.

Comprehension

1. When did this story take place? Why do you think so?
2. What is a "christening?"
3. Albert Edward Foreman says he was "in service" before he became the verger of Saint Peter's, Neville Square. What does he mean?
4. Why hadn't Albert Edward Foreman learned to read or write?
5. Why would it be important that "Albert should be able to read and write as a verger?"
6. What can we determine about Albert Edward Foreman based upon his spoken English?
7. What does it mean to "make money hand over fist?"
8. What might "gilt-edged securities" be?
9. What is ironical about "The Verger?"
10. Is there a moral to this story? Does this moral hold true today?

Further Study

Works of irony

- *"Charles"* by Shirley Jackson
- *Oedipus the King* by Sophocles

Works by James Thurber

- *My Life and Hard Times*
- *"The Secret Life of Walter Mitty"*

Works by Somerset Maugham

- *The Moon and the Six Pence*
- *"Rain"*
- *Of Human Bondage*

Unit 6

The Choice of Words

Unit Goals

☞ To learn to write in clear and concise English by avoiding:
- hackneyed metaphors
- long-winded expressions
- vague and high sounding words

☞ To choose the right word for precision

Before Reading

Think and Discuss

1. Do you sometimes find it hard to express precisely what you want to say?
2. What exactly are your difficulties when deciding which word to choose in writing or speaking? How do you usually solve the problems?
3. What do you usually do when confronted with several words but are not certain which to choose?
4. Do you think a large vocabulary will guarantee using the right word? Why or why not?
5. What do you know about style in writing? In your opinion, what contributes to appropriateness in style?
6. Is it correct to consider one style to be superior to another? (For instance, to regard formal style superior to informal style.)
7. What do you think are the criteria of good writing?

A Glimpse into the Text

There is a saying in English: "Everyone complains about the weather, but no one does anything about it!" The same seems true of the English language itself, especially in its written form. It is commonly complained that English is being poorly written these days, and yet it seems that nothing can be done about it. In this article, one of the greatest English writers of the 20th century, George Orwell[1], takes up the subject to argue, on the contrary, that something can be done about it if we apply some basic rules and stick to the general principle of "letting meaning choose the word, and not the other way about."

Text A

Politics and the English Language[2]
George Orwell
(Abridged and Edited)

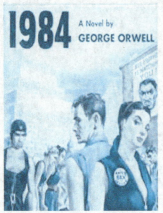

Most people who bother with the matter at all would admit that the English language is in a bad way, but it is generally assumed that we cannot by conscious action do anything about it. Our civilization is decadent and our
5 language—so the argument runs—must inevitably share in the general collapse. It follows that any struggle against the abuse of language is a sentimental archaism, like preferring candles to electric light or hansom cabs[3] to aeroplanes. Underneath this lies the half-conscious belief that language
10 is a natural growth and not an instrument which we shape for our own purposes.

Now, it is clear that the decline of a language must ultimately have political and economic causes: it is not due simply to the bad influence of this or that individual writer. But an effect can become a cause, reinforcing the original cause and
15 producing the same effect in an intensified form, and so on indefinitely. A man may take to drink because he feels himself to be a failure, and then fail all the more completely because he drinks. It is rather the same thing that is happening to the English language. It becomes ugly and inaccurate because our thoughts are foolish, but the slovenliness of our language makes it easier for us to have foolish thoughts. The point is that the process is reversible. Modern
20 English, especially written English, is full of bad habits which spread by imitation and which can be avoided if one is willing to take the necessary trouble. If one gets rid of these habits one can think more clearly, and to think clearly is a necessary first step toward political regeneration: so that the fight against bad English is not frivolous and is not the exclusive concern of professional writers.

25 Here are some specimens of the English language as it is now habitually written.

(1) I am not, indeed, sure whether it is not true to say that the Milton who once seemed not unlike a seventeenth-century
30 Shelley had not become, out of an experience ever more bitter in each year, more alien to the founder of that Jesuit sect which nothing could induce him to tolerate.

35 —Professor Harold Laski
(Essay in Freedom of Expression)

(2) Above all, we cannot play ducks and drakes with a native battery[4] of idioms

---

archaism /ˈɑːkeɪɪzəm/ *n.* a very old word or phrase that is no longer used
slovenly /ˈslʌvənli/ *adj.* careless, untidy or dirty in appearance or habits
reversible /rɪˈvɜːsəbl/ *adj.* (of a process, an action or a disease) that can be changed so that sth. returns to its original state or situation
regenerate /rɪˈdʒenəreɪt/ *v.* 1) to make an area, institution, etc. develop and grow strong again 2) to grow again; to make sth. grow again
frivolous /ˈfrɪvələs/ *adj.* (of people or their behaviour) silly or amusing, especially when such behaviour is not suitable
specimen /ˈspesɪmɪn/ *n.* a small amount of sth. that shows what the rest of it is like

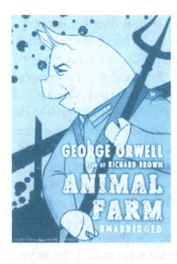

40 which prescribes such egregious collocations of vocables as the Basic *put up with* for *tolerate* or *put at a loss* for *bewilder*.

—Professor Lancelot Hogben *(Interglossa)*

(3) If a new spirit is to be infused into this old country, there is one thorny and contentious reform which
45 must be tackled, and that is the humanization and galvanization of the B.B.C. Timidity here will bespeak canker and atrophy of the soul. The heart of Britain may be sound and of strong beat, for instance, but the British lion's roar at present is
50 like that of Bottom in Shakespeare's *Midsummer Night's Dream*—as gentle as any sucking dove ....

—Letter in *Tribune*

Each of these passages has faults of its own, but, quite apart from avoidable ugliness, two qualities are common to all of them. The first is staleness of imagery; the other is lack of
55 precision. The writer either had a meaning and cannot express it, or he inadvertently says something else, or he is almost indifferent as to whether his words mean anything or not. This mixture of vagueness and sheer incompetence is the most marked characteristic of modern English prose, and especially of any kind of political writing. As soon as certain topics are raised, the concrete melts into the abstract and no one seems able to think of terms of speech
60 that are not hackneyed: prose consists less and less of *words* chosen for the sake of their meaning, and more and more of *phrases* tacked together like the sections of prefabricated hen-house.

I said earlier that the decadence of our language is probably curable. Those who deny this would argue, if they produced an argument at all, that language merely reflects existing social
65 conditions, and that we cannot influence its development by any direct tinkering with words and constructions. So far as the general tone or spirit of a language goes, this may be true, but it is not true in detail. Silly words and expressions have often disappeared, not through any evolutionary process but owing to the conscious action of a minority. Two recent examples were *explore every avenue* and *leave no stone unturned*, which were killed by the jeers of a
70 few journalists. There is a long list of flyblown metaphors which could similarly be got rid of if enough people would interest themselves in the job; and it should
75 also be possible to laugh the *not un-*formation[5] out of existence, to reduce the amount of Latin and Greek in the average sentence, to drive out foreign phrases and strayed scientific
80 words, and in general, to make pretentiousness unfashionable. But all these are minor points. The defence of the English language

inadvertently /ˌmədˈvɜːtəntli/ *adv.* by accident; without intending to
hackneyed /ˈhæknɪd/ *adj.* used too often and therefore boring
prefabricated /ˌpriːˈfæbrɪkeɪtɪd/ *adj.* (especially of a building) made in sections that can be put together later
decadence /ˈdekədəns/ *n.* behaviour, attitudes, etc. which show a fall in standards, especially moral ones
tinker /ˈtɪŋkə/ *v.* to make small changes to sth. in order to repair or improve it, especially in a way that may not be helpful
jeer /dʒɪə/ *n.* a rude remark that sb. shouts at sb. else to show that they do not respect or like them
flyblown /ˈflaɪbləʊn/ *adj.* dirty and in bad condition; not fit to eat
strayed /streɪ/ *adj.* that has gone astray or lost
pretentiousness /prɪˈtenʃəsnɪs/ *n.* trying to appear important, intelligent, etc. in order to impress other people; trying to be sth. that you are not, in order to impress

implies more than this, and perhaps it is best to start by saying what it does *not* imply.

85　　To begin with it has nothing to do with archaism, with the salvaging of obsolete words and turns of speech, or with the setting up of a "standard English" which must never be departed from. On the contrary, it is especially concerned with the scrapping of every word or idiom which has outworn its usefulness. It has nothing to do with correct grammar and syntax, which are of no importance so long as one makes one's meaning clear, or with the
90　avoidance of Americanisms, or with having what is called a "good prose style." On the other hand it is not concerned with fake simplicity and the attempt to make written English colloquial. Nor does it even imply in every case preferring the Saxon word to the Latin one, though it does imply using the fewest and shortest words that will cover one's meaning. What is above all needed is to let the meaning choose the word, and not the other way about. In prose, the
95　worst thing one can do with words is to surrender to them. When you think of a concrete object, you think wordlessly, and then, if you want to describe the thing you have been visualizing you probably hunt about till you find the exact words that seem to fit it. When you think of something abstract you are more inclined to use words from the start, and unless you make a conscious effort to prevent it, the existing dialect will come rushing in and do the job
100 for you, at the expense of blurring or even changing your meaning. Probably it is better to put off using words as long as possible and get one's meaning as clear as one can through pictures or sensations. Afterwards one can choose—not simply *accept*—the phrases that will best cover the meaning, and then switch round and decide what impression one's words are likely to make on another person. This last effort of the mind cuts out all stale or mixed
105 images, all prefabricated phrases, needless repetitions, and humbug and vagueness generally. But one can often be in doubt about the effect of a word or a phrase, and one needs rules that one can rely on when instinct fails. I think the following rules will cover most cases:

　　1. Never use a metaphor, simile or other figure of speech which you are used to seeing in print.
110　2. Never use a long word where a short one will do.
　　3. If it is possible to cut a word out, always cut it out
　　4. Never use the passive where you can use the active.
　　5. Never use a foreign phrase, scientific word or a jargon word if you can think of an everyday English equivalent.
115　6. Break any of these rules sooner than say anything outright barbarous.

　　These rules sound elementary, and so they are, but they demand a deep change of attitude in anyone who has grown used to writing in the style
120 now fashionable. One could keep all of them and still write bad English, but one could not write the kind of stuff that I quoted in those specimens at the beginning of this article.

125　　I have not here been considering the literary use of language, but merely language as an instrument for expressing

salvage /ˈsælvɪdʒ/ *v.* 1) to save parts or property from a damaged ship or from a fire, etc. 2) to manage to rescue sth. from a difficult situation; to stop a bad situation from being a complete failure
obsolete /ˈɒbsəliːt/ *adj.* no longer used because sth. new has been invented
scrap /skræp/ *v.* to cancel or get rid of sth. that is no longer practical or useful
blur /blɜː/ *v.* to become or make sth. become difficult to distinguish clearly
stale /steɪl/ *adj.* something that has been said or done too many times before and is no longer interesting or exciting
humbug /ˈhʌmbʌɡ/ *n.* dishonest language or behaviour that is intended to deceive people

and not for concealing or preventing thought. Stuart Chase⁶ and others have come near to claiming that all abstract words are meaningless, and have used this as a pretext for advocating a kind of political quietism. Since you don't know what Fascism is, how can you struggle against Fascism? One need not swallow such absurdities as this, but one ought to recognize the present political chaos is connected with the decay of language, and that one can probably bring about some improvement by starting at the verbal end. If you simplify your English, you are freed from the worst follies of orthodoxy. You cannot speak any of the necessary dialects, and when you make a stupid remark its stupidity will be obvious, even to yourself. Political language—and with variations this is true of all political parties, from Conservatives to Anarchists—is designed to make lies sound truthful and murder respectable, and to give an appearance of solidity to pure wind. One cannot change this all in a moment, but one can at least change one's own habits, and from time to time one can even, if one jeers loudly enough, send some worn-out and useless phrase—some *jackboot, Achilles' heel,*⁷ *hotbed, melting pot, acid test, veritable inferno* or other lump of verbal refuse—into the dustbin where it belongs.

> **pretext** /ˈpriːtekst/ *n.* a false reason for doing sth., usually bad, in order to hide the real reason; an excuse
> **advocate** /ˈædvəkeɪt/ *v.* to support sth. publicly
> **quietism** /ˈkwaɪətɪz(ə)m/ *n.* an attitude to life which makes you calmly accept things as they are rather than try to change them
> **absurdity** /əbˈsɜːdɪti/ *n.* behavior that shows a lack of thought or good judgement
> **chaos** /ˈkeɪɒs/ *n.* a state of complete confusion
> **decay** /dɪˈkeɪ/ *n.* 1) the process or result of being destroyed by natural causes or by not being cared for (= of decaying) 2) the gradual destruction of a society, an institution, a system, etc.
> **verbal** /ˈvɜːbəl/ *adj.* 1) spoken, not written; 2) relating to words
> **orthodoxy** /ˈɔːθədɒksi/ *n.* (pl. -ies) an idea or view that is generally accepted

More about the Text

1. George Orwell

George Orwell (1903—1950) was born Eric Arthur Blair in Bengal, brought to England at an early age, and educated at Cyprian's and then at Eton. Orwell saw himself primarily as a political writer, a democratic socialist who avoided party labels. His plain, colloquial style made him highly effective as pamphleteer and journalist. He wrote documentaries, essays, and criticism during the 1930s but his most popular works were his political satires *Animal Farm* (1945) and *Nineteen Eighty-four* (1949) which brought inevitable comparisons with Jonathan Swift, the well-known 18th Century political satirist. Orwell became one of the most important and influential voices of the century. [See *George Orwell: A life* by Bernard Crick (1980).]

2. Politics and the English Language

Politics and the English Language was published in April 1946, when Orwell had just finished collaborating with the B.B.C. against fascists in India in World War II. He wrote this text in part to justify the work his journalism had done for the Empire. The passage has become widely influential, with Orwell's claimed connection between the corrupted (and corruptive) language and political manipulation. Orwell believed that "ugly" language, characterized with a staleness of imagery and lack of precision, contributes to muddy or "foolish" thinking; in return, foolish thinking produces even uglier language, and the reversible cycle continues. For Orwell, this was not a purely philosophical or academic issue. The political chaos at the time, according to Orwell, was linked to the decay of language, and to improve politics, therefore, one may well begin with the improvement of the language.

3. hansom cabs

A hansom cab is a carriage with two wheels, pulled by one horse and used in the past to carry two passengers.

4. battery

A battery (of sth.) is a large number of things or people of the same type.

5. not un-formation

One can cure oneself of the "not-un-formation" by jeering at this sentence: A not *unblack dog was chasing a not unsmall rabbit across a not ungreen field.*

6. Stuart Chase

Stuart Chase (1888—1985) was an American economist and engineer trained at Massachusetts Institute of Technology (MIT). His writings cover diverse topics.

7. Achilles' heel

According to Greek mythology. Thetis, the daughter of a God of the sea, was married to a mortal human being. They had a son called Achilles who was also a mortal human being. Thetis wanted her son to become immortal, so she dipped the infant Achilles in the river Styx, holding onto him by his heel, and he became invulnerable where the waters touched him—that is, everywhere but the areas covered by her thumb and forefinger—implying that only a heel wound could have been his downfall. In Trojan War, Achilles died from a heel wound. Based on this mythology, Achilles' heel means a fatal weakness in spite of overall strength, actually or potentially leading to downfall.

Check Your Understanding

1. The author argues that language is not a natural growth but a socially determined growth. Would you agree with this view? Why or why not?
2. According to Orwell, how are politics connected with language?
3. What are the two qualities Orwell claims each of his specimens of poor writing illustrates? What problem can you discern in each?
4. Why is Orwell so against staleness of imagery and imprecision with words?
5. According to Orwell, what is the general problem with modern English prose?
6. According to Orwell, what is the general solution to the problems with written English that he perceives?
7. Which of the six basic rules suggested by the author do you consciously follow when writing in English, and which do you least adhere to?
8. Orwell's first rule for good writing is "Never use a metaphor, simile or other figures of speech which you are used to seeing in print." Can you find any metaphor, simile or other figures of speech that Orwell uses in his article? Have you seen his figure of speech

before?
9. What does Orwell suggest concerning word or phrase choice? How can writers improve their word or phrase choice, according to Orwell?
10. In your opinion, has Orwell followed his own advice in this article? Was the article clear in meaning to you? Expand on your answer, giving examples.

Paraphrasing

1. When you think of something abstract you are more inclined to use words from the start, and unless you make a conscious effort to prevent it, the existing dialect will come rushing in and do the job for you, at the expense of blurring or even changing your meaning.
2. Break any of these rules sooner than say anything outright barbarous.
3. One need not swallow such absurdities as this, but one ought to recognize the present political chaos is connected with the decay of language, and that one can probably bring about some improvement by starting at the verbal end.
4. If you simplify your English, you are freed from the worst follies of orthodoxy.
5. Political language—and with variations this is true of all political parties, from Conservatives to Anarchists—is designed to make lies sound truthful and murder respectable, and to give an appearance of solidity to pure wind.

Some Information about English Style

1. Writing in clear and concise English

Tastes may change in language, but some basic principles of good writing have remained unchanged. Among them are principles of **Accuracy**, **Brevity** and **Clarity**, appropriately abbreviated into ABC. Of the three principles, the one that relates most directly to the goal of communication is **Clarity**. When you write, you need to let your readers know from the very beginning what you want to say. You need not attempt to dazzle them with multi-syllable words and long, involved sentences. Graceful phrasing certainly contributes to good writing, but you need to strive first for clarity. It is ill-mannered to make your readers rack their brains trying to understand you. Nothing will annoy readers more than having to waste their time plowing through a cluttered paragraph because you neglected to spend your time cleaning it up.

In the text, Orwell argues that we can improve our writing by getting rid of hackneyed metaphors, long-winded expressions and vague, high-sounding words. Be very careful, then, with over-used expressions such as the following:

hackneyed metaphors:
- as busy as a bee
- by leaps and bounds
- as clear as crystal
- face the music
- play with fire
- as cool as a cucumber
- like a needle in a haystack

clichés
- last but not least
- lucky dog
- no pains, no gains
- a piece of cake
- from the bottom of my heart
- from every walk of life
- the other side of the coin
- few and far between
- bite off more than you can chew

big, long words
- endeavor (*attempt, try*)
- repercussions (*results / effects*)
- transmit (*send*)
- materialize (*happen, occur*)
- commence (*begin, start*)
- blueprint (*plan*)
- terminate (*end*)
- assistance (*help*)
- expenditure (*cost*)
- necessitate (*need, demand*)
- indebtedness (*thanks, gratitude*)

circumlocutions
- a limited number (*few*)
- a sizable percentage of ... (*many*)
- be of the opinion that ... (*think*)

archaism
- prior to (*before*)
- as per (*according to*)

2. Using the right word

Words are many and it is not always easy choosing the right one.

First, words that look similar may have different meanings. For example:

human: of, or relating to man, as in *human being; human nature; human rights*

humane: be characterized by kindness, mercy, or compassion, as in *a humane judge/office; a humane killer* (very different from a *human killer*!)

singularity: (of mind) oddity, peculiarity, something that singles a person out from others

singleness: (of mind) holding steadfastly to the purpose in mind, without being drawn aside by less worthy objects

Secondly, words that have the same meaning may be used in different situations and different styles. For example, in each of the following sets, words of the same notion are used at different levels of formality.

{	**poor**	(general)	{	**face**	(general)
	penniless	(informal)		**visage**	(formal & literary)
	broke	(casual)		**mug**	(slangy)

{ **start** (general)
  initiate (more formal)
  commence (formal)

Thirdly, words that have similar meaning may carry different associations. For example, the following words have different connotations in addition to their shades of difference in meaning.

{ **happiness:** most general term, implying any degree of well-being from mere contentment to the most intense joy.
  bliss: pointing to complete, ecstatic happiness or to great contentment, in the religious sense referring to a state of absolute felicity brought about by the submergence of the self into a divine infinity.
  blessedness: intense spiritual bliss, so profound as to be attributed to a deity, used with religious associations
  rapture: a feeling of extreme pleasure and happiness, may carry sexual connotation

In addition, there are cultural differences in word choice.

We need to think about the various aspects of a word when deciding which to choose. Choosing the right word is, therefore, a process of clarifying and defining our thoughts. Unless we have found the exact words to verbalize our own thoughts, we can never be very sure of what our thoughts are. Without words, our thoughts can not be defined or stated in a clear and precise manner.

3. Logical reasoning in argumentative writing

Read the following excerpts from Orwell's article and take special note of the underlined parts.

Most people who bother with the matter at all <u>would admit that</u> the English language is in a bad way, <u>but it is generally assumed that</u> we cannot by conscious action do anything about it. Our civilization is decadent and our language—<u>so the argument runs</u>—must inevitably share in the general collapse. <u>It follows</u> that any struggle against the abuse of language is a sentimental archaism, like preferring candles to electric light or hansom cabs to aeroplanes. <u>Underneath this lies the half-conscious belief that</u> language is a natural growth and not an instrument which we shape for our own purposes.

Structures used:

- Most people would admit that .... (Making a concession.)
- But it is generally assumed that .... (Showing partial disagreement.)
- So the argument runs. (Showing tentative agreement.)
- It follows that .... (Showing tentative agreement.)
- Underneath this lies the belief that .... (Showing tentative agreement.)

<u>Those who deny this would argue</u>, if they produced an argument at all, <u>that</u> language merely reflects existing social conditions, <u>and that</u> we cannot influence its development by any direct tinkering with words and constructions. <u>So far as</u> the general tone or spirit of a

language goes, this may be true, but it is not true in detail.

Structures used:

- Those who ... would argue that ..., and that .... (Citing other people's opinions.)
- So far as ... goes, this may be true, but it is not true in that .... (Showing disagreement after making a concession.)

To begin with it has nothing to do with archaism, with the salvaging of obsolete words and turns of speech, or with the setting up of a "standard English" which must never be departed from. On the contrary, it is especially concerned with the scrapping of every word or idiom which has outworn its usefulness. It has nothing to do with correct grammar and syntax, which are of no importance so long as one makes one's meaning clear, or with the avoidance of Americanisms, or with having what is called a "good prose style." On the other hand it is not concerned with fake simplicity and the attempt to make written English colloquial. Nor does it even imply in every case preferring the Saxon word to the Latin one, though it does imply using the fewest and shortest words that will cover one's meaning. What is above all needed is to let the meaning choose the word, and not the other way about.

Structures used:

- It has nothing to do with ..., with ..., or with ..., On the contrary, it is concerned with …. (Showing disagreement after clarifying several misconceptions.)
- It has nothing to do with ... or with ..., or with .... Nor does it imply ..., though it does imply .... (Showing disagreement after clarifying several misconceptions.)
- What is above all is .... (Expressing one's view emphatically.)

I have not here been considering the literary use of language, but merely language as an instrument for expressing and not for concealing or preventing thought.

- I have not been considering ... but merely .... (Making one's stand clearly by clarifying misconception.)

As shown, points of view may be expressed cautiously or tentatively, forcefully or emphatically, depending on your feelings and purpose of the writing. Agreement or disagreement may be total or partial. Here are further ways to express views:

1. Introducing your own point of view

It is a fact
There is no doubt → that ….
I believe / contend

2. Showing agreement

I agree with X when he/she → writes / says / argues → that ….

3. Showing cautious agreement

X may be correct → when he/she says that in that …. in saying that ….

4. Showing emphatic agreement

X is certainly correct → when he/she → maintains / says / writes → that ....

5. Showing disagreement

I disagree with ....
To me, this is not true.
In my opinion, the reverse/opposite is the case.

6. Showing partial disagreement

One of the main arguments → in favour of / against → X is that ... → but .... / however / on the other hand

Practice

Building word power

1. Fill in each blank with the best answer by choosing A, B, C or D.

(1) He _____ that the purchase had been a mistake.
   A. admitted   B. acknowledged   C. conceded   D. confessed
(2) We should _____ that a person is innocent until proven guilty.
   A. assume   B. presume   C. presuppose   D. suppose
(3) The furniture received a lot of _____ from the ten kids in the family.
   A. abuse   B. misuse   C. mistreat   D. maltreat
(4) After being away for so long, he feels _____ in his own country now.
   A. foreign   B. alien   C. exotic   D. strange
(5) There is a fatal _____ in your reasoning.
   A. fault   B. flaw   C. defect   D. blemish
(6) Frustrated by _____ instructions, the parents were never able to assemble the new toy.
   A. vague   B. fuzzy   C. ambiguous   D. equivocal
(7) His account _____ the story that they had gotten earlier.
   A. deny   B. gainsay   C. contradict   D. negate
(8) Years ago people would have _____ at the idea that cars would be built by robots.
   A. scoffed   B. jeered   C. sneered   D. flouted
(9) You'll have to _____ the amount of money you spend on CDs if you want to have any money left for college.
   A. reduce   B. dwindle   C. decrease   D. diminish
(10) Determined to give up smoking, she so far has not _____ to her continuing desire to have a cigarette.
   A. surrendered B. yielded   C. submitted   D. succumbed
(11) Tall shrubs _____ the actor's home from the curious.
   A. conceal   B. hide   C. screen   D. cloak

(12) My parents _____ the local schools both by volunteering and by fiercely opposing funding cuts at town meetings.
   A. support   B. uphold   C. advocate   D. back

2. Fill in each blank with an appropriate word by adding to the given word in brackets the necessary prefix or suffix or both as is required.
   (1) _____ is when a person is unable to respond to people and other stimuli around him or her. (conscious)
   (2) We were impressed by the _____ of the children's work. (original)
   (3) Unprecedented and maybe _____ effects of Arctic warming, linked to human intervention, have been discovered by a team of international researchers. (reversible)
   (4) In today's financial environment obtaining a home loan is far easier than the bad old days when grovelling to the bank was a(n) _____ unpleasant task. (avoid)
   (5) _____ education (or learning by doing) is the process of actively engaging students in an authentic experience that will have benefits and consequences. (experience)
   (6) At a time when Congress remains divided over tax cuts and how to handle an ailing economy, these reports offer sound _____ for economic renewal—challenging beliefs and policies advanced by both political parties. (prescribe)
   (7) The high crime rate is a _____ of the violent society. (reflect)
   (8) Chinese is a _____ language in which changes in pitch lead to changes in word meaning. (tone)
   (9) A(n) _____ observer is not merely impartial, but has nothing to gain from taking a stand on an issue. It implies neutrality, not lack of concern. (interest)
   (10) There can be no _____ from the rules. (depart)
   (11) AutoWeek Magazine delivers the most complete _____ of all the major auto shows. (cover)
   (12) Angus Deayton, host of the BBC's satirical news quiz *Have I Got News for You*, has been fired following a new round of _____ tabloid news stories about his private life. (sensation)

Grammar and Usage

Translate the following sentences into English by using the key words in the brackets.
   (1) 不要为了区区小事而如此焦虑。(bother)
   (2) 她吃素,所以她总是那么苗条。(follow)
   (3) 每向前一步,就是向奇迹迈进了一步。(step)
   (4) 你怎能面对饥民的疾苦无动于衷？(indifferent)
   (5) 警察要求司机把事故讲述得更详细些。(detail)
   (6) 那儿的村民用水全靠井。(rely on)
   (7) 玛丽一点儿也不吝啬。正相反,她很慷慨。(contrary)
   (8) 这件事对我们来说至关重要。(importance)
   (9) 若能设想自己成功,你就一定会成功。(visualize)
   (10) 他倾向于放手让他们干。(inclined)
   (11) 降低价格绝不能以牺牲质量为代价。(expense)

(12) 很可能她会接受这份工作。(likely)
(13) 整个事情仍然未见分晓。(doubt)
(14) 这届政府没有腐败现象。(free)
(15) 语言的学习需要付出极大努力，对其他课程的学习也一样。(true)

Improving your writing style

1. Rewrite the following sentences by getting rid of abstract and vague expressions.

Example:
   Food consumption has been dominated by the world supply situation.
   People have had to eat what they can get.

(1) The cessation of house building operated over a period of five years.

(2) From a cleaning point of view the shelving is too high.

(3) The problem is likely to continue in existence for an indefinite period ahead.

(4) The children were evacuated to alternative accommodation.

2. Tidy the following sentences by eliminating verbiage.

Example:
■ It is believed by a number of persons in this country that the young people of today do not assume as much responsibility toward society as it might be hoped that they would. (33 words)

Revised:
   Today many believe that our young people assume too little responsibility toward society. (13 words)

(1) It has been in the most recent past that society has viewed the poor as being closely akin to the criminal.

(2) There came a time when there was a feeling that, at least on my part, based upon what I had been reading, the food we buy at the supermarket to eat is genuinely poisonous.

(3) In my opinion there are many diverse elements about this problem that we probably ought to think about before arriving at an opinion on this terribly complex matter.

(4) Government policy-makers should as a matter of course consider the widely varied and diverse opinions of those qualified people outside government, as well as the ideas of people in their own departments and agencies.

(5) We stand ready, willing and able to be of assistance and service to you in the near future.

Writing task

Write a passage on "My opinion of good writing". Here are some questions to set you to tlink.

- On what major points do the two authors of this unit—Orwell and Gowers—agree on what constitutes good writing?
- In your opinion, which of the two authors in this unit has expressed his meaning more clearly—Orwell or Gowers?
- Which of the two authors in this unit has been more helpful to you in improving the quality of your own written English—Orwell or Gowers? Why?
- In your opinion, have the elements of good writing changed in the half-century since these articles were published in 1946 and 1956?
- Based on your personal reading of English literature, would you agree with the two authors in this unit that the quality of written English is declining? Give examples.

Text B

The Choice of Words

Sir Ernest Gowers[1]
(Abridged and Edited)

One of the most esteemed books ever written on the subject of writing in English is *The Elements of Style* (1959), by William Strunk, Jr. and E.B. White. In their book, White wrote that "a fox cannot tell you what a chicken looks like, but it knows one when it sees one." So too it was, explained White, with well-written English. It is difficult to describe, but one knows good writing when one sees it. In the excerpt[2] below, the author implores us to be more critically perceptive of our own written English and thereby improve its quality.

> The craftsman is proud and careful of his tools: the surgeon does not operate with an old razor – blade: the sportsman fusses happily and longs over the choice of rod, gun, club, or racquet. But the man who is working in words, unless he is a professional writer (and not always then), is singularly neglectful of his instruments.
> —Ivor Brown[3]

Here we come to the most important part of our subject. Correctness is not enough. The words used may all be words approved by the dictionary and the idiom above reproach. Yet what is written may still fail to convey a ready and precise meaning to the reader.

racquet /ˈrækɪt/ *n.* a piece of sports equipment used for hitting the ball, etc. in the game of tennis or badminton
singularly /ˈsɪŋɡjʊləli/ *adv.* very; in an unusual way

That it does so fail is the charge brought against much of what is written nowadays, including much of what is written by officials. Matthew Arnold[4] said that the secret of style was to have something to say and to say it as clearly as you can. The basic fault of present-day writing is a tendency to say what one has to say in as complicated a way as possible. Instead of being simple, terse, and direct, it is stilted, long-winded and circumlocutory; instead of choosing the simple word it prefers the unusual; instead of the plain phrase the cliché.

Ivor Brown, a connoisseur of words, has invented several names for this sort of writing. In one book he calls it "jargantuan", in another "barnacular" and in another "pudder.[5]" The Americans have a word for it—"gobbledygook."[6] Its nature can be studied not only in the original, but also in translation. Ivor Brown has translated the Lord's Prayer, Sir Alan Herbert[7] Catechism, and George Orwell the passage in Ecclesiastes[8].... It may be significant that all these critics of pudder have gone to the Bible or Prayer Book to find their greatest contrasts with it. English style must have been immeasurably influenced by everyone's intimate knowledge of those two books, whose cadences were heard every day at family prayer and every Sunday at matins and evensong[9]. Now family prayers are said no longer, and few go to church.

Why do so many writers prefer pudder to simplicity? Officials are far from being the only offenders. It seems to be a morbid condition contracted in early manhood. Children show no signs of it. Here, for example, is the response of a child of ten to an invitation to write an essay on a bird and a beast:

> The bird that I am going to write about is the owl. The owl cannot see at all by day and at night is as blind as a bat.
>
> I do not know much about the owl, so I will go on to the beast which I am going to choose. It is the cow. The cow is a mammal. It has six sides—right, left, an upper and below. At the back it has a tail on which hangs a brush. With this it sends the flies away so that they do not fall into the milk. The head is for the purpose of growing horns and so that the mouth is to moo with. Under the cow hangs the milk. It is arranged for milking. When people milk, the milk comes and there is never an end to the supply. How the cow does it I have not yet realized, but it makes more and more. The cow has a fine sense of smell; one can smell it far away. This is the reason for the fresh air in the country.
>
> The man cow is called an ox. It is not a mammal. The cow does not eat much, but what it eats it eats twice, so that it gets enough. When it is hungry it moos, and when it says nothing it is because its inside is all full up with grass.

The writer had something to say and said it as clearly as he could, and so has unconsciously achieved style. But

---

terse /tɜːs/ *adj.* (of language) brief, concise, to the point

stilted /ˈstɪltɪd/ *adj.* (of a way of speaking or writing) not natural or relaxed; too formal

long-winded /ˌlɒŋˈwɪndɪd/ *adj.* (especially of talking or writing) continuing for too long and therefore boring

circumlocutory /ˌsɜːkəmˈlɒkjʊtəri/ *adj.* using more words than are necessary, instead of speaking or writing in a clear, direct way

cliché /ˈkliːʃeɪ/ *n.* a phrase or an idea that has been used so often that it no longer has much meaning and is not interesting

connoisseur /ˌkɒnəˈsɜː/ *n.* an expert on matters involving the judgment of beauty, quality or skill in art, food or music

Catechism /ˈkætɪkɪzəm/ a set of questions and answers that are used for teaching people about the beliefs of the Christian religion

cadence /ˈkeɪdəns/ *n.* the rise and fall of the voice in speaking

morbid /ˈmɔːbɪd/ *adj.* having or expressing a strong interest in sad or unpleasant things, especially disease or death

contract /kənˈtrækt/ *v.* to get an illness or virus

why do we write, when we are ten, "so that the mouth can be somewhere" and perhaps when we are thirty " in order to ensure that the mouth may be appropriately positioned environmentally?" What barnacular song do the puddering sirens sing, to lure the writer into the land of jargantua? That, as we know, is the sort of question which though puzzling, is not beyond all conjecture. I will hazard one or two.

The first affects only the official. It is a temptation to cling too long to outworn words and phrases. The British Constitution, as everyone knows, has been shaped by retaining old forms and putting them to new uses. Among the old forms that we are reluctant to abandon are those of expressing ourselves in State documents. Every Bill begins with the words: "Be it enacted by the Queen's most Excellent Majesty by and with the advice and consent of the Lords Spiritual and Temporal and Commons in this present ...."[10] It ends its career as a Bill, and becomes an Act, when the Clerk of the Parliaments is authorized by the Queen to declare "La Reine le vault."[11] That is all very well, because no one ever reads these traditional phrases; they are no longer intended to convey thought from one brain to another. But the official, living in this atmosphere, properly proud of the ancient traditions of his service, sometimes allows his style of letter-writing to be affected by it—*adverting* and *acquainting* and *causing to be informed*. There may even be produced in his mind a feeling that all common words lack the dignity that he is bound to maintain.

That, I think, is one song the sirens sing to the official. Another they certainly sing to all of us. Ivor Brown reminds us how Well's Mr. Polly[12] "revelled in sesquippledan verboojuice,"[13] and comments that he was behaving like William Shakespeare before him. There is something of Mr. Polly in most of us, especially when we are young. All young people of sensibility feel the lure of rippling or reverberating polysyllables. "Evacuated to alternative accommodation" can give a satisfaction that cannot be got from "taken to another house;" "ablution facilities" strikes a chord that does not vibrate to "wash-basins." Far-fetched words are by definition "recherché"[14] words, and are thought to give distinction; thus such words as allergic, ambivalent, and viable acquire their vogue. A newly-discovered metaphor shines like a jewel in a drab vocabulary; thus *blueprint, bottleneck, ceiling,* and *target* are eagerly seized, and the dust settles on their discarded predecessors— *plan, hold-up, limit,* and *objective*....

Another song I am sure the sirens have in their repertoire—a call to the instinct of self-preservation. It is sometimes dangerous to be precise. "Mistiness is the mother of safety," said Newman[15]. Politicians have long known

siren /ˈsaɪərən/ *n.* 1) a sweet singer; 2) a device that makes a long loud sound as a signal or warning
lure /lʊə/ *v.* to persuade or trick sb. to go somewhere or to do sth. by promising them a reward
conjecture /kənˈdʒektʃə/ *n.* the forming of an opinion or idea that is not based on definite knowledge
hazard /ˈhæzəd/ *v.* 1) to make a suggestion or guess which you know may be wrong; 2) to risk sth. or put it in danger
enact /ɪˈnækt/ *v.* to pass a law
reverberate /rɪˈvɜːbəreɪt/ *v.* (of a sound) to be repeated several times as it is reflected off different surfaces
ablution /əˈbluːʃən/ *n.* the act of washing yourself
vibrate /vaɪˈbreɪt/ *v.* to move or make sth. move from side to side very quickly and with small movements
far-fetched /ˈfɑːˈfetʃt/ *adj.* very difficult to believe
allergic /əˈlɜːdʒɪk/ *adj.* having an allergy to; having a strong dislike of
ambivalent /æmˈbɪvələnt/ *adj.* having or showing both good and bad feelings about sb./sth.
viable /ˈvaɪəbəl/ *adj.* that can be done; that will be successful
discard /dɪsˈkɑːd/ *v.* to get rid of sth. that is no longer wanted or needed
repertoire /ˈrepətwɑː/ *n.* 1) all the plays, songs, pieces of music, etc. that a performer knows and can perform; 2) a stock of all regularly performed pieces, regular techniques

the dangers of precision of statement, especially at election time. As Mr. Stuart Chase testifies:

A Senator, distinguished, powerful, an astute leader with surpassing skill in political management, told me that Americanism was to be this year's campaign issue. When I asked him what Americanism meant, he said he did not know, but that it was a damned good word with which to carry an election.[16]

When the official does not know his Minister's mind, or his Minister does not know his own mind, or the Minister thinks it wiser not to speak his mind, the official must sometimes cover his utterance with a mist of vagueness …. Ministers are under daily attack, and their reputations are largely in the hands of their staff. Only if he has full and explicit authority from his Minister can a civil servant show in an important matter that promptness and boldness which are said to be the attributes of men of business.

The words which he writes will go on record, possibly for all time, certainly for a great many years. They may have to be published, and may have a wide circulation. They may even mean something in international relationships. So, even though mathematical accuracy may in the nature of things be unattainable, identifiable inaccuracy must at least be avoided. The hackneyed official phrase, the wide circumlocution, the vague promise, the implied qualification, are comfortingly to hand. Only those who have been exposed to the temptation to use them know how hard it is to resist. But with all the sympathy that such understanding may mean, it is still possible to hold that something might be done to purge official style and caution, necessary and desirable in themselves, of their worst extravagances.

This is a quotation from a leading article in *The Times*. It arose out of a correspondent's ridicule of this extract from a letter written by a Government Department to its Advisory Council:

In transmitting this matter to the council the Minister feels that it may be of assistance to them to learn that, as at present advised, he is inclined to the view that, in existing circumstances, there is, *prima facie*[17], a case for....

It is as easy to slip into this sort of thing without noticing it, as to see the absurdity of it when pointed out. One may surmise that the writer felt himself to be in a dilemma: he wanted the Advisory Council to advise the Minister in a certain way, but did not want them to think that the Minister had made up his mind before getting their advice. But he might have done this without piling qualification on qualification and reservation on reservation, all that he needed to say was that the Minister thought so-and-so but wanted to know what the Advisory Committee thought before taking a decision....

There is often a real need for caution, and it is a temptation to hedging and obscurity.

astute /əˈstjuːt/ *adj.* very clever and quick at seeing what to do in a particular situation, especially how to get an advantage
purge /pɜːdʒ/ *v.* to make sb. or sth. pure, healthy or clean by getting rid of bad thoughts or feelings
extravagance /ɪkˈstrævəɡəns/ *n.* 1) the act or habit of spending more money than one can afford or necessary; 2) sth. that is impressive or noticeable because it is unusual or extreme
surmise /ˈsəːmaɪz/ *v.* to guess or suppose sth. using the evidence you have, without definitely knowing
hedge /hedʒ/ *v.* to avoid giving a direct answer to a question or promising to support a particular idea, etc.

160 But it is no excuse for them. A frank admission that an answer cannot be given is better than an answer that looks as if it meant something but really means nothing. Such a reply *exasperates* the reader and brings the Service into discredit.

> **exasperate** /ɪɡˈzɑːspəreɪt/ *v.* to annoy or irritate sb. very much

Notes

1. Sir Ernest Gowers

Sir Ernest Gowers (1880—1966) was educated at Rugby School and Clare College, Cambridge. He entered the Inland Revenue Department of the British government and served 27 years before becoming the chairman of the Coal Mines Reorganization Commission (later the Coal Commission). During the Second World War he was London Regional Commissioner for Civil Defense. Since then he has been chairman of numerous committees and commissions on a wide variety of subjects, including the admission of women into the Foreign Service, the conditions of work in shops and offices, the preservation of historic houses, foot-and-mouth disease, and capital punishment. He is now best known for work on style guides for maintaining standards of clear English, especially in official prose.

2. the excerpt

The present text is selected from *The Complete Plain Words*, a reconstruction of Gowers' two previous books, *Plain Words* (1948) and *ABC of Plain Words* (1951), written at the invitation of the British Treasury as a contribution to what they were doing to improve official English. *The Complete Plain Words* makes no claim to be a grammar of the English Language; the book is wholly concerned with the choice and arrangement of words in such a way as to get ideas as exactly as possible out of one mind into another. The book is intended primarily for those who use words as tools of their trade, in administration or business.

3. Ivor Brown

Ivor Brown (1891—1974) was a British journalist. He wrote for *The Manchester Guardian* from 1919 to 1935, for the *London Saturday Review* from 1923 to 1930, for *The Observer* (of which he was the editor from 1942 to 1948) from 1929 to 1954, and for *Punch* from 1940 to 1942. His writing included editorials and sports criticism but drama criticism was his specialty.

4. Matthew Arnold

Matthew Arnold (1822—1988) was born in Laleham-on-Thames, England and educated at Balliol College, Oxford, where he became a close friend of the poet Arthur Clough, whom he later eulogized in "Thysris" (1866). In 1851 Arnold became an inspector of schools, a position he held for 35 years. His writing on education advocated the study of the Bible and the humanities as the remedy for what he saw as the Philistinism and insularity of the times, and he worked indefatigably to improve standards and to introduce rigor into the school curriculum.

5. "jargantuan", "barnacular" and "pudder"

"Jargantuan", "barnacular" and "pudder" are self-explanatory; pudder is taken from Lear's prayer to 'the gods who keep this dreadful pudder o'er our heads.'

6. gobbledygook

Gobbledygook (*informal*), complicated language that is difficult to understand, especially when used in official documents.

7. Sir Alan Herbert

Sir Alan Herbert (1890—1971) was an English humourist, novelist, playwright and law reform activist.

8. Ecclesiastes

This is a book of the Apocrypha, also called "Wisdom of Jesus: the son of Sirach" containing moral and practical maxims and probably composed or compiled in the early 2nd Century. AD.

9. matins and evensongs

Matins and evensongs are the service of morning and evening prayer, especially in the Anglican Church.

10. Be it enacted by the Queen's ...in this present.

This may be understood as: Be it enacted by the Crown, the Church and the Parliament.

11. "La Reine le vault"

This is French for "the Queen desires (it)."

12. Mr. Polly

Mr. Polly is the hero of a 1910 comic novel by H. G. Wells.

13. "sesquippledon verboojuice"

The phrase is a satire of bad style. Somebody who uses long words is a sesquipedalianist, and this style of writing is sesquipedalianism.

14. recherché

Recherché is French, meaning unusual and not easy to understand, chosen in order to impress people.

15. Newman

John Henry Newman (1801—1891) was the English prelate and theologian who (with John Keble and Edward Pusey) founded the Oxford Movement; Newman later turned to Roman Catholicism and became a cardinal.

16. A Senator, ...to carry an election.

This is a quotation from *The Tyranny of Words* (Methuen, 7th ed., 1950) by Stuart Chase.

17. prima facie

"Prima facie" is from Latin, meaning "at first sight", "from a first impression."

Comprehension

1. In the opening quotation to this 1956 article, the author suggests that writers are sometimes neglectful of their instruments of writing. What might the "instruments of writing" refer to?
2. What does the author believe is the main problem with written English?
3. Where does the author suggest good examples of simple, terse, and direct English can be found?

4. What possible reason does the author forward for the decline of written English?
5. Why might it be that children's writing is often clearer in meaning than adult writing?
6. Can you paraphrase the author's sentence "All young people of sensibility feel the lure of rippling or reverberating polysyllables" in simpler and more direct English?
7. Does the author approve or not of the metaphors "blueprint" (in place of "plan"), "bottleneck" (in place of "holdup"), "ceiling" (in place of "limit"), and "target" (in place of "objective")? Which forms do you prefer?
8. Why do so many people prefer "pudder" to simplicity, according to the author?

*F*urther *Study*

In the omitted section of *Politics and the English Language*, Orwell lists with notes and examples some features of bad style, including:

- dying metaphors
- operators or verbal false limbs
- pretentious diction
- meaningless words

Orwell claims that you may well find the problems he details in his own essay because they are so pervasive. Now go back to the text and read it carefully and see if you can find any such problems. Can you find examples of the flaws in prose you are reading in your textbooks or in newspapers? Find as many as you can and classify them according to Orwell's categories.

Go to the library and find more about the English style. Here are three well-known books to start with:

a) *A Short Guide to English Style* (1961) by Alan Warner.
b) *The Elements of Style* (1959) by William Strunk, Jr. and E.B. White.
c) *Twenty Questions for the Writer* by Jacqueline Berke.

Unit 7

Nature and Civilization

Unit Goals

☞ To develop students' awareness of the paradox of modern civilization and its relationship with nature
☞ To provide a sample essay for an in-depth, reflective movie review
☞ To examine the satirical use of language

Before Reading

1. Who is X. J. Kennedy, the author of the following text? What other contributions has he made to the literary world? What is the most prominent style in his writing?
2. Search on the Internet for information about the movie King Kong, and try to find the remaking history of this movie: when it was first screened and when its latest version was, and how the viewers and reviewers respond to it.
3. Have you seen this movie? If you have, how would you answer the question raised by the title of Kennedy's essay?
4. What other movies have you seen that have an enduring appeal? Share your knowledge and views with your partner.

A Glimpse into the Text

There are few American cultural icons as enduring as that of King Kong. More than seventy years have passed since the original motion picture was released in 1933, and yet the image of Kong atop the Empire State Building (at the time the tallest in the world) remains as resilient in the collective imagination of Americans as any created by Hollywood—as durable as the famous photograph of Marilyn Monroe standing over a subway vent in New York City, but with a fame much more complicated to explain. In 1960, only twenty-six years after King Kong was first screened, the author of this article attempts to understand its phenomenal popularity.

Text A

Who Killed King Kong?

X.J. Kennedy[1]
(Abridged and edited)

The ordeal and spectacular death of King Kong, the giant ape, undoubtedly have been witnessed by more Americans than have ever seen a performance of *Hamlet, Iphigenia at Aulis*[2], or even *Tobacco Road*[3]. Since RKO-Radio Pictures[4] first released *King Kong* [1933], a quarter-century has gone by; yet year after year, from prints that grow more rain-beaten[5], from sound tracks that grow more tinny, ticket-buyers by the thousands still pursue Kong's luckless fight against the forces of technology, tabloid[6] journalism, and the DAR[7]. They see him chloroformed to sleep, see him whisked from his jungle isle to New York and placed on show, see him burst his chains to roam the city (lugging a frightened blonde), at last to plunge from the spire of the Empire State Building,[8] machine-gunned by model airplanes.

Though Kong may die, one begins to think his legend unkillable. No clearer proof of his hold upon the popular imagination may be seen than what emerged one catastrophic week in March 1955, when New York WOR-TV[9] programmed *Kong* for seven evenings in a row. Many a rival network vice-president must have scowled when surveys showed that *Kong*—the 1933 B-picture[10]—had lured away fat segments of the viewing populace from such powerful competitors as Ed Sullivan, Groucho Marx, and Bishop Sheen[11].

But even television has failed to run *King Kong* into oblivion. Coffee-in-the-lobby cinemas still show the old hunk of hokum,[12] with the apology that in its use of composite shots[13] and animated models the film remains technically interesting. And no other monster in movie history has won so devoted a popular audience. None of the plodding mummies, the stultified draculas,[14] the whitecoated Lugosis[15] with their shiny pinball-machine[16] laboratories, none of the invisible stranglers, berserk robots, or menaces from Mars has ever enjoyed so many resurrections.

Why does the American public refuse to let King Kong rest in peace? It

---

tinny /'tɪni/ *adj.* (disapproving, especially BrE) having a high thin sound like small pieces of metal hitting each other

chloroform /'klɔ(ː)rəfɔːm/ *v.* to administer a liquid in order to anesthetize, make unconscious, or kill

whisk /wɪsk/ *v.* to take sb./sth. somewhere very quickly and suddenly

lug /lʌɡ/ *v.* (informal) to carry or drag sth. heavy with a lot of effort

in a row if sth. happens for several days, etc. **in a row**, it happens on each of those days

scowl /skaʊl/ *v.* ~ **(at sb./sth.)** to look at sb./sth. in an angry or annoyed way

hunk /hʌŋk/ *n.* a large piece of sth., especially food, that has been cut or broken from a larger piece

apology /ə'pɒlədʒi/ *n.* explanation or defence

composite /'kɒmpəzɪt/ *adj.* made of different parts or materials

stultify /'stʌltɪfaɪ/ *v.* (formal) cause (sb.) to feel dull, bored, etc.

stultifying /'stʌltɪfaɪɪŋ/ *adj.* (formal) making you feel very bored and unable to think of new ideas

berserk /bə(ː)'sɜːk/ *adj.* very angry

is true, I'll admit, that *Kong* outdid every monster movie before or since in sheer carnage.
Producers Cooper and Schoedsack crammed into it dinosaurs, headhunters, riots, aerial battles, bullets, bombs, bloodletting. Heroine Fay Wray, whose function is mainly to scream, shuts her mouth for hardly one uninterrupted minute from first reel to last. It is also true that *Kong* is larded with good healthy sadism, for those whose joy it is to see the frantic girl dangled from cliffs and harried by pterodactyls[17]. But it seems to me that the abiding appeal of the giant ape rests on other foundations.

Kong has, first of all, the attraction of being manlike. His simian[18] nature gives him one huge advantage over giant ants and walking vegetables in that an audience may conceivably identify with him. Kong's appeal has the quality that established the Tarzan[19] series as American myth—for what man doesn't secretly imagine himself a huge hairy howler against whom no other monster has a chance? If Tarzan recalls the ape in us, then Kong may well appeal to that great-granddaddy primordial brute from whose tribe we have all deteriorated.

Intentionally or not, the producers of *King Kong* encourage this identification by etching the character of Kong with keen sympathy. For the ape is a figure in a tradition familiar to moviegoers: the pitiable monster. We think of Lon Chaney in the role of Quasimodo,[20] of Karloff in the original Frankenstein.[21] As we watch the Frankenstein monster's fumbling and disastrous attempts to befriend a flower-picking child, our sympathies are enlisted with the monster in his impenetrable loneliness. And so with Kong. As he roars in his chains, while barkers sell tickets to boobs who gape at him, we perhaps feel something more deep than pathos. We begin to sense something of the problem that engaged Eugene O'Neill[22] in *The Hairy ape*: the dilemma of a displaced animal spirit forced to live in a jungle built by machines.

King Kong, it is true, had special relevance in 1933. Landscapes of the depression are glimpsed early in the film when an impresario,[23] seeking some desperate pretty girl to play the lead in a jungle movie, visits souplines[24] and a Woman's Home Mission.[25] In Fay Wray— who's been caught snitching an apple from a fruitstand—his search is ended. When he gives her a big feed and a movie contract, the girl is magic-carpeted out of the world of the National Recovery Act.[26] And when, in the film's climax, Kong smashes that very Third Avenue[27] landscape in which Fay has wandered hungry, audiences of 1933 may well have felt a personal satisfaction.

What is curious is that audiences of 1960 remain hooked. For in the heart of urban man, one suspects, lurks the impulse to fling a bomb. Though machines speed him to the scene of his daily grind, though IBM comptometers ("freeing the human mind from drudgery") enable him to drudge more efficiently once he arrives, there comes a moment when he wishes to turn upon his

---

carnage /ˈkɑːnɪdʒ/ *n.* the violent killing of a large number of people

lard /lɑːd/ *v.* to put small pieces of fat on or into sth. before cooking it

lard sth. with sth. [usually passive] (often disapproving) to include a lot of a particular kind of word or expressions in a speech or in a piece of writing

harry /ˈhæri/ *v.* to make repeated attacks on an enemy

etch /etʃ/ *v.* to make a strong clear mark or pattern on sth.

fumbling /ˈfʌmblɪŋ/ *adj.* awkward, uncertain or hesitating

enlist /ɪnˈlɪst/ *v.* to persuade sb. to help you or to join you in doing sth.

barker /ˈbɑːkə/ barker is a person who stands outside a place where there is entertainment and shouts to people to go in

boob /buːb/ a boob is a stupid or silly person

gape /ɡeɪp/ *v.* ~ **(at sb./sth.)** to stare at sb./sth. with your mouth open because you are shocked or surprised

pathos /ˈpeɪθɒs/ *n.* (in writing, speech and plays) the power of a performance, description, etc. to produce feelings of sadness and sympathy

machines and kick hell out of them.²⁸ He wants to hurl his combination radio-alarm-clock out
the bedroom window and listen to its smash. What subway commuter wouldn't love—just
for once—to see the downtown express smack head-on into the uptown local?²⁹ Such a wish
is gratified in that memorable scene in *Kong* that opens with a wide-angle shot:³⁰ interior of a
railway car on the Third Avenue EL.³¹ Straphangers³² are nodding, the literate refold their
newspapers. Unknown to them, Kong has torn away a section of trestle toward which the train
now speeds. The motorman spies Kong up ahead, jams on the brakes.³³ Passengers hurtle
together like so many peas in a pail. In a window of the car appear Kong's bloodshot eyes.
Women shriek. Kong picks up the railway car as if it were a rat, flips it to the street and
ties knots in it, or something. To any commuter the scene must appear one of the most
satisfactory pieces of celluloid ever exposed.

    Yet however violent his acts, Kong remains a gentleman. Remarkable is his sense of
chivalry. Whenever a fresh boa constrictor threatens Fay, Kong first sees that the lady is safely
parked, then manfully thrashes her attacker. (And she, the ingrate, runs away every time his
back is turned.) Atop the Empire State Building, ignoring his pursuers, Kong places Fay on a
ledge as tenderly as if she were a dozen eggs. He fondles her, then turns to face the Army
Air-Force. And Kong is perhaps the most disinterested lover since Cyrano:³⁴ his attentions to the
lady are utterly without hope of reward. After all, between a five-foot blonde and a fifty-foot
ape, love can hardly be more than an intellectual flirtation.³⁵ In his simian way King Kong is
the hopelessly yearning lover of Petrarchan convention.³⁶ His forced exit from his jungle, in
chains, results directly from his single-minded pursuit of Fay. He smashes a Broadway theater
when the notion enters his dull brain that the flashbulbs of photographers somehow endanger
the lady. His perilous shinnying up a skyscraper to pluck Fay from her boudoir is an act of the
kindliest of hearts. He's impossible to discourage even though the love of his life can't lay
eyes on him without shrieking murder.³⁷

    The tragedy of King Kong then, is to be the beast who at the end of the fable fails to turn
into the handsome prince. This is the conviction that the scriptwriters would leave with us
in the film's closing line. As Kong's corpse lies blocking traffic in the street, the entrepreneur
who brought him to New York turns to the assembled reporters and proclaims: "That's your
story, boys—it was Beauty killed the Beast!" But greater forces than those of the screaming Lady have combined to lay Kong low,³⁸ if you ask me. Kong lives for a time as one of those persecuted near-animal souls bewildered in the middle of an industrial order, whose simple desires are thwarted at every turn. He climbs the Empire State Building because in all New York it's the closest thing he can find to the clifftop of his jungle isle. He dies, a pitiful dolt, and the army brass and publicity-men cackle over him. His death is the only possible outcome to as neat a traffic dilemma as you can ask for.³⁹ The machine-guns

---

hurtle /'hɜːtl/ *v.* to move or make sb./sth. move very fast in a particular direction

celluloid /'seljulɔɪd/ *n.* a) is a thin transparent plastic material made in sheets, used in past for photographic film; b) films/movies

chivalry /'ʃɪvəlri/ *n.* the polite and kind behaviour that shows a sense of honour, especially by men towards women

thrash /θræʃ/ *v.* (informal, especially BrE) to defeat sb. very easily in a game

fondle /'fɒndl/ *v.* to touch and move your hand gently over sb./sth., especially in a sexual way, or in order to show love

shinny /'ʃɪni/ *v.* (AmE)=shin, to climb up or down sth. quickly, using your hands and legs

boudoir /'buːdwɑː/ *n.* a woman's small private room or bedroom

dolt /dəʊlt/ *n.* a stupid person

brass /brɑːs/ *n.* important people

cackle /'kækəl/ *v.* to laugh in a loud unpleasant way

neat /niːt/ (AmE, informal) good; excellent

do him in, while the manicured human hero (a nice clean Dartmouth[40] boy) carries away Kong's sweetheart to the altar. O, the misery of it all.

A Negro friend from Atlanta tells me that in colored neighborhoods throughout the South, *Kong* does a constant business. They show the thing in Atlanta at least every year, presumably to the same audiences. Perhaps this popularity may simply be due to the fact that Kong is one of the most watchable movies ever constructed, but I wonder whether Negro audiences may not find some archetypical appeal in this seriocomic tale of a huge black powerful free spirit whom all the hardworking white policemen are out to kill.

Every day in the week on a screen somewhere in the world, King Kong relives his agony. Again and again he expires on the Empire State Building, as audiences of the devout assist his sacrifice. We watch him die, and by extension kill the ape within our bones, but these little deaths of ours occur in prosaic surroundings. We do not die on a tower, New York before our feet, nor do we give our lives to smash a few flying machines. It is not for us to bring to a momentary standstill the civilization in which we move. King Kong does this for us. And so we kill him again and again, in much-spliced celluloid, while the ape in us expires from day to day, obscure, in desperation.[41]

> **do sb. in** (informal) to kill sb.
> **manicured** /ˈmænɪkjʊəd/ *adj.* (of hands or fingers) with nails that are neatly cut and polished
> **seriocomic** /ˌsɪərɪəʊˈkɒmɪk/ *adj.* partly serious and partly comic
> **prosaic** /prəʊˈzeɪ-ɪk/ *adj.* (written, often disapproving) dull; not romantic

More about the Text

1. X. J. Kennedy

X. J. Kennedy (born on 21 August, 1929, Dover, New Jersey) is a prominent formalist poet, translator, anthologist, editor, and writer of children's literature. He professes himself as writing for "three separate audiences: children, college students (who use textbooks), and that small band of people who still read poetry." But there is unity in all of Kennedy's writings —underlying it is a love of poetry and meter, a playfulness verging on the absurd, and a fervent regard for the possibilities of language.

Among his works, *One Winter Night in August* (1975), a collection of children's verse, is his first book for children. *An Introduction to Poetry* (1966) is his most famous textbook, and *Literature: An Introduction to Fiction, Poetry, and Drama* (1976) is very popular with Chinese students of English literature and serves as a useful handbook for their understanding of some of the masterpieces in world literature.

When studying this present essay by X. J. Kennedy, bear in mind that it was written in 1960, and many references to American culture of that era may be unfamiliar to contemporary Chinese readers. Still, it is an excellent model of a reflective essay, and an interesting reading of the 1933 movie *King Kong*. Moreover, Kennedy in his essay sees Kong as a human-like beast, trapped by civilization, whose roars of battle we instinctively understand, and whose feat of turning a modern city into a chaotic scene we secretly feel gratified by. In this sense, the essay is not only a movie review, but also a mild satire on Western civilization, in which the glory and glamour of a city based on technological advancement is brought to a standstill by a primitive violent impulse, "the impulse to fling a bomb" lurking "in the heart of urban man."

2. Iphigenia at Aulis

A play written by Greek playwright Euripides (410 B.C.E). Iphigenia: daughter of Agamemnon, King of Mycenae. Aulis: anchorage on the eastern coast of Greece, opposite the island of Euboea (Éνvoια). In Greek mythology, it was the point of departure for the Greek expedition against Troy.

3. Tobacco Road

This is a novel by Erskine Caldwell, published in 1932. It depicts the oppressed and degraded life of a poverty-stricken sharecropper, Jeeter Lester, and his miserable family in the squalid backcountry of contemporary Georgia. The sensational dramatization by Jack Kirkland (1933) had a continuous run of 3128 Broadway performances.

4. RKO-Radio Pictures

US film studio created in 1928. "RKO-Radio" was a company that was originally involved in producing radio programs but later produced motion pictures as well.

5. rain-beaten

Worn out by rain.

6. tabloid

Tabloid is a newspaper with small pages (usually half the size of those in larger papers). Tabloids usually have short articles and a lot of pictures and stories about famous people, and are thought of as less serious than other newspapers.

7. DAR

"Daughters of the American Revolution"—an ultra-conservative association of women (predominantly white and wealthy) whose family roots in America go back to the mid-1700s or earlier. The DAR was notoriously critical of "un-American activities"—which they essentially saw as anything that threatened the status quo (for example socialism, homosexuality, non-Christian religions, feminism, and even immigration). So conservative was this group that by 1960 (when this article was written) they had become the target of jokes by liberally-minded people, since they appeared to be virtually opposed to anything out of the ordinary. The reference here is an example of such a joke. That is, although there is no mention of the DAR in the movie itself, the author is humorously suggesting that Kong would certainly have been persecuted by the women of the organization since he would have been definitely socially unacceptable to them.

8. Empire State Building

Built in 1931 (two years before *King Kong* was released), the Empire State Building was the tallest structure in New York City (102 Floors, 381 meters) until the completion of the World Trade Center in 1975. It is still a primary tourist attraction in the city—a "must see" like the Statue of Liberty.

9. New York WOR-TV

This is a television station in New York City.

10. B-pictures

B-pictures are low-budget movies.

11. Ed Sullivan, Groucho Marx, and Bishop Sheen

Ed Sullivan was the host of a TV variety program called "The Ed Sullivan Show." It aired nationally every Sunday evening, and it was the program on which The Beatles first performed in America. Groucho Marx (of the comedy team the Marx Brothers) had a comedy TV game show in the late 1950s called "You Bet Your Life." Bishop Fulton Sheen was the host of a Catholic TV program also in the late 1950s called "Life is Worth Living." All three TV programs aired nationally and were very popular.

12. hokum

Hokum is a film/movie, play, etc. that is not realistic and has no artistic qualities.

13. composite shots

In filmmaking jargon, a composite shot is a scene composed by filming actors in front of a screen on which another film is being back-projected, giving the impression that the actions of the actors and those on the screen are happening simultaneously and together.

14. Dracula

Count Dracula was the blood sucking vampire who first appeared in the 1920s German film *Nosferatu*. There have been countless remakes of the Dracula legend since then.

15. whitecoated Lugosis

Bella Lugosi was a Hollywood actor who frequently appeared in movies as a mad scientist dressed in a white lab coat, such as doctors wear. It became a stereotype for mad scientists in Hollywood movies ever after to wear a white lab coat just like Lugosi's.

16. pinball-machine

It is a device in which the player operates a plunger to shoot a ball down a slanted surface.

17. pterodactyls

It is a dragon with feather or wing.

18. simian

It is connected with or similar to a monkey or ape.

19. Tarzan

First a comic-strip character, later a movie character, "Tarzan of the Apes" was a boy with British aristocratic roots who was raised by apes in Africa to become the Lord of the Jungle. In the original Hollywood version Tarzan speaks the immortal words: "Me Tarzan; you Jane."

20. Lon Chaney in the role of Quasimodo

Lon Chaney was the actor who played the role of the ill-fated hunchbacked, bell-ringer in the 1930s Hollywood version of *The Hunchback of Notre Dame*.

21. Karloff in the original Frankenstein

Boris Karloff was the American actor who played the role of *Frankenstein's Monster* in the 1930s Hollywood version of the book. Frankenstein (1818): A Gothic tale of terror by the English writer Mary Shelly, wife of the famous English Romantic poet, Percy Bysshe Sherry. The tale inspired many film versions, and has been regarded as the origin of modern science fiction.

22. Eugene O'Neill

Eugene O'Neill (1888—1953) is acknowledged as the foremost creative American playwright, and was awarded Nobel Prize in 1936.

The Hairy ape: expressionist play by O'Neill, produced and published in 1922. It is symbolic of the perversion of human strength by technological progress.

23. impresario

Impresario is a person who arranges plays in the theatre, etc., especially a person who manages a theatre, opera or ballet company.

24. souplines

During the depression, homeless people lined up for free meals of soup and bread that were provided by charities.

25. Woman's Home Mission

A home for destitute women provided by charities during the depression.

26. the girl is magic-carpeted out of the world of the National Recovery Act

Magic carpet (in stories) is a carpet that can fly and carry people. **National Recovery Act:** the federal government program instituted by the administration of President Franklin Delano Roosevelt to put people back to work during the depression. The sentence humorously implies that the girl's fate seemed to have suddenly changed for the better.

27. Third Avenue

Third Avenue is a major road in Manhattan, New York City.

28. Though machines... kick hell out of them.

In this sentence, the author is humorously suggesting that we are all subconsciously "Luddites," that is, anti-progress and anti-machine, and secretly wishing to destroy these things.

29. What subway commuter... uptown local?

This sentence is another joke, humorously suggesting that a collision of subway trains would amuse us.

30. a wide-angle shot

It is the camera lens that captures a wide picture.

31. Third Avenue EL

This refers to the Third Avenue electric line in New York in the 1930s. Along the line, horses of the surface cans and of wagons jogged along, people looked into shop windows and not to the sky, and the only difference was the train, having more room on each side and did not make so much noise.

32. straphanger

It refers to the standing passenger in a bus, train, etc. who supports himself by holding onto a strap attached to the ceiling; commuter.

33. Straphangers... brakes.

This is an actual scene from the movie.

34. Cyrano

Cyrano de Bergerac is a famous French literary character who was totally unattractive to women because of his large nose. He wrote love poems for a friend to attract a beautiful woman named Roxanne—though Cyrano himself was deeply in love with her.

35. love can hardly be more than an intellectual flirtation
Physical love is impossible.

36. Petrarchan convention
From a Shakespeare sonnet—a despairing lover writes to a lovely, unattainable lady in words of adoration and reverent praise.

37. shrieking murder
Screaming wildly. In the movie, the heroine is constantly screaming in the presence of Kong.

38. to lay Kong low
To kill him.

39. His death is the only possible outcome to as neat a traffic dilemma as you can ask for.
Kong's presence in New York City wreaks havoc in the streets.

40. Dartmouth
A town of southeast Massachusetts on Buzzards Bay southwest of New Bedford. Formerly a shipbuilding center, it is now a tourist resort.

41. while the ape in us expires from day to day, obscure, in desperation
The true nature of men is crushed day by day by civilization, desperate to survive, to fight back—thus the popularity of *King Kong*.

Check Your Understanding

1. Who or what is King Kong? Where is King Kong's natural home? How does King Kong arrive in America?
2. What does Kennedy accomplish for his readers in the first paragraph?
3. What is the topic sentence of the second paragraph? What evidence does Kennedy use to support the point?
4. What is the reason for the movie's immediate popularity with the 1933 American audience?
5. What are some of the more superficial reasons given by the author for the movie's enduring popularity?
6. What, according to Kennedy, is the tragedy of King Kong?
7. Why does the author think the movie is especially popular with black audiences?
8. According to the author, what psychological effect might King Kong's violence and death have on movie-goers in general?
9. According to the author, who is actually responsible for killing King Kong?
10. What other forms of entertainment and literature does Kennedy refer to in making his argument? How many genres does he name? What does he gain through all these allusions?

Paraphrasing

1. His (Kong's) simian nature gives him one huge advantage over giant ants and walking vegetables in that an audience may conceivably identify with him.
2. If Tarzan recalls the ape in us, then Kong may well appeal to that great-granddaddy primordial brute from whose tribe we have all deteriorated.
3. Intentionally or not, the producers of *King Kong* encourage this identification by etching the character of Kong with keen sympathy.
4. What is curious is that audiences of 1960 remain hooked. For in the heart of urban man, one suspects, lurks the impulse to fling a bomb. Though machines speed him to the scene of his daily grind, though IBM comptometers ("freeing the human mind from drudgery") enable him to drudge more efficiently once he arrives, there comes a moment when he wishes to turn upon his machines and kick hell out of them.
5. Kong is perhaps the most disinterested lover since Cyrano.
6. In his simian way King Kong is the hopelessly yearning lover of Petrarchan convention.
7. His death is the only possible outcome to as neat a traffic dilemma as you can ask for.
8. Every day in the week on a screen somewhere in the world, King Kong relives his agony. Again and again he expires on the Empire State Building, as audiences of the devout assist his sacrifice. We watch him die, and by extension kill the ape within our bones, but these little deaths of ours occur in prosaic surroundings.

Some Information about English Style

1. How to write a reflective essay on a movie

The present text is an excellent example of a reflective essay on a movie. Apart from his grasp of the details of the movie, the reflection is characterized by the author's passion, insight, humor, familiarity with literary heritage and cinematic art, as well as his understanding of the concerns and psychology of American society and his adroitness in applying and relating all these to his comments on *King Kong*. Through his review, we not only see the movie as a commercial success or a sensational thriller, but also what is truly "classic" about the movie, thus setting us thinking upon matters such as the role of modern civilization and the relationship between man and nature in the light of technological progress.

Below are some techniques the author follows in his essay to make his review both enjoyable and thought-provoking. Can you find some specific examples from the text to illustrate each?

   (1) Comparison: comparing *King Kong* with other cinema performances, especially popular monster movies and TV programs during the same period to show how popular the movie was.

   (2) Detailing: presenting details from scenes of the movie to show the gripping power of the film.

   (3) Cause-effect analysis: Why does *King Kong* have such enduring appeal to an audience?

      a. It is a successful thriller

         i. Kong outdid every monster movie before or since in sheer carnage.

ii. Kong gratifies audience with "good healthy sadism."
b. Kong has the attraction of being humanlike so that an audience may identify with him.
c. *King Kong* had special relevance in 1933 with its landscape of the Great Depression, which the audiences of the 1930s were well familiar with.
d. Kong's violent acts against New York city were still meaningful for audiences of the 1960s, since the urban citizens of the 1960s man lived in an ever encompassing jungle of machines, and had developed a more uninhibited secret impulse for destruction, which finds its gratification or catharsis in *King Kong*.
e. Kong remains charming, with his remarkable sense of chivalry, and romantic with his single-minded devotion to the object of his love.
f. Negro audiences may find some archetypical appeal in this seriocomic tale of a huge black powerful free spirit that white policemen are trying to kill.
(4) Abundant references to other famous movie characters to highlight Kong's special hold on the audience's imagination.
(5) Tone of voice is filled with passion, occasionally tinged with satirical humor, to elicit readers' emotions and engage their interest.

2. Satire

As in most of his creative works, Kennedy in this argumentative essay demonstrates his particular talent for satire.

Satire is an artistic form in which human or individual vices, follies, abuses, or shortcomings are held up to censure by means of ridicule, derision, burlesque, irony, caustic wit or other methods, sometimes with an intent to bring about improvement. Literature and drama are its chief vehicles, but it is also found in such mediums as film, the visual arts (e.g., caricatures), and political cartoons. Though present in Greek literature, notably in the works of Aristophanes, satire generally follows the example of either of two Romans, Horace or Juvenal. To Horace the satirist is an urbane man of the world who sees folly everywhere but is moved to gentle laughter rather than to rage. Juvenal's satirist is an upright man who is horrified and angered by corruption. Their different perspectives produced the subgenres of satire identified by John Dryden as comic satire and tragic satire. Shakespeare later wrote Horatian satire, which is usually comic, and Jonathan Swift wrote Juvenalian satire, which borders on the tragic.

In the present text, Kennedy's satire is more Horatian than Juvenalian. That is to say, though he does launch a serious attack on the myth of modern civilization with its proud indifference to and greedy exploitation of nature, he is not so much angered by as detached from the folly and vice he attacks. In achieving the satirical effect Kennedy in his essay uses various rhetorical devices, such as anticlimax, oxymoron, rhetorical questions, irony, metonymy, paradox, exclamation, etc. Try to identify the meaning of each of these terms and find examples from the text to illustrate these devices.

3. Comparison and contrast

Though the present text is not a comparison and contrast essay in the overall sense, during the process of making his argument the author presents a number of comparisons and contrasts to convince his readers that *King Kong* was better received than many other highly-reputed movies. The comparisons and contrasts are presented either through sentence structures containing adverbial phrases of comparatives or superlatives, or through references to other compatible categories. Through these devices the author gives the readers a more concrete notion of why and how *King Kong* outdid many of its competitors and enjoyed an enduring appeal to its viewers. For instance, the essay begins with the following sentence: "The ordeal and spectacular death of King Kong, the giant ape, undoubtedly have been witnessed by <u>more</u> Americans <u>than</u> have ever seen a performance of *Hamlet, Iphigenia at Aulis*, or even *Tobacco Road*." By comparing the tragic end of *King Kong* with three other classic tragedies the author successfully illustrates that *King Kong* is even more popular than those equally well-acclaimed and powerful productions. "<u>And no other</u> monster in movie history has won <u>so</u> devoted a popular audience. <u>None</u> of the plodding mummies, the stultified draculas, the whitecoated Lugosis with their shiny pinball-machine laboratories, <u>none</u> of the invisible stranglers, berserk robots, or menaces from Mars has <u>ever</u> enjoyed <u>so</u> many resurrections." These sentences with the "no other... so" and "none... ever... so" structures further emphasize that Kong is one of the most appealing monster characters in all movie history.

Can you find other examples from the text to show how, through direct and indirect comparisons and contrasts, the unique power of *King Kong* is convincingly conveyed to readers?

Practice

📖 Building word power

1. **Differentiate the words in each bracket and choose the appropriate one to complete the sentence.**

   (1) During the interview he _____ (fumbled, mumbled) helplessly for words.
   (2) He _____ (fumbled; mumbled) something to me which I didn't quite catch.
   (3) I'm fed up with the _____ (mundane; prosaic) style of that article.
   (4) I lead a pretty _____ (mundane; prosaic) life; nothing interesting ever happens to me.
   (5) His _____ (forgetfulness; oblivion) is well known; better tell him again.
   (6) _____ (Forgetfulness; Oblivion) is the fate of most writers.
   (7) I find his ideas very _____ (appealing; attractive); I like them.
   (8) She looked at him with _____ (appealing; attractive) eyes.
   (9) She was _____ (gratified; satisfied) to find that they had followed her advice.
   (10) Most of the people were _____ (gratified; satisfied) with the result.
   (11) Seeing the sack of gold coins under his roof, the miser rubbed his hands and _____ (cackled, chuckled) with delight.
   (12) Father always _____ (cackles, chuckles) when he reads the funny papers.
   (13) This information is not available to the _____ (populace, population, public) at large.
   (14) The law was intended for the good of the general _____ (populace, population, public).
   (15) There has been a steady fall in the _____ (populace, population, public) of Scotland since 1945.

2. Choose the appropriate words from the list below and complete the following passage.

influential	innovative	offered	cinematography
Beauty	effects	astounded	Virtually
making	course	star	legend
unequalled	awesome	trick	primitive
to	hits	witnessing	version

How many films can truly be said to be definitive? The answer is probably "not many," but the original 1933 _____ (1) of King Kong is certainly one of them. For its time, every aspect is _____ (2). First-of-their-kind special effects, first-of-its-kind plot, famous performances and a final sequence that remains _____ (3) as an eye-popping cinematic experience. The quality of _____ (4) and visual trickery has progressed a long way since 1933—so the special _____ (5) obviously look rather _____ (6) to 21st Century eyes—but anyone with a shred of common sense will still be _____ (7) by what they see. This is movie history in the _____ (8) . Had this never been made, the whole history of film may have taken a different _____ (9) .

Ace film director Carl Denham (Robert Armstrong) hires an unemployed, attractive New York woman Ann Darrow (Fay Wray) to _____ (10) in his new picture. He takes her by boat to remote Skull Island where, according to _____ (11) , there lives an _____ (12) god-like beast named Kong. Denham's plan is to shoot a variation of the _____ (13) and the Beast story, using Ann as his beauty and Kong as his beast. Everyone involved gets more than they bargained for when Ann is kidnapped by the island natives and _____ (14) as a sacrifice to Kong. She is kidnapped by a gigantic prehistoric ape and saved only by the courage of ship's mate Jack Driscoll (Bruce Cabot). But Denham has one more _____ (15) up his sleeve when he captures Kong and takes the beast back to New York. You don't really think those chains will hold him, do you?

_____ (16) every monster movie ever made owes something _____ (17) King Kong—even colossal modern _____ (18) like Jurassic Park, The Lost World and Godzilla (not to mention thousands of small scale homages such as The Land Unknown and Gorgo). It is arguably the most _____ (19) film of all-time. I genuinely envy people who were lucky enough to experience this film during its 1933 opening week—what must they have thought? Did they realize they were _____ (20) something utterly extraordinary? I could go on all day giving reasons why you should see it, but it would be pointless. It can all be summed up in one sentence: if you have even the slightest interest in movies SEE THIS FILM!

Grammar and Usage

Translate the following sentences with the words or phrases given.
(1) 恐怕这个姑娘真的被那个青年迷住了。(hook)
(2) 那次事件多年来一直铭刻在她心中。(etch)
(3) 她摸黑找灯的开关。(fumble)
(4) 他继续工作着,完全忘却了时间的流逝。(oblivious)

(5) 在顾客服务方面，有时小企业可能优于大企业。(outdo)
(6) 看到他忧心忡忡的样子，我恍然明白了他内心的真实感受。(glimpse)
(7) 我不喜欢这本书，因为我无法与书中任何一个主要角色产生共鸣。(identify)
(8) 想不出有什么理由把他提升到她的上面。(conceivable)
(9) 我们像罐头里的沙丁鱼一般紧紧挤在一起。(jam)
(10) 平静的河流里隐藏着危机。(lurk)

Improving your writing style

1. List at least five examples to illustrate the satirical use of the language in the essay.
2. Can you identify any other stylistic features in Kennedy's use of language in this essay? Write them down and illustrate with examples.

Writing task

Write a reflective essay of about 800 words on the Hollywood 2005 version of King Kong. In your writing make sure that you perform the following tasks:

- stating your opinion;
- giving an outline;
- highlighting a key moment or idea;
- commenting on the performance of the actors and actresses, the technical elements such as cinematography and lighting;
- summarizing your general evaluation of the movie.

Text B

Yellow Woman and a Beauty of the Spirit
Leslie Marmon Silko[1]
(Abridged and Edited)

Prior to the late-1960s, almost all published fiction about the American Indian was written by white males, who most often portrayed the Indians in a negative light—hostile, sometimes brutal, or at best when civilized to some degree, servile. This state of affairs changed along with the rise of second-wave feminism. When women found their voices, so too were various minority groups at last able to express theirs, as publishers and readers alike became receptive to authenticity rather than misrepresentation. In this story, the author, who is an American Indian and feminist, presents her personal picture of a native Indian community—one that is tolerant, vibrant, in harmony with *the natural world, and puzzled by a foreign culture that lacks these virtues and yet assumes authority over it.*

From the time I was a small child, I was aware that I was different. I looked different from my playmates. My two sisters looked different too. We didn't quite look like the other Laguna Pueblo[2] children, but we didn't look quite white either.

I spent a great deal of time with my great-grandmother. Her house was next to our house, and I used to wake up at dawn, hours before my parents or younger sisters, and I'd go wait on the porch swing or on the back steps by her kitchen door. She got up at dawn, but she was more than eighty years old, so she needed a little while to get dressed and to get the fire going in the cook stove. I had been carefully instructed by my parents not to bother her and to behave, and to try to help her any way I could. I always loved the early mornings when the air was so cool with a hint of rain smell in the breeze. In the dry New Mexico air, the least hint of dampness smells sweet.

Grandma A'mooh would tell about the old days, family stories about relatives who had been killed by Apache[3] raiders who stole the sheep our relatives had been herding near Swahnee. Sometimes she read Bible stories that we kids liked because of the illustrations of Jonah in the mouth of a whale and Daniel surrounded by lions.[4] Grandma A'mooh would send me home when she took her nap, but when the sun got low and the afternoon began to cool off, I would be back on the porch swing, waiting for her to come out to water the plants and to haul in firewood for the evening. When Grandma was eighty-five, she still chopped her own kindling. She used to let me carry it in the coal bucket for her, but she would not allow me to use the ax. I carried armloads of kindling too, and I learned to be proud of my strength.

I was allowed to listen quietly when Aunt Susie or Aunt Alice came to visit Grandma. When I got old enough to cross the road alone, I went and visited them almost daily. They were vigorous women who valued books and writing. They were usually busy chopping wood or cooking but never hesitated to take time to answer my questions. Best of all they told me the *hummah-hah* stories,[5] about an earlier time when animals and humans shared a common language. In the old days, the Pueblo people had educated their children in this manner; adults took time out to talk to and teach young people. Everyone was a teacher, and every activity had the potential to teach the child.

But as soon as I started kindergarten at the Bureau of Indian Affairs day school, I began to learn more about the differences between the Laguna Pueblo world and the outside world. It was at school that I learned just how different I looked from my classmates. Sometimes tourists driving past on Route 66 would stop by Laguna Day School at recess time to take photographs of us kids. One day, when I was in the first grade, we all crowded around the smiling white tourists, who peered at our faces. We all wanted to be in the picture because

raider /ˈreɪdə/ *n.* a person who makes a criminal attack on a place
herd /hɜːd/ *v.* to make animals move together as a group
illustration /ˌɪləsˈtreɪʃən/ *n.* a drawing or picture in a book, magazine, etc. especially one th at explains sth.
armload /ˈɑːmləʊd/ *n.* = armful, a quantity that you can carry in one or both arms
kindling /ˈkɪndlɪŋ/ *n.* small dry pieces of wood, etc. used to start a fire
bureau /ˈbjʊərəʊ/ *n.* (in the US) a government department or part of a government department
recess /rɪˈses/ *n.* (AmE) = break, a period of time between lessons at school
peer /pɪə/ *v.* to look closely or carefully at sth., especially when you cannot see it clearly

afterward the tourists sometimes gave us each a penny. Just as we were all posed and ready to have our picture taken, the tourist man looked at me. "Not you," he said and motioned for me to step away from my classmates. I felt so embarrassed that I wanted to disappear. My classmates were puzzled by the tourists' behavior, but I knew the tourists didn't want me in their snapshot because I looked different, because I was part white.

My grandmother was dark and handsome. Her expression in photographs is one of confidence and strength. I do not know if white people then or now would consider her beautiful. I do not know if old-time Laguna Pueblo people considered her beautiful or if the old-time people even thought in those terms. To the Pueblo way of thinking, the act of comparing one living being with another was silly, because each living being or thing is unique and therefore incomparably valuable because it is the only one of its kind. The old-time people thought it was crazy to attach such importance to a person's appearance. I understood very early that there were two distinct ways of interpreting the world. There was the white people's way and there was the Laguna way. In the Laguna way, it was bad manners to make comparisons that might hurt another person's feelings.

The old stories demonstrate the interrelationships that the Pueblo people have maintained with their plant and animal clanspeople. "Kochininako"—Yellow Woman—represents all women in the old stories. Her deeds span the spectrum of human behavior and are mostly heroic acts, though in at least one story, she chooses to join the secret Destroyer Clan, which worships destruction and death. Because Laguna Pueblo cosmology features a female Creator, the status of women is equal with the status of men, and women appear as often as men in the old stories as hero figures. Yellow Woman is my favorite because she dares to cross traditional boundaries of ordinary behavior during times of crisis in order to save the Pueblo; her power lies in her courage and her uninhibited sexuality, which the old-time Pueblo stories celebrate again and again because fertility was so highly valued.

The old stories always say that Yellow Woman was beautiful, but remember that the old-time people were not so much thinking about physical appearances. In each story, the beauty that Yellow Woman possesses is the beauty of her passion, her daring, and her sheer strength to act when catastrophe is imminent. In one story, the people are suffering during a great drought and accompanying famine. Each day, Kochininako has to walk farther and farther from the village to find fresh water for her husband and children. One day she travels far, far to the east, to the plains, and she finally locates a freshwater spring. But when she reaches the pool, the water is churning violently as if something large had just gotten out of the pool. Kochininako does not want to see what huge creature had been at the pool, but just as she fills her water jar and turns to hurry away, a strong, sexy man in buffalo-skin leggings appears by the pool. Little drops of

---

motion /ˈməʊʃən/ v. ~ to sb. (to do sth.) to make a movement, usually with your hand or head to show sb. what you want them to do

snapshot /ˈsnæpʃɒt/ n. = snap, a photograph, especially one taken quickly

clanspeople /ˈklænzˌpiːpl/ n. = clansman, a member of a clan

spectrum /ˈspektrəm/ n. (written) a complete or wide range of related qualities, ideas, etc.

clan /klæn/ n. a group of families who are related to each other, especially in Scotland

cosmology /kɒzˈmɒlədʒi/ n. the scientific study of the universe and its origin and development

feature /ˈfiːtʃə/ v. to include a particular person or thing as a special feature

imminent /ˈɪmɪnənt/ adj. (especially of sth. unpleasant) likely to happen very soon

churn /tʃɜːn/ v. if water, mud, etc. churns, or if sth. churns it (up), it moves or is moved around violently

leggings /ˈleɡɪŋz/ n. protective outer coverings for the legs

water glisten on his chest. She cannot help but look at him because he is so strong and so good to look at. Able to transform himself from human to buffalo in the wink of an eye, Buffalo Man gallops away with her on his back. Kochininako falls in love with Buffalo Man and, because of this liaison, the Buffalo People agree to give their bodies to the hunters to feed the starving Pueblo. Thus Kochininako's fearless sensuality results in the salvation of the people of her village, who are saved by the meat the Buffalo People "give" to them.

> in the wink of an eye = in the twinkling of an eye, very quickly
> gallop /ˈɡæləp/ v. (informal) (of a person) to run very quickly
> liaison /liˈeɪzɑːn/ n. a secret sexual relationship, especially if one or both partners are married
> presence of mind the ability to react quickly and stay calm in a difficult or dangerous situation
> outwit /aʊtˈwɪt/ v. to defeat sb./sth. or gain an advantage over them by doing sth. clever
> fling /flɪŋ/ n. a short sexual relationship with sb.
> tote /təʊt/ v. carrying the thing mentioned

The Kochininako stories were always my favorite because Yellow Woman had so many adventures. In one story, as she hunts rabbits to feed her family, a giant monster pursues her, but she has the courage and the presence of mind to outwit it. In another story, Kochininako has a fling with Whirlwind Man and returns to her husband ten months later with twin baby boys. The twin boys grow up to be great heroes of the people. The stories about Kochininako made me aware that sometimes an individual must act despite disapproval, or concern for appearances or what others may say. From Yellow Woman's adventures, I learned to be comfortable with my differences. I even imagined that Yellow Woman had yellow skin, brown hair, and green eyes like mine, although her name does not refer to her color, but rather to the ritual color of the east.

There have been many other moments like the one with the camera toting tourist in the schoolyard. But the old-time people always say, remember the stories, the stories will help you be strong. So all these years I have depended on Kochininako and the stories of her adventures. Kochininako is beautiful because she has courage to act in times of great peril, and her triumph is achieved by her sensuality, not through violence and destruction. For these qualities of the spirit, Yellow Woman and all women are beautiful.

Notes

1. Leslie Marmon Silko

Leslie Marmon Silko was born on March 5, 1948, in Albuquerque, New Mexico. Raised on the Laguna Pueblo Reservation in northern New Mexico, Silko's cultural and ethnic heritage was a mix of Laguna Pueblo, Plains Indian, Mexican, and Anglo-American. As a native-American writer Silko is perhaps best known for her first novel, *Ceremony* (1977), a coming-of-age story about a young man of mixed Native American and white ancestry. Many of Silko's works contrast the values of the white world with those of native-American tradition. Silko's emergence in the 1970s coincided with a revival of interest in Native American culture in North America.

The present text is taken from the author's essay collection entitled *Yellow Woman and a Beauty of Spirit: Essays on Native American Life Today* (1996).

It collects a number of Silko's previously published essays on the life, culture, and societal position of modern Native Americans. In this collection Silko begins with the land and relates it to the remaining three elements of focus: human identity, imagination, and storytelling. Drawing on her background of oral tradition, Silko weaves these four elements together in such a way as to both identify herself with, and allow the reader a broader sense of, the related fusions and conflicts many modern native-Americans face.

2. Laguna Pueblo

Pueblo (people) (Spanish *pueblo*, "village"), Native Americans living in compact, apartment-like villages of stone or adobe in northwestern New Mexico and northeastern Arizona. They belong to four distinct linguistic groups, but the cultures of the different villages are closely related.

Laguna, Pueblo tribe of Keresan stock, living on a pueblo in Valencia County, New Mexico, near Albuquerque. The Laguna Pueblo contains the largest settlement of Pueblo peoples in the United States. It is a part of the Laguna Indian Reservation, which comprises more than 50,000 hectares (125,000 acres) of grazing and irrigated farming lands. The Laguna culture is typical of that of the Pueblo peoples, modified in recent times by improvements of lands and modernization of buildings and equipment. Like other Keresan tribes, the Laguna practice a religion based on ancestor worship and nature gods. They use wrapped ears of corn as clan fetishes, depositing them in houses that become clan centers. Their annual harvest dances, held in September, are a major tourist attraction in the Southwest. In the 2000 U.S. census about 6,200 people identified themselves as Laguna only; an additional 1,200 people reported being part Laguna.

3. Apache

A formerly nomadic tribe of North American Indians inhabiting the southwestern United States and northern Mexico.

4. Jonah in the mouth of a whale and Daniel surrounded by lions

The stories come from two of the Old Testament books: Book of Jonah and Book of Daniel.

5. hummah-hah stories

In *Storyteller*, Leslie Marmon Silko offers such directions: "The Laguna people always begin their stories with 'humma-hah' that means 'long ago.' And the ones who are listening say 'aaaa-eh.'"

Comprehension

1. Why does the narrator of the story appear different from her playmates as a child?
2. Would you describe the narrator as more white or Indian? Why do you think so?
3. Based upon the narrative, how would you describe the climate of New Mexico? What in the story indicates this?
4. Does the narrator's great-grandmother live a traditional-Indian or modern lifestyle?
5. Is the narrator a feminist? How do you know?
6. Why do you suppose the white tourists do not want the narrator in their picture?

7. The tourist who says "Not you" is a white male. Is this coincidental or a conscious decision made by the author? Why do you think so?
8. Who is "Yellow Woman" and why is she powerful in the narrator's view?
9. What are the predominant themes of the Yellow Woman stories?
10. What moral does the author wish readers to draw from her narrative?

Further Study

- X. J. Kennedy: *Literature*: *An Introduction to Fiction, Poetry, and Drama* (1976)
- Leslie Marmon Silko: *Yellow Woman and a Beauty of Spirit: Essays on Native American Life Today* (1996)
- Read the following passage from Silko's *Yellow Woman and a Beauty of the Spirit* and try to get a better understanding of her native-American background.

From a High Arid Plateau in New Mexico

You see that, after a thing is dead, it dries up. It might take weeks or years, but eventually, if you touch the thing, it crumbles under your fingers. It goes back to dust. The soul of the thing has long since departed. With the plants and wild game the soul may have already been born back into bones and blood or thick green stalks and leaves. Nothing is wasted. What cannot be eaten by people or in some way used must then be left where other living creatures may benefit. What domestic animals or wild scavengers can't eat will be fed to the plants. The plants feed on the dust of these few remains.

The ancient Pueblo people buried the dead in vacant rooms or in partially collapsed rooms adjacent to the main living quarters. Sand and clay, used to construct the roof, make layers many inches deep once the roof has collapsed. The layers of sand and clay make for easy grave digging. The vacant room fills with cast-off objects and debris. When a vacant room has filled deep enough, a shallow but adequate grave can be scooped in a far corner. Archaeologists have remarked over formal burials complete with elaborate funerary objects excavated in trash middens of abandoned rooms. But the rocks and adobe mortar of collapsed walls were valued by the ancient people, because each rock had been carefully selected for size and shape, then chiseled to an even face. Even the pink clay adobe melting with each rainstorm had to be prayed over, then dug and carried some distance. Corn-cobs and husks, the rinds and stalks and animal bones were not regarded by the ancient people as filth or garbage. The remains were merely resting at a midpoint in their journey back to dust. Human remains are not so different. They should rest with the bones and rinds where they all may benefit living creatures—small rodents and insects—until their return is completed. The remains of things—animals and plants, the clay and stones—were treated with respect, because for the ancient people all these things had spirit and being.

The antelope merely consents to return home with the hunter. All phases of the hunt are conducted with love: the love the hunter and the people have for the Antelope People, and the love of the antelope who agree to give up their meat and blood so that human beings will not starve. Waste of meat or even the thoughtless handling of bones cooked bare will offend the antelope spirits. Next year the hunters will vainly search the dry plains for antelope. Thus, it is necessary to return carefully the bones and hair and the stalks and leaves to the earth, who first created them. The spirits remain close by. They do not leave us.

The dead become dust, and in this becoming they are once more joined with the Mother. The ancient Pueblo people called the earth the Mother Creator of all things in this world. Her sister, the Corn Mother, occasionally merges with her because all succulent green life rises out of the depths of the earth.

Rocks and clay are part of the Mother. They emerge in various forms, but at some time before they were smaller particles of great boulders. At a later time they may again become what they once were: dust.

A rock shares this fate with us and with animals and plants as well. A rock has being or spirit, although we may not understand it. The spirit may differ from the spirit we know in animals or plants or in ourselves. In the end we all originate from the depths of the earth. Perhaps this is how all beings share in the spirit of the Creator. We do not know. ("Interior and Exterior Landscapes: The Pueblo Migration Stories" from *Yellow Woman and a Beauty of the Spirit: Essays on Native American Life Today* by Leslie Marmon Silko)

Unit

Women's Consciousness

Unit Goals

- To keep track of women's consciousness
- To learn to write in chronological order
- To effect transition through comparison and contrast
- To use intermittent repetition for coherence

Before Reading

1. Virginia Woolf was a famous writer. Have you ever read anything by her? Check a literary encyclopedia to find what she was famous for in her time.
2. Work within a group of four; list all the women writers that you know of from the 16th to the 19th century and their works.

A Glimpse into the Text

By the mid-nineteenth century and increasingly into the early twentieth century, women were making substantial contributions to English literature—among them Jane Austen, the Brontë Sisters, George Eliot, Katherine Mansfield, and of course, Virginia Woolf, the author of several modern classics, including her historical survey of British women authors, *A Room of One's Own*. In this excerpt from the latter work, Woolf, with a keen eye to both social history and publishing, discerns the essential shifts that have occurred in women's lives and their writing from the seventeenth through nineteenth centuries.

Text A

A Room of One's Own
Virginia Woolf[1]
(Abridged)

That one would find any woman in that state of mind in the sixteenth century was obviously impossible. One has only to think of the Elizabethan[2] tombstones with all those children kneeling with clasped hands; and their early deaths; and to see their houses with their dark, cramped rooms, to realize that no woman could have written poetry then. What one would expect to find would be that rather later perhaps some great lady would take advantage of her comparative freedom and comfort to publish something with her name to it and risk being thought a monster. Men, of course, are not snobs, but they appreciate with sympathy for the most part the efforts of a countess to write verse. One would expect to find a lady of title meeting with far greater encouragement than an unknown Miss Austen or a Miss Brontë at that time would have met with. But one would also expect to find that her mind was disturbed by alien emotions like fear and hatred and that her poems showed traces of that disturbance. Here is Lady Winchilsea³, for example, I thought, taking down her poems. She was born in the year 1661; she was noble both by birth and by marriage; she was childless; she wrote poetry, and one has only to open her poetry to find her bursting out in indignation against the position of women:

Woolf's home in East Sussex

> How we are fallen! fallen by mistaken rules,
> And Education's more than Nature's fools;
> Debarred from all improvements of the mind,
> And to be dull, expected and designed;
> And if someone would soar above the rest,
> With warmer fancy, and ambition pressed,
> So strong the opposing faction still appears,
> The hopes to thrive can ne'er outweigh the fears.⁴

The human race is split up for her into two parties. Men are the "opposing faction"; men are hated and feared, because they have the power to bar her way to what she wants to do—which is to write.

It was a thousand pities that the woman who could write like that, whose mind was tuned to nature and reflection, should have been forced to anger and bitterness. But how could she have helped herself? I asked, imagining the sneers and the laughter, the adulation of the toadies, the scepticism of the professional poet. She must have shut herself up in a room in the country to write, and been torn asunder by bitterness and scruples perhaps, though her husband was of the kindest, and their married life perfection. She "must have," I say, because when one comes to seek out the facts about Lady Winchilsea, one finds, as usual, that almost nothing is known about her.

Putting her back on the shelf, I turned to the other great lady, the Duchess whom Lamb loved, harebrained, fantastical Margaret of Newcastle⁵. They were very different, but alike in this that both were noble and both childless, and both were married to

---

cramped /kræmpt/ *adj.* a cramped room, etc. does not have enough space for the people in it
countess /ˈkaʊntɪs/ *n.* [C] a woman who has the rank of a count or an earl; the wife of a count or an earl
alien /ˈeɪliən/ *adj.* strange and frightening
debar /dɪˈbɑː/ *v.* ~ sb. (from sth./from doing sth.) (formal) to prevent sb. from doing sth., joining sth., etc.
thrive /θraɪv/ *v.* to become, and continue to be, successful, strong, healthy, etc.
ne'er /neə/ (poetic) never
outweigh /aʊtˈweɪ/ *v.* to be greater or more important than sth.
faction /ˈfækʃən/ *n.* [C] a small group of people within a larger one whose members have some different aims and beliefs to those of the larger group
tune /tjuːn/ *v.* ~ sth. (to sth.) to prepare or adjust sth. so that it is suitable for a particular situation
toady /ˈtəʊdi/ *n.* (disapproving) a person who treats sb. more important with special kindness or respect in order to gain their favour or help
asunder /əˈsʌndə/ *adv.* (old-fashioned or literary) into pieces; apart
scruple /ˈskruːpəl/ *n.* a feeling that prevents you from doing sth. that you think may be morally wrong
harebrained /ˈheəbreɪnd/ *adj.* (informal) crazy and unlikely to succeed

the best of husbands. In both burnt the same passion for poetry and both are disfigured and deformed by the same causes. Open the Duchess and one finds the same outburst of rage. "Women live like Bats or Owls, labour like Beasts, and die like Worms...."[6] Margaret too might have been a poet. She should have had a microscope put in her hand. She should have been taught to look at the stars and reason scientifically. Her wits were turned with solitude and freedom. No one checked her. No one taught her. The professors fawned on her. At Court they jeered at her. She shut herself up at Welbeck alone.

Here, I remembered, putting away the Duchess and opening Dorothy Osborne's[7] letters. The strange thing is, what a gift that untaught and solitary girl had for the framing of a sentence, for the fashioning of a scene. Listen to her running on:

most commonly when we are in the middest of our discourse one looks aboute her and spyes her Cow's goeing into the Corne and then away they all run, as if they had wing's at theire heels. I that am not soe nimble stay behinde, and when I see them driveing home theire Cattle I think tis time for mee to retyre too.

One could have sworn that she had the makings of a writer in her. And so we come, I continued, replacing the single short volume of Dorothy Osborne's letters upon the shelf, to Mrs Behn.[8]

And with Mrs Behn we turn a very important corner on the road. We leave behind, shut up in their parks among their folios, those solitary great ladies who wrote without audience or criticism, for their own delight alone. We come to town and rub shoulders with ordinary people in the streets. Mrs Behn was a middle-class woman with all the plebeian virtues of humour, vitality and courage; a woman forced by the death of her husband and some unfortunate adventures of her own to make her living by her wits. She had to work on equal terms with men. She made, by working very hard, enough to live on. The importance of that fact outweighs anything that she actually wrote, even the splendid "A Thousand Martyrs I have made,"[9] or "Love in Fantastic Triumph sat,"[10] for here begins the freedom of the mind, or rather the possibility that in the course of time the mind will be free to write what it likes.

Aphra Behn proved that money could be made by writing at the sacrifice, perhaps, of certain agreeable qualities; and so by degrees writing became not merely a sign of folly and a distracted mind, but was of practical importance. A husband might die, or some disaster overtakes the family. Hundreds of women began as the eighteenth century drew on to add to their pin money, or to come to the rescue of their families by making translations or writing the innumerable novels which have ceased to be recorded even in text-books, but are to be picked up in the fourpenny boxes in the Charing Cross Road.[11] The extreme activity of mind which showed itself in the later eighteenth century among women—the talking, and the meeting, the writing of essays on Shakespeare, the translating of the classics—was founded on the solid fact that women could make money by writing. Money dignifies what is frivolous if unpaid for. Thus, towards the end of the eighteenth century a change came about which, if I were rewriting history, I should describe more fully and think of greater importance than the

> **duchess** /'dʌtʃɪs/ *n.* [C] a woman who has the rank of a duke; the wife of a duke
> **fawn** /fɔːn/ *v.* ~ **(on/over sb.)** (disapproving) to try to please sb. by praising her/him or paying her/him too much attention
> **folio** /'fəʊliəʊ/ *n.* a book made with large sheets of paper eopecially as used in early printing
> **rub shoulders with sb.** to meet and spend time with a famous person, socially or as part of one's job
> **plebeian** /plɪ'biːən/ *adj.* connected with ordinary people or people of the lower social classes

Crusades or the Wars of the Roses.¹²

The middle-class woman began to write. For if PRIDE AND PREJUDICE¹³ matters, and MIDDLEMARCH and VILLETTE and WUTHERING HEIGHTS matter, then it matters far more than I can prove in an hour's discourse that women generally, and not merely the lonely aristocrat shut up in her country house among her folios and her flatterers, took to writing. All women together ought to let flowers fall upon the tomb of Aphra Behn in Westminster Abbey¹⁴ for it was she who earned them the right to speak their minds. It is she—shady and amorous as she was—who makes it not quite fantastic for me to say to you to-night: Earn five hundred a year by your wits.

Here, then, one had reached the early nineteenth century. And here, for the first time, I found several shelves given up entirely to the works of women. But why, I could not help asking, as I ran my eyes over them, were they, with very few exceptions, all novels? Looking at the four famous names, what had George Eliot in common with Emily Brontë? Did not Charlotte Brontë fail entirely to understand Jane Austen? Save for the possibly relevant fact that not one of them had a child, four more incongruous characters could not have met together in a room so much so that it is tempting to invent a meeting and a dialogue between them. Yet by some strange force they were all compelled when they wrote, to write novels. Had it something to do with being born of the middle class? As Miss Emily Davies¹⁵ was so strikingly to demonstrate, that the middle-class family in the early nineteenth century was possessed only of a single sitting-room between them. If a woman wrote, she would have to write in the common sitting-room. She was always interrupted. Still it would be easier to write prose and fiction there than to write poetry or a play. Less concentration is required. Jane Austen wrote like that to the end of her days. "How she was able to effect all this," her nephew writes in his Memoir, "is surprising, for she had no separate study to repair to, and most of the work must have been done in the general sitting-room, subject to all kinds of casual interruptions. She was careful that her occupation should not be suspected by servants or visitors or any persons beyond her own family party." Jane Austen hid her manuscripts or covered them with a piece of blotting-paper. Then, again, all the literary training that a woman had in the early nineteenth century was training in the observation of character, in the analysis of emotion. Her sensibility had been educated for centuries by the influences of the common sitting-room. People's feelings were impressed on her; personal relations were always before her eyes. Therefore, when the middle-class woman took to writing, she naturally wrote novels, even though, as seems evident enough, two of the four famous women here named were not by nature novelists. Emily Brontë should have written poetic plays; the overflow of George Eliot's capacious mind should have spread itself when the creative impulse was spent upon history or biography.

> Crusade /kruːˈseɪd/ n. any of the wars fought in Palestine by European Christian countries against the Muslims in the Middle Ages
> incongruous /ɪnˈkɒŋgruəs/ adj. strange, and not suitable in a particular situation
> memoir /ˈmemwɑː/ n. a written account of sb's life, a place or an event, written by sb. who knows it well
> repair to (formal or humorous) to go to a particular place
> capacious /kəˈpeɪʃəs/ adj. (formal) having a lot of space to put things in

More about the Text

1. Virginia Woolf

Virginia Woolf (1882—1941), famous English novelist, essayist, critic of Modernism. As a novelist Woolf's primary was not on plot or characterization but on a character's consciousness, his/her thoughts and feelings, which she brilliantly illuminated by the stream of consciousness technique. Her most famous novels include *Mrs. Dalloway, To the Lighthouse* and *Orlando*.

A Room of One's Own is an extended essay, based on Woolf's lectures at Cambridge University in 1928. In it, Wolfe addresses her thoughts on "the question of women and fiction." Her chief standing on it is "a woman must have money and a room of her own if she is going to write." The excerpt is the condensation of Chapter Four of the essay.

2. Elizabethan

Of, relating to, or characteristic of Elizabeth I of England or her reign (1558—1603).

3. Lady Winchilsea

Anne, daughter of Sir William Kingsmill of Sidmonton, married colonel Heneage Finch, afterwards Earl of Winchilsea. In 1690, Ardelia (her name as authoress) settled at beautiful Eastwell and began to write verses for circulation among her noble friends.

4. 'The hopes to thrive can ne'er outweigh the fears.'

This selection is from Lady Winchilsea's poem entitled *The Introduction*.

5. Margaret of Newcastle

Margaret Cavendish (1623—1673) is unique among women writers of the seventeenth century both in the scale of her output and in her aspiration to create a philosophical system.

6. 'Women live like Bats or Owls, labour like Beasts, and die like worms....'

This line is from Margaret Cavendish's poem entitled *Female Orations* (1662).

7. Dorothy Osborne

Dorothy Osborne (1627—1695) afterwards Lady Temple, wife of Sir William Temple, has become known for the letters she wrote to her future husband before their marriage. These letters, written in a conversational style, present a vivid picture of the life of a young gentlewoman in the middle of the seventeenth century.

8. Mrs Behn

Aphra Behn (1640—1689) was the first professional woman writer in English.

9. 'A Thousand Martyrs I have made'

This line is from Behn's poem entitled *The Libertine*.

10. 'Love in Fantastic Triumph sat'

This line is from Behn's poem entitled *Song from Abdelazar*.

11. Charing Cross Road

Charing Cross Road is a street in London lined with numerous bookstores.

12. The Wars of the Roses

The Wars of the Roses are a series of civil wars fought in medieval England from 1455 to 1487 between the House of Lancaster and the House of York. The name "Wars of the Roses" is based on the badges used by the two sides, the red rose for the Lancastrians and the white rose for the Yorkists.

13. PRIDE AND PREJUDICE

This is a novel by Jane Austin. MIDDLEMARCH by George Eliot, VILLETTE by Charlotte Brontë, WUTHERING HEIGHTS by Emily Brontë.

14. Westminster Abbey

Westminster Abbey is the famous church located in London. Almost all English monarchs since William the Conqueror have been crowned there. Distinguished English subjects are buried there.

15. Emily Davies (Sarah Emily Davies)

Emily Davies (1830—1921) British feminist, co-founder of Girton College, Cambridge. From 1866 she was closely associated with the English woman-suffrage movement and was active in organizing the first woman-suffrage petition presented to Parliament by John Stuart Mill in 1866.

Check Your Understanding

1. Why does Woolf conclude that no woman could have written poetry in the 16th Century?
2. What does Lady Winchilsea mean by writing "We are fallen by mistaken rules, and education's more than nature's fools?" What alien emotions does Lady Winchilsea possess toward the male faction? Why is very little known about Lady Winchilsea's life?
3. What subject does the author suggest Margaret of Newcastle should have been taught?
4. What is Dorothy Osborne's literary genius?
5. According to Woolf, what is important about Mrs. Behn in the history of women's writings?
6. What contributed to the extreme activity of the mind in women of the late 18th century?
7. Paraphrase Woolf's claim that "Money dignifies what is frivolous if unpaid for."
8. Why does Woolf believe that middle-class women in the 1800s took to writing novels and prose rather than poetry and plays?
9. Why did Jane Austen hide her manuscripts or cover them with a piece of blotting-paper?
10. What does the author suggest Geroge Eliot should have written?

Paraphrasing

1. One **has only to** think of the Elizabethan tombstones with all those children kneeling with clasped hands; and their early deaths; and to see their houses with their dark, cramped rooms, **to** realize that no woman could have written poetry then.
2. She must have shut herself up in a room in the country to write, and been **torn asunder** by bitterness and scruples perhaps, though her husband was of the kindest, and their married life perfection.

3. And here, for the first time, I found several shelves **given up entirely to** the works of women.
4. It was **a thousand** pities that the woman who could write like that, whose mind was **tuned to** nature and reflection, should have been forced to anger and bitterness.
5. The **overflow** of George Eliot's capacious mind should have **spread itself** when the creative impulse was spent upon history or biography.

Some Information about English Style

1. Writing in chronological order

"Chronos" is a Greek word meaning time. Chronological order, therefore, means a way of organizing ideas according to their occurrence in time. In the present text, Woolf examines the literary history of women writers from the 16th to the 19th century in a chronological order, which is convenient for narration. She uses certain discourse marks to indicate the time sequence, such as *the sixteenth century, rather later, in the year 1661, in the later eighteenth century, towards the end of the eighteenth century,* and *in the early nineteenth century*, so that the historical development of women writing is clear to the reader.

Certain other linking words are useful to join sentences and paragraphs when writing in a chronological order, e.g. *first, next, then, later, finally, while, before, after, since*, etc.

2. Transition through comparison and contrast

Transition between paragraphs is like threads piecing together ideas to show the logical connections between them. Transitions are effected through many devices such as addition, emphasizing, contrasting, qualification, exemplification, cause and effect, conclusion, etc. In the text, Woolf uses comparison and contrast to connect different women writers. Notice the transitional signals used in the text:

■ *They were very different, but **alike** in this that **both** were noble and both childless, and **both** were married to the best of husbands. In **both** burnt the same passion for poetry and **both** are disfigured and deformed by the same causes.*

(The word "alike" and a parallel usage of "both" show the similarity between Lady Winchilsea and Margaret of Newcastle.)

■ *And with Mrs Behn we **turn a very important corner** on the road. We leave behind, shut up in their parks among their folios, those solitary great ladies who wrote without audience or criticism, for their own delight alone. We come to town and rub shoulders with ordinary people in the streets.*

(The phrase "we turn a very important corner" is a semantic marker to indicate contrast, showing a major turning point in women writers from ladies in the 17th century to ordinary women in the 18th century.)

■ *Save for the possibly relevant fact that not one of them had a child, four more **incongruous** characters could not have met together in a room so much so that it is tempting to invent a meeting and a dialogue between them. **Yet** by some strange force they were **all** compelled when they wrote, to write novels.*

(While "incongruous" shows semantically the difference among the four women writers, the word "yet" functions as a transitional link to shift to similarities among the four; and "all" is another indicator of similarity.)

Other conventional devices for transition through comparison and contrast include "also," "in the same way," "just as... so too," "likewise," "similarly," "on the one hand... on the other hand," "in contrast," "by contrast," "whereas," "on the contrary"... etc.

3. Intermittent repetition as a cohesive device in a paragraph

Intermittent repetition is another technique to achieve cohesion in a lengthy paragraph. To help the reader follow the logical reasoning of the author, or more often for the sake of emphasis, the author deliberately repeats the key words or structure to keep his ideas flowing. Certain repetitions are special cases of parallelism.

Examples from the text:

- ***She** was born in the year 1661; **she** was noble both by birth and by marriage; **she** was childless; **she** wrote poetry, and one has only to open her poetry to find her bursting out in indignation against the position of women. (Repetition of "she".)*

- *That **one would find** any woman in that state of mind in the sixteenth century was obviously impossible. One has only to think of the Elizabethan tombstones with all those children kneeling with clasped hands; and their early deaths; and to see their houses with their dark, cramped rooms, to realize that no woman could have written poetry then. What **one would expect to find** would be that rather later perhaps some great lady would take advantage of her comparative freedom and comfort to publish something with her name to it and risk being thought a monster. Men, of course, are not snobs, but they appreciate with sympathy for the most part the efforts of a countess to write verse. **One would expect to find** a lady of title meeting with far greater encouragement than an unknown Miss Austen or a Miss Bront? at that time would have met with. But **one would also expect to find** that her mind was disturbed by alien emotions like fear and hatred and that her poems showed traces of that disturbance. (Repetition of the structure "one would....")*

- *They were very different, but alike in this that **both** were noble and **both** childless, and **both** were married to the best of husbands. In **both** burnt the same passion for poetry and **both** are disfigured and deformed by the same causes. (Repetition of "both".)*

Practice

📖 Building word power

1. Work with your partner to talk about the following situation, using the words provided.
  (1) Describe somebody of a dominant nature. What does he/she want you to do? What is your response, physical and emotional? (debar, alien, bar, freedom, discomfort)
  (2) Describe a toady using examples. (adulate, discriminate, sneer)
  (3) Compare and contrast a pair of twins. (both, alike)
  (4) Defend your hobby which seems trivial to others. (frivolous, distracted, folly)

2. Work out the antonyms
  (1) social—_____; symmetry—_____;
  (2) social—_____; body—_____; clockwise—_____;
  (3) centralize—_____; form—_____; code—_____; color—_____;

(4) current—_____; act—_____
(5) appear—_____; honest—_____; obey—_____; order—_____
(6) able—_____; arm—_____; color—_____;
(7) legal—_____; legitimate—_____; regular—_____; literate—_____; logical—_____
(8) possible—_____; mutable—_____; partial—_____; potent —_____
(9) numerable—_____; congruous—_____; imitable—_____;
(10) essential—_____; existent—_____; alcoholic—_____; sense—_____; violent—_____; traditional—_____
(11) biased—_____; certain—_____; common—_____; acceptable_____; official—_____; conditional—_____
(12) bind—_____; fold—_____; pack—_____; tie—_____; veil—_____

3. **Make sentences with each of the words provided**
(1) _____ (outweigh)
(2) _____ (outdo)
(3) _____ (outwit)
(4) _____ (outlive)
(5) _____ (outnumber)
(6) _____ (outrun)

Grammar and Usage

Translate the following sentences into English by using the key words in the brackets.
(1) 商业管理不好是兴旺不起来的。(thrive)
(2) 他的思想适合时代的潮流。(tune)
(3) 皮大衣和游泳衣是不相称的。(incongruous)
(4) 她具有当音乐家的禀赋。(makings)
(5) 孩子往往很难对付,对此我们都非常清楚。(know)

Improving your writing style

1. Complete the following passage by choosing an appropriate time indicator from the list below:

in the nineteenth century / December, 1903 / while / in 1899 / Later / as early as the fifteenth century

It was _____(1), in the southeastern United States. A group of men were standing near a strange machine. One of them, whose name was Wilbur Wright, began to push the machine _____(2) his brother Orville, lay on the lower wing and held the simple controls.

Only five persons were there to see the clumsy craft rise from the ground, fly 120 feet and touch down again. Man had flown the first successful airplane with a gasoline engine.

The Wright brothers had made use of the knowledge of many people before them. _____(3), an Italian named Leonardo da Vinci, had designed flying machines. _____(4), men had experimented with balloons. One of them, a Brazilian, had flown a dirigible near Paris _____(5). Other inventors experimenting with gliders _____(6) had learned much about designing airplane bodies.

Since the days of the Wright brothers, planes have steadily improved.

2. Fill in each blank with an appropriate transitional word or expression.

■ Some militant Indian groups oppose the use of the word *tribe* to refer to their people, claiming that it suggests savagery and brutality. _____(1), most Indian populations in the United States willingly apply the term to themselves. _____(2), they feel that *tribe* is a far better word than *nation or organization*. A tribal society, they say, suggests warmth and humanity, _____(3) the coldness and commercialism of modern U.S. society.

(1) _____ (2) _____ (3) _____

■ _____(4) —most people's opinions, the ocean is a relatively safe place to swim. The natural action of the ocean tends to push swimmers toward shore. _____(5), it is more difficult to drown in salt water than in fresh water, since the salt helps to keep swimmers afloat. _____(6), few people know how to swim properly in the ocean. _____(7), about twenty people a day drowns at ocean beaches this summer.

(4) _____ (5) _____ (6) _____ (7) _____

3. Add a concluding sentence to the following paragraph by using the given opening word. Can you explain the different logical relation that results in each case?

To be successful in a job interview (or for that matter in almost any interview situation), you should demonstrate certain personal and professional qualities. You need to create a good image in the limited time available, usually from 20 to 30 minutes. Furthermore, you must make a positive impression which the interviewer will remember while he interviews other applicants.

_____

Example:
However, precautions should be taken that too much showcasing would give an impression that you are more a talker than a doer. (Contrast)
Accordingly, _____
Moreover, _____
Indeed, _____
For example, _____
Finally, _____

4. Read the following paragraph. Write a similar paragraph on the topic "I need a friend...." or "We must embrace life...."

I want a wife who will take care of my physical needs. I want a wife who will keep my house clean. A wife who will pick up after my children, a wife who will pick up after me. I want a wife who will keep my clothes clean, ironed, mended, replaced when need be, and who will see to it that my personal things are kept in their proper place so that I can find what I need the minute I need it. I want a wife who will plan the menus, do the necessary grocery shopping, prepare the meals, serve them pleasantly, and then do the cleaning up while I do my studying. I want a wife who will care for me when I am sick and sympathize with my pain and loss of time from school. I want a wife to go along when our family takes a vacation so that someone can continue to care for me and my children when I need a rest and a change of scene.

—"Why I want a Wife" by Judy Syphers, in *Radical Feminism* (1973)

Writing task

Write a passage on the history of the European Union with the given time-line. (The first paragraph has been written for you.)

The beginnings of the EU date from May 9th 1950, when Robert Schuman, France's Foreign Minister, proposed that France and Germany should combine their coal and steel industries under an independent, 'supranational' authority. This led to the establishment of the European Coal and Steel Community (E.C.S.C.) in 1952. In addition to France and Germany, Belgium, Italy, Luxemburg and the Netherlands also became members.

9 May 1950	Robert Schuman's proposal
1952	European Coal and Steel Community (ECSC)
25 March 1957	Treaty of Rome EEC (European Economic Community, same six member states as in ECSC)
1973	Denmark, R. Ireland joined in
1980s	Greece, Spain, Portugal joined in
7 February 1992	Treaty on European Union, signed in Maastricht
1 Jan 1993	Maastricht Treaty came into effect E.E.C renamed as EU (from economical entity to economical and political entity)
1 Jan 1999	Euro introduced in 11 countries (joined by Greece in 2001) as a common currency
1 May 2004	Ten more countries joined in (totaling 25 member states)

| 16 Feb 2006 | The European Parliament approved a report for new legislation, opening the Internal market also in the field of services. |
| 1 Jan 2007 | Bulgaria and Romania joined in (totaling 27 member states) |

Text B

Feminist Consciousness after the Women's Movement

Barbara Epstein[1]
(Abridged and Edited)

What happens to a social movement after it has entered public consciousness and its principles have become generally accepted? Why do some social movements come to an end while others are perpetuated? Barbara Epstein's scholarship has consistently been about social movements and the problems that they face. This article looks at the present condition of feminist consciousness in the West following the initial success of the mass women's movement in the 1970s and 1980s.

National Organization for Women calls on young women to join her

There is no longer an organized feminist movement in the United States that influences the lives and actions of millions of women and engages their political support. There are many organizations, ranging from the National Organization for Women to women's caucuses in labor unions and professional groups, which fight for women's rights, and there are many more organizations, many of them including men as well as women, whose priorities include women's issues. But the mass women's movement of the late sixties, seventies, and early eighties no longer exists. Few, among the many women who regard themselves as feminists, have anything to do with feminist organizations other than reading about them in the newspapers. Young women who are drawn to political activism do not, for the most part, join women's groups. They are much more likely to join anticorporate, antiglobalization, or social justice groups. These young women are likely to regard themselves as feminists, and in the groups that they join a feminist perspective is likely to affect the way in which issues are defined and addressed. But this is not the same thing as a mass movement of women for gender equality.

A similar dynamic has taken place in other circles as well.

The extent of feminist or protofeminist

feminist /ˈfemɪnst/ *n.* a person who supports the belief that women should have the same rights and opportunities as men
caucus /ˈkɔːkəs/ *n.* a group of people with similar interests, often within a larger organization or political party
activism /ˈæktɪvɪzəm/ *n.* the theory, doctrine, or practice of assertive, often militant action, such as mass demonstrations or strikes, used as a means of opposing or supporting a controversial issue, entity, or person
gender /ˈdʒendə/ *n.* [C, U] the fact of being male or female
dynamic /daɪˈnæmɪk/ *n.* [sing.] (formal) a force that produces change, action or effects

consciousness, by which I mean an awareness of the inequality of women and a determination to resist it, now existing in the United States, is an accomplishment of the women's movement. But it is also something of an anomaly, since it is no longer linked to the movement that produced it. When the first wave of the women's movement in the United States went into decline, after woman suffrage was won in 1921, feminism went into decline with it. By the 1950s, feminism had almost entirely disappeared, not only as an organized movement, but also as an ideology and a political and social sensibility. Even in the early sixties, in the New Left,[2] to describe oneself as a feminist was to invite raised eyebrows and probably more extreme reactions. Now, for a second time in U.S. history, the memory of a movement that engages the energy of very large numbers of women is receding into the past. But this time feminist consciousness has if anything become more widespread. This raises the question: what accounts for this difference? How and what does feminism change when it becomes a cultural current rather than a movement for social change?

In part this different history may have to do with the disparities between the first and second waves of feminism. The first wave of feminism began, in the 1840s, as a demand for women's equality generally. The women's movement emerged out of the abolitionist movement, and at first feminism was part of an egalitarian world view, closely connected to antislavery and antiracism. But in the last decade of the nineteenth century, and to an even greater degree over the first two decades of the twentieth, feminism narrowed to the demand for woman suffrage. Leading feminists, mostly middle-and upper-middle-class, native-born white women, even made racist and anti-immigrant arguments for woman suffrage. Though the women's movement also included working-class women, many of them socialists, for whom feminism remained a part of a broader commitment to social equality, by the second decade of the twentieth century, radicalism was a minor current within the women's movement. For most feminists, and for the public, feminism had come to mean the vote for women and little more. Once suffrage was won, feminism lost its raison d'etre and so had little future either as a movement or as consciousness.

The second wave of the women's movement turned out differently. It did not narrow ideologically, nor did it run into any dead end, as its predecessor had. If anything, over time the radical currents within the movement gained influence; women who had entered the movement thinking that women's equality would not require major social changes tended to become convinced that gender inequality was linked to other dimensions of inequality, especially class and race. The women's movement declined, in the eighties and nineties, few feminists thought that the aims of the women's movement had been accomplished. Many thought that they could continue to work towards these aims in the arenas, mostly professional, that they were entering. Feminist consciousness was sustained.

In the wake of the September 11 attacks,

---

anomaly /ə'nɒməli/ n. a thing, situation, etc. that is different from what is normal or expected

suffrage /'sʌfrɪdʒ/ n. the right to vote in political elections

current /'kʌrənt/ n. the fact of particular ideas, opinions or feelings being present in a group of people

abolitionist /ˌæbə'lɪʃənɪst/ n. a person who is in favour of the abolition of sth.

egalitarian /ɪˌɡælɪ'teərɪən/ adj. based on, or holding, the belief that everyone is equal and should have the same rights and opportunities

mainstream /'meɪnstriːm/ n. [sing.] the ideas and opinions that are thought to be normal because they are shared by most

raison d'etre (French) reason to exist

arena /ə'riːnə/ n. (written) an area of activity that concerns the public, especially one where there is a lot of opposition between different commentator groups or countries some commentators have argued that the inequality of women in the Arab world is a sign of the deep cultural gap involved: to reject feminism is to reject modernity and the West. For instance, Laura Bush, speaking on the weekly presidential radio address, on November 17, 2001, supported the Bush administration's attack on Afghanistan on grounds of the denial of women's rights by the Taliban. In the sixties, probably even in the seventies, such an argument would have been unthinkable. Many feminists, especially radical feminists, thought that their challenge to male supremacy was also a challenge to the existing social order. Many, who regarded themselves as guardians of that social order, agreed.

The feminist goal of gender equality has not been achieved; not only do women still earn less than men, but in the ranks of the poor, single women and their children have come to predominate. The prejudices that discourage women from entering traditionally male fields remain and violence against women persists. Though the nuclear family of the forties and fifties was based on male supremacy, the increasing instability of family life has hardly been a blessing for women. But women's equality has become a publicly accepted principle. Glaring deviations from this principle are open to challenge, and very large numbers of women are ready to make such challenges when necessary. This in itself is an enormous and transforming advance.

So, over the last two decades feminist consciousness has spread even as the organized women's movement has contracted. This is partly because of the increasing numbers of women in the labor force, and in other areas of public life, who, in talking to each other and giving each other support, spread and redefined feminism, even if they do not call themselves feminists or use the word. It was possible for the first wave of feminism to disappear because the women's movement that it was associated with had come to an end without the majority of American women having gained access to arenas outside the home. The fact that women are now in the labor force and the public arena to stay makes it hard to imagine that feminism and what it stands for could disappear again. This is a measure of progress. Probably feminism will continue to be a major political current in the United States, though perhaps not based in any movement, and in that sense a cultural as well as a political phenomenon.

It does not seem likely that another mass women's movement will emerge any time soon. But feminism is being given new vitality by its association with the range of activist groups that make up the antiglobalization and anticorporate movements. Young women in these movements are very likely to describe themselves as feminists; feminism is accepted as one of the ideological currents that shape these movements, along with anarchism, environmentalism, and the struggle against white supremacy. Inside these groups, women tend to take for granted the equality that women of the movements of the sixties and seventies fought for. If the labor movement makes headway in its effort to organize the unorganized, feminism will inevitably become part of the culture that develops within it, because so many of the unorganized are women. Such movement-based versions of feminism

---

modernity /məˈdɜːnəti/ *n.* [U] (written) the condition of being new and modern
supremacy /sjuˈpreməsi/ *n.* [U] (written) a position in which you have more power, authority or status than anyone else
guardian /ˈɡɑːdiən/ *n.* a person who protects sth.
glaring /ˈɡleərɪŋ/ *adj.* [usually before noun] (of sth. bad) very easily seen
deviation /ˌdiːviˈeɪʃən/ *n.* ~ **(from sth.)** the act of moving away from what is normal or acceptable; a difference from what is expected or acceptable
anarchism /ˈænəkɪzəm/ *n.* the political belief that laws and governments are not necessary
to make headway (idiom) to make progress, especially when this is slow or difficult

could introduce radicalism into wider feminist discussions.

Over the last two decades other movements have followed the same trajectory as the women's movement. The environmental movement is a clear case: once consisting of large numbers of people engaged in political activity, it now consists on the one hand of a series of staff-driven organizations, and on the other, of a large sector of people who consider themselves environmentalist, or who have an environmental consciousness, but who take action on environmental issues largely in individual ways, such as in their shopping habits and in recycling. A similar argument could be made about the African-American movement, whose organizations have shriveled while militant forms of racial and ethnic consciousness have expanded, at least culturally, among young people. To some degree this expansion of various forms of consciousness going way beyond the borders of the movements in which they first emerged shows the lasting influence of those movements. But it also has to do with what appears to be the decline of political and protest movements, and the difficulty of finding compelling forms of political engagement. The tendency of the political to collapse into the cultural, even as it connotes a measure of triumph, weakens the left.

> trajectory /trəˈdʒektəri/ *n.* (technical) the curved path of sth. that has been fired, hit or thrown into the air
> shrivel /ˈʃrɪvəl/ *v.* become or make sth. dry and wrinkled from heat, cold or old age
> connote /kəˈnəʊt/ *v.* (formal) to suggest a feeling, an idea, etc. as well as the main meaning
> measure /ˈmeʒə/ *n.* [sing.] a particular amount of sth., especially a fairly large amount

Notes

1. Barbara Epstein

Barbara Epstein teaches in the History of Consciousness program at the University of California at Santa Cruz. Barbara Epstein's scholarship has consistently been about social movements and the problems that they face. The present essay is taken from an article of the same title published in *Monthly Review* September, 2002. The article looks at the present situation of feminist consciousness in the US after the mass women's movement has declined and waned.

2. New Left

A political movement originating in the United States in the 1960s, especially among college students, marked by advocacy of radical changes in government, politics, and society.

Comprehension

1. What evidence does the author give that feminism is now a permanent feature of Western social thinking?
2. According to the author, what is the difference between "feminist consciousness" and "the women's movement?"

3. What was "woman suffrage?" Who were the "suffragettes?"
4. What is the difference between the first and the second waves of women's movement in view of their impact?
5. What example is cited as a feminist argument for support of political action?
6. What gender inequalities does the author suggest still exist in the United States?
7. Why has feminist consciousness spread over the last two decades even as the organized women's movement has contracted?
8. According to the author, the environmental movement "has followed the same trajectory as the women's movement." What does she mean by this?

Further Study

The web page http://etext.library.adelaide.edu.au/w/woolf/virginia/ provides free downloadable works by Virginia Woolf, including the complete essay of "A Room of One's Own."

Students interested in the Bloomsbury group, with which Virginia Woolf was closely associated, may search the web page http://bloomsbury.denise-randle.co.uk/intro.htm for further information.

Unit 9

National Character

Unit Goals

☞ To learn about American and British national character
☞ To appreciate the use of paradox as a figure of speech and its difference from oxymoron
☞ To understand social commentary as a literary genre

Before Reading

1. Search an encyclopedia or the Internet for information about the life, major works, and themes of John Steinbeck. If possible, view films adapted from his novels, such as *Of Mice and Man*, and *The Grapes of Wrath*.
2. Find some other literature about American national character and share these with your classmates.

A Glimpse into the Text

Winner of the Nobel Prize for Literature in 1962, John Steinbeck (1902—1968) was a keen observer of the national character of America—a gift best demonstrated by his masterwork, *The Grapes of Wrath*. In this article, Steinbeck turns his power of scrutiny upon a particular manifestation of the "American Way of Life" and the paradoxes inherent in it—the dream of owning a home.

Text A

Paradox and Dream

John Steinbeck[1]
(Abridged and edited)

One of the generalities most often noted about Americans is that we are a restless, a dissatisfied, a
5 searching people. We bridle

> paradox /ˈpærədɒks/ n. [C] a person, thing or situation that has two opposite features and therefore seems strange
> generality /ˌdʒenəˈrælɪti/ n. [C, usually pl.] a statement that discusses general examples
> bridle /ˈbraɪdl/ v. (literary) to show that you are annoyed and/or offended at sth., especially by moving your head up and backwards in a proud way

129

and buck under failure, and we go mad with dissatisfaction in the face of success. We spend our time searching for security, and hate it when we get it. For the most part we are an intemperate people: we eat too much when we can, drink too much, indulge our senses too much. Even in our so-called virtues we are intemperate: a teetotaler is not content to not drink—he must stop all the drinking in the world; a vegetarian among us would outlaw the eating of meat. We work too hard, and many die under the strain; and then to make up for that we play with a violence as suicidal.

The result is that we seem to be in a state of turmoil all the time, both physically and mentally. We are able to believe that our government is weak, stupid, overbearing, dishonest, and inefficient, and at the same time we are deeply convinced that it is the best government in the world, and we would like to impose it upon everyone else. We speak of the American Way of Life as though it involved the ground rules for the governance of heaven. A man hungry and unemployed through his own stupidity and that of others, a man beaten by a brutal policeman, a woman forced into prostitution by her own laziness, high prices, availability, and despair—all bow with reverence toward the American Way of Life, although each one would look puzzled and angry if he were asked to define it. We scramble and scrabble² up the stony path toward the pot of gold² we have taken to mean security. We trample friends, relatives, and strangers who get in our way of achieving it; and once we get it we shower it on psychoanalysts to try to find out why we are unhappy, and finally—if we have enough of the gold—we contribute it back to the nation in the form of foundations and charities.

We fight our way in, and try to buy our way out. We are alert, curious, hopeful, and we take more drugs designed to make us unaware than any other people. We are self-reliant and at the same time completely dependent. We are aggressive and defenseless. Americans overindulge their children and do not like them; the children in turn are overly dependent and full of hate for their parents. We are complacent in our possessions, in our houses, in our education; but it is hard to find a man or woman who does not want something better for the next generation. Americans are remarkably kind and hospitable and open with both guests and strangers; and yet they will make a wide circle around the man dying on the pavement. Fortunes are spent getting cats out of trees and dogs out of sewer pipes; but a girl screaming for help in the street draws only slammed doors, closed windows, and silence.

---

buck /bʌk/ v. to resist stubbornly and obstinately; balk

intemperate /ɪnˈtempərɪt/ adj. (formal) showing a lack of control over yourself

indulge /ɪnˈdʌldʒ/ v. satisfy (a perhaps unwarranted or illicit desire) ~ **oneself/sb. (with sth.)**, allow oneself/sb. to have whatever one/he likes or wants

teetotaler /tiːˈtəʊtələ(r)/ n. a person who does not drink alcohol

turmoil /ˈtɜːmɔɪl/ n. [U, sing.] a state of great anxiety, confusion and uncertainty

overbearing /ˌəʊvəˈbeərɪŋ/ adj. (disapproving) trying to control other people in an unpleasant way

ground rules a basic rule of procedure or behaviour, often used in the plural

governance /ˈgʌvənəns/ n. [U] (technical) the activity of governing a country or controlling a company or an organization; the way in which a country is governed or a company or institution is controlled

scrabble /ˈskræbəl/ v. to climb with scrambling, disorderly haste; clamber

trample /ˈtræmpl/ v. to tread heavily on sth./sb. so as to cause damage or destruction

complacent /kəmˈpleɪsənt/ adj. (usually disapproving) too satisfied with yourself or with a situation, so that you do not feel that any change is necessary; showing or feeling complacency

Americans seem to live and breathe and function by paradox; but in nothing are we so paradoxical as in our passionate beliefs in our own myths. We truly believe ourselves to be natural-born mechanics and do-it-yourselfers. We spend our lives in motor cars, yet most of us—a great many of us at least—do not know enough about a car to look in the gas tank when the motor fails. Our lives as we live them would not function without electricity, but it is a rare man or woman who, when the power goes off, knows how to look for a burned-out fuse and replace it. We believe implicitly that we are the heirs of the pioneers; that we have inherited self-sufficiency and the ability to take care of ourselves, particularly in relation to nature. There isn't a man among us in ten thousand who knows how to butcher a cow or a pig and cut it up for eating, let alone a wild animal. By natural endowment, we are great rifle shots and great hunters—but when hunting season opens there is a slaughter of farm animals and humans by men and women who couldn't hit a real target if they could see it. Americans treasure the knowledge that they live close to nature, but fewer and fewer farmers feed more and more people; and as soon as we can afford to we eat out of cans, buy frozen TV dinners, and haunt the delicatessens. Affluence means moving to the suburbs, but the American suburbanite sees, if anything, less of the country than the city apartment dweller with his window boxes and his African violets[3] tended under lights. In no country are more seeds and plants and equipment purchased, and less flowers and vegetables raised.

The paradoxes are everywhere: We shout that we are a nation of laws, not men—and then proceed to break every law we can if we can get away with it. We proudly insist that we base our political positions on the issues—and we will vote against a man because of his religion, his name, or the shape of his nose.

Sometimes we seem to be a nation of public puritans and private profligates. There surely can be no excesses like those committed by good family men away from home at a convention. We believe in the manliness of our men and the womanliness of our women, but we go to extremes of expense and discomfort to cover any natural evidence that we are either. From puberty we are preoccupied with sex; but our courts, our counselors, and our psychiatrists are dealing constantly with cases of sexual failure or charges of frigidity or impotence.

We fancy ourselves as hard-headed realists, but we will buy anything we see advertised, particularly on television; and we buy it not with reference to the quality or the value of the product, but directly as a result of the number of times we have heard it mentioned. The most arrant nonsense about a product is never questioned. We are afraid to be awake, afraid to be alone, afraid to be a moment without the noise and confusion we call entertainment. We boast of our dislike of highbrow art and music, and we have more and better-attended symphonies, art galleries, and theaters than any country in the world. We detest abstract art and

---

haunt /hɔːnt/ *v.* to visit often, frequent

delicatessen (also **deli**) /ˌdelɪkəˈtesən/ *n.* a shop/store or part of one that sells cooked meats and cheeses, and special or unusual foods that come from other countries

profligate /ˈprɒflɪgɪt/ *n.* a recklessly wasteful person

puberty /ˈpjuːbəti/ *n.* the stage in a person's life when they develop from a child into an adult because of changes in their body that make them able to have children

frigidity /frɪˈdʒɪdəti/ *n.* (of a woman) the state of having difficulty in becoming sexually excited

impotence /ˈɪmpətəns/ *n.* (of a man) the state of being unable to have sex because his penis cannot harden or stay hard

hard-headed /ˈhɑːdˈhedɪd/ *adj.* determined and not allowing your emotions to affect your decisions

arrant /ˈærənt/ *adj.* [only before n.] (old-fashioned) used to emphasize how bad sth./sb. is

highbrow /ˈhaɪbraʊ/ *adj.* (sometimes disapproving) concerned with or interested in serious artistic or cultural ideas

produce more of it than all the rest of the world put together.

One of the characteristics most puzzling to a foreign observer is the strong and imperishable dream the American carries. On inspection, it is found that the dream has little to do with reality in American life. Consider the dream of and the hunger for a home. The very word can reduce nearly all of my compatriots to tears. Builders and developers never build houses—they build homes. The dream home is either in a small town or in a suburban area where grass and trees simulate the country. This dream home is not rented but owned. It is a center where a man and his wife grow graciously old, warmed by the radiance of well-washed children and grandchildren. Many thousands of these homes are built every year; built, planned, advertised, and sold—and yet, the American family rarely stays in one place for more than five years. The home and its equipment are purchased on time and heavily mortgaged. The earning power of the father is almost always overextended, so that after a few years he is not able to keep up the payments on his loans. But suppose the earner is successful and his income increases. Right away the house is not big enough, or in the proper neighborhood. Or perhaps suburban life palls, and the family moves to the city, where excitement and convenience beckon.

The home dream is only one of the deepest American illusions which, since they can't be changed, function as cohesive principles to bind the nation together and make it different from all other nations. It occurs to me that all dreams, waking and sleeping, are powerful and prominent memories of something real, of something that really happened. I believe these memories—some of them, at least—can be inherited; our generalized dreams of water and warmth, of falling, of monsters, of danger and premonitions may have been pre-recorded on some kind of genetic tape in the species out of which we evolved or mutated, just as some of our organs which no longer function seem to be physical memories of other, earlier processes. The national dream of Americans is a whole pattern of thinking and feeling and may well be a historic memory surprisingly little distorted. This pattern of thought and conduct which is the national character is absorbed even by the children of immigrants born in America, but it never comes to the immigrants themselves, no matter how they may wish it; birth on American soil seems to be required.

For Americans, the wider and more general dream has a name. It is called "the American Way of Life." No one can define it or point to any one person or group who lives it, but it is very real nevertheless, perhaps more real than that equally remote dream the Russians call Communism. These dreams describe our vague yearnings toward what we wish we were and hope we may be: wise, just, compassionate, and noble. The fact that we have this dream at all is perhaps an indication of its possibility.

(From *America and Americans*)

---

imperishable /ɪmˈperɪʃəbəl/ *adj.* (formal or literary) that will last for a long time or forever
compatriot /kəmˈpætrɪət/ *n.* a person who was born in, or is a citizen of, the same country as sb. else
simulate /ˈsɪmjʊleɪt/ *v.* to take on the appearance of (sth./sb.).
pall (on sb.) /pɔːl/ *v.* become uninteresting or boring by being experienced too often
premonition /ˌpreməˈnɪʃən/ *n.* ~ (of sth./that...) a feeling that sth. is going to happen, especially sth. unpleasant
mutate /mjuːˈteɪt/ *v.* ~ (into sth.) to develop or make sth. develop a new form or structure, because of a genetic change

More about the Text

1. John Steinbeck

John Ernst Steinbeck (1902—1968), American writer of short stories and novels. A winner of the Nobel Prize for Literature in 1962, he is best known for his novel *Of Mice and Men* (1937) and his Pulitzer Prize-winning novel *The Grapes of Wrath* (1939), both of which examine the lives of the working class and the migrant workers during the Great Depression. Seventeen of his works, including *Cannery Row* (1945) and *The Pearl* (1947), became Hollywood films, and Steinbeck himself achieved success as a Hollywood writer, garnering an Academy Award nomination for Best Writing for Alfred Hitchcock's *Lifeboat*, in 1945. The present selection is an excerpt from *America and Americans* (1966), in  which Steinbeck's text accompanied by photographs renders the many faces of America, its scenic beauty as well as its human varieties. Selections from the book first appeared in *The Saturday Evening Post* July 2, 1966.

2. pot of gold

The old story goes that he who follows the rainbow to the end will find a pot of gold. It is but a legend, for there is no end to find. Rainbows we now know are an artifact of optics.

3. African violet

Any of various East African herbs, having a basal leaf rosette and a showy cluster of violet or sometimes pink or white flowers. African violets are grown as indoor ornamentals.

Check Your Understanding

1. Can you find examples in the text to illustrate that Americans are a restless, dissatisfied, and searching people?
2. What do Americans think of their government, according to Steinbeck? Do you agree with him?
3. What do Americans think of security? What do they do to achieve it, according to Steinbeck? Do you think Steinbeck is fair in saying so?
4. What do you think are the major reasons for the rich and famous to give money back to society in the form of foundations and charities?
5. Are Americans generous, kind and hospitable people? Explain your answer.
6. Do you think the dream home and the American dream are the same thing?
7. What drives American people to move into bigger and better homes?
8. What are the dreams of Americans you know about?
9. What is your understanding of "the American Way of Life?" What do you think are the values of the American way of life?
10. Do immigrants share the same American dream as native Americans?

Paraphrasing

1. We speak of the American Way of Life as though it involved the ground rules for the governance of heaven.
2. Americans seem to live and breathe and function by paradox; but in nothing are we so paradoxical as in our passionate beliefs in our own myths.
3. The home dream is only one of the deepest American illusions which, since they can't be changed, function as cohesive principles to bind the nation together and make it different from all other nations.
4. I believe these memories—some of them, at least—can be inherited; our generalized dreams of water and warmth, of falling, of monsters, of danger and premonitions may have been pre-recorded on some kind of genetic tape in the species out of which we evolved or mutated, just as some of our organs which no longer function seem to be physical memories of other, earlier processes.
5. These dreams describe our vague yearnings toward what we wish we were and hope we may be: wise, just, compassionate, and noble. The fact that we have this dream at all is perhaps an indication of its possibility.

Some Information about English Style

1. Paradox as a literary device

The term paradox is from the Greek *paradoxos*, *para*-(beyond) + *doxa*(opinion), meaning "contrary to received opinion" or "conflicting with expectation." A paradox is a statement that appears to be self-contradictory or opposed to common sense at first but upon closer inspection contains some degree of truth or validity. The purpose of a paradox is to arrest attention and provoke fresh thought, as in the saying "More haste, less speed." Another example is "The child is father to the man." Rationally, a child cannot be a father, but one can propose in this figurative way that the nature of one's early life affects later ideas and attitudes.

In ordinary conversation, we might use a paradox, such as "Deep down he's really very shallow." Paradox is frequently used in literature. For example, Juliet describes Romeo by saying "O serpent heart, hid with a flowering face!" (III ii 75) While Juliet knows that Romeo is not a serpent nor does he have a face full of flowers, her use of these descriptions show how paradoxically he is her lover and the murderer of her cousin at the same time. *A Tale of Two Cities* opens with the famous paradox, "It was the best of times, it was the worst of times." Such a statement seems contradictory, unbelievable, or absurd, but it challenges deeper thought on the matter. "What a pity that youth must be wasted on the young," a quotation from George Bernard Shaw, seems to be opposed to common sense at first, but contains some truth in it. "It is only very shallow people," observed Oscar Wilde, "who do not judge by appearances." What the words state conflicts with the conventional view that shallow people judge by appearances and wise people look beneath the appearance to the reality beneath. However, after a few moments' thought, we might be led to recognize that shallow people do not realize that appearances are as much a part of things as what lies underneath, and that there is no reason to think that they are a less significant part. After all, appearances are produced by the things of which they are appearances. Experience and wisdom tell us that if the appearance is wrong to start with, it is usually the case that everything else is wrong as well. Then we may accept Wilde's statement.

In the present selection, paradox is the most significant strategy, enabling Steinbeck to reconcile contrasts in ideas. For example, in his discussion of the US government, he notes that "We are able to believe that our government is weak, stupid, overbearing, dishonest, and inefficient, and at the same time we are deeply convinced that it is the best government in the world, and we would like to impose it upon everyone else." Paradoxical as it seems at first, the statement arrests the reader's attention to the contrast and arouses his curiosity to discover the truth of it. Paradox is employed in his discussions of nearly every aspect of America and Americans, attitudes toward success, work, children, law, art, and music, to name but a few. With all the paradoxes, the reader is persuaded that Americans live, breathe, and function by paradox, which is the central theme of this reading.

2. Paradox and oxymoron

Paradox is sometimes confused with oxymoron. The term oxymoron comes from the Greek *oxumoros*, meaning pointedly foolish. The Greek word is formed by combining *oxus* (sharp) and *moros* (foolish). Oxymoron is combination of two seemingly contradictory or incongruous words, as in the line by the English poet Sir Philip Sidney in which lovers are said to speak of "*living deaths, dear wounds, fair storms, and freezing fires.*" Oxymoron is similar to paradox in that both figures of speech use contradictions to state a truth. However, unlike paradox, oxymoron places opposing words side by side, as in "*sweet sorrow*" and "*hellish paradise.*" Oxymoron is used for effect, to emphasize contrasts, incongruities, hypocrisy, or simply the complex nature of reality. The following speech from William Shakespeare's *Romeo and Juliet* uses several oxymorons:

Why, then, O brawling love! O loving hate!
O anything, of nothing first create!
O heavy lightness! serious vanity!
Mis-shapen chaos of well-seeming forms!
Feather of lead, bright smoke, cold fire, sick health!
This love feel I, that feel no love in this.

In this speech Romeo described love using several oxymorons to suggest its contradictory nature. Oxymorons abound in English, such as "wise fool," "ignorantly learned," "laughing sadness," and "pious hate."

3. Social commentary

A social commentary expresses an opinion on the nature of society. Social commentaries are often made in an attempt to bring about or promote change by informing the general public of a given problem and appealing to people's sense of justice. Two examples of strong and bitter social commentary are the writings of Jonathan Swift and Martin Luther. Swift exposed and decried the appalling poverty in Ireland at the time; Luther initiated the Protestant Reformation against practices of the Catholic Church.

The most common social commentary is found in the editorial section of newspapers, where columnists give their opinion on current affairs. The letters section of newspapers allows a similar platform for members of the public. The topics of written social commentaries vary widely, from religious issues (e.g. Martin Luther's treatises) to philosophical probing (e.g. Plato's *Republic*). Most public speaking constitutes social commentary of some form. For instance, many sermons describe the ills of society and offer religious solutions, and many politicians speak in a similar manner. Allegorical fictional works such as *Animal Farm* clearly contain a social commentary and one can find some degree of social commentary in almost any novel. Fictional works in radio, television, and film have a similar scope. Radio and television talk shows also allow some discussion and sometimes debate on social issues. The Internet performs a similar function to the letters section in newspapers, with discussion and debate occurring in many blogs, forums, and chat rooms because they allow the dissemination of ideas by anyone with a computer to a potentially enormous audience and may initiate instant comment and discussion.

The present reading is a social commentary that deals with paradoxes and the "home dream" in American life. While it is difficult to define the "American Way of Life," Steinbeck is at home with his commentary on various aspects of American life. Through these comments, the reader can catch a glimpse of what Americans are like and how they live their lives.

Practice

Building word power

1. Below are a list of words from the reading selection and ten pairs of sentences. The blank in sentence a of each pair can be filled in with a word in its proper form as is used in the reading selection. The blank in sentence b can be filled in with the same word, but with a different meaning. After you have finished, compare your answers with a classmate.

   (1) a. He's been under a lot of _____ recently.
       b. The hurricane put such a _____ on the bridge that it collapsed.
   (2) a. He _____ her with emeralds and furs.
       b. I _____ every morning.
   (3) a. He _____ himself as a bit of a singer.
       b. I just _____ a drink.
   (4) a. He argues that the Congress and President Clinton _____ the constitutional rights of legal immigrants in the new welfare reform law.
       b. Many people were _____ in the panic that followed.
   (5) a. They risk losing their homes because they can no longer _____ the repayments.
       b. He started to walk faster and the children had to run to _____.
   (6) a. For many young people, the bright lights of London _____, though a lot of them ended up sleeping on the streets.
       b. Hughes _____ him to sit down on a sofa.
   (7) a. The lights mysteriously _____, and we stumbled around in complete darkness.
       b. When I looked down and saw how far I had to jump, my courage _____ me.
   (8) a. If I criticize him, he gets _____ and starts shouting.
       b. He is respected as a very _____ and competitive executive.

(9) a. There are tests which can establish a baby's genetic _____.
   b. The college has received a(n) _____ of land and investments.
(10) a. We were all surprised at the _____ of his anger.
   b. The report documents the staggering amount of domestic _____ against women.
(11) a. The attentions of the media _____ her to tears.
   b. I'd run out of cigarettes and was _____ to smoking the butts left in the ashtrays.
(12) a. He _____ down before the king and begged for mercy.
   b. Grief _____ them down.

2. **Fill in each blank with the best answer for each of the following sentences by choosing A, B, C or D.**
   (1) A _____ child is a teacher's delight.
      A. curious   B. inquisitive   C. meddlesome   D. prying
   (2) Although business is improving we cannot afford to be _____ —there is still a lot of hard work to be done.
      A. complacent   B. self-satisfied   C. haughty   D. arrogant
   (3) The two brothers were very different—the older one was _____ and good-natured, while the younger one was very quick-tempered.
      A. friendly   B. amiable   C. genial   D. hospitable
   (4) Once cockroaches get into a building, it's very difficult to _____ them.
      A. butcher   B. slaughter   C. massacre   D. exterminate
   (5) Consumer goods are a symbol of prestige in a(n) _____ society.
      A. rich   B. wealthy   C. affluent   D. prosperous
   (6) I _____ warm milk—it makes me feel sick.
      A. hate   B. abhor   C. detest   D. abominate
   (7) Her new book _____ the cause of social discontent.
      A. examines   B. studies   C. inspects   D. scrutinizes
   (8) These organizations have fought very hard for the rights and _____ of immigrants.
      A. safety   B. refuge   C. security   D. welfare
   (9) Employers seem to share the general _____ that young people are more efficient than old.
      A. fallacy   B. illusion   C. delusion   D. misconception
   (10) The chairman's serious public _____ is in sharp contrast with that of his humourous deputy.
      A. behaviour   B. conduct   C. manner   D. demeanour
   (11) Justice must be a(n) _____ of an ideal society.
      A. character   B. characteristic   C. attribute   D. property
   (12) The chiefs of big corporations occupy a _____ position in society.
      A. strong   B. powerful   C. influential   D. dominant

Grammar and Usage

1. The following is a list of idioms and phrasal verbs from the reading selection. Translate the following sentences by using one of them.

for the most part	let alone	get/be in the way
in the face of	go off	in relation to
if anything	in turn	with reference to
get away with	impose on	make up for

(1) 面对逆境他们仍面带微笑。
(2) 教授通常专注于教学而不是科研。
(3) 有趣的工作能弥补微薄的工资吗?
(4) 那些小贩把古董赝品强行兜售给外国游客。
(5) 增加生产会继而增加利润。
(6) 她决心要成功,不会让任何事情妨碍自己。
(7) 水从窗户进来时,所有的灯都熄灭了。
(8) 他 1 万米都跑不了,更别提马拉松了。
(9) 与工资相比,物价似乎偏高。
(10) 如果我想着干了坏事不会被发觉,我会任何税都不交的。
(11) 这家报纸对这一事件进行了详尽的报道,但并未指明消息的来源。
(12) 他并不勤奋。恰恰相反,他非常懒惰。

2. Fill in the blanks with appropriate prepositions or adverbs.

Today, _____ (1) the ancient American tendency to look for greener pastures still very much alive, the mobile home has become the new dream. It is not a trailer; it is a house, long and narrow in shape, and equipped with wheels so that it can, if necessary, be transported over the highway to a new area. In a mobile home, a man doesn't have to take a loss when he moves; his home goes with him. Until recently, when the local authorities have set _____ (2) finding means of making Mr. Mobile pay his way, a mobile home owner living in a rented space in a trailer park could avoid local taxes and local duties while making use of the public schools and all the other facilities American towns set up for their people. The mobile way of life is not a new thing in the world, of course. It is more than probable that humans lived this way for hundreds of thousands of years before they ever conceived _____ (3) settling down—the herdsmen followed the herds, the hunters followed the game, and everybody ran _____ (4) the weather. The Tartars moved whole villages on wheels, and the die-hard gypsies have never left their caravans. No, people go back to mobility with enthusiasm for something they recognize, and if they can double the dream—have a symbolic home and mobility at the same time—they have it made. And now there are huge settlements of these metal houses clustered _____ (5) the edges of our cities. Plots of grass and shrubs are planted, awnings stretched out, and garden chairs appear. A community life soon springs up— a life having all the signs of status, the standards of success or failure that exist elsewhere in America.

Of course, the home dream can be acted _____ (6) almost anywhere. A number of years ago, when I lived on East 51st Street in New York City, I saw an instance of it every day on my morning walk, near Third Avenue, where great numbers of old red brick buildings were the small, walk-up cold-water flats in which so many New Yorkers lived. Every summer morning about nine o'clock a stout and benign-looking lady came down the stairs from her flat to the pavement carrying the great outdoors in her arms. She set out a canvas deck chair, and _____ (7) it mounted a beach umbrella—one of the kind which has a little cocktail table around it—and then, smiling happily, this benign and robust woman rolled out a little lawn made of green rafia in front of her chair, set out two pots of red geraniums and an artificial palm, brought a little cabinet filled with cold drinks—Coca-Cola, Pepsi-Cola—in a small icebox; she laid her folded copy of the Daily News on the table, arranged her equipment, and sank back _____ (8) the chair—and she was in the country. She nodded and smiled to everyone who went _____ (9), and somehow she conveyed her dream to everyone who saw her, and everyone who saw her was delighted _____ (10) her. For some reason I was overwhelmed with a desire to contribute to this sylvan retreat, and so one day when she had stepped inside for a moment, I deposited on her table a potted fern and a little bowl with two goldfish; and the next morning, I was pleased to see that these had been added to the permanent equipment. Every day through that summer the fern and the goldfish were part of the scene.

Improving your writing style

1. Complete the following paradoxes with an appropriate word.

(1) What is mature love? It is union under the condition of preserving one's integrity, one's individuality. In love the paradox occurs that two beings become one and yet remain _____. (Erich Fromm)

(2) Freedom is not doing what you want, freedom is _____ to do what you have to do... this kind of freedom is always rooted in practised habit. (Northrop Frye)

(3) Things are simultaneously knowable and _____.

(4) Sometimes it proves the highest understanding not to _____.

(5) The opposite of a correct statement is a _____ statement. But the opposite of a profound truth may well be another profound truth. (Niels Bohr)

(6) Madness may be defined as using mental activity so as to reach mental _____. (G. K. Chesterton)

(7) To believe with certainty we must begin with _____. (King Stanislaw II)

(8) Rivals grow more alike with every new attempt to be _____ and this causes them to intensify their conflict.

(9) The paradox of courage is that a man must be a little _____ of his life even in order to keep it. (G. K. Chesterton)

(10) Each new power won by man (over Nature) is a power over man as well. Each advance leaves him weaker as well as _____. (C. S. Lewis)

2. The following are well-known oxymorons. Can you complete them with appropriate words and then compare your work with your classmates?

_____ secret	_____ silence	_____ reality
pretty _____	_____ estimate	_____ comedy
genuine _____	_____ choice	_____ kindness
_____ life	_____ dead	_____ gas

Writing task

Reflect on Western/American influences on China and write an essay which answers this question: Is there any similarity between the way things American were beginning to have a big impact in Europe at the time when Alistair Cooke wrote the letter and the way things Western, which largely mean American, have been having an impact on China over the last couple of decades? Support your opinion with examples.

Text B

The European's America (23 October 1952)

Alistair Cooke[1]
(Abridged and Edited)

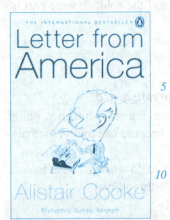

"*Otherness*" is an important concept in cultural studies. Otherness is a means by which a society is defined by distinguishing what attributes it possesses that other cultures lack or, conversely, what attributes other cultures possess that it lacks. In this light-hearted article by the British social commentator, Alistair Cooke, the otherness of American culture is used to convey his general impressions of 1950s America to European readers.

It is the fall. The fall of the year, an American institution now so well known, and even respected, in Europe that you no doubt expect me to take off, as I annually do, about the scarlet maples pouring like a fire through New England, the brilliant light everywhere, the thin milky trails of woodsmoke that rise into a bottomless blue sky. Well, once you've created a stereotype, it is time to demolish it. The fall has refinements, even perils, that the autumn in other countries does not share. Once you've learned the big clichés of a country, which are true and which are not, it is the off-beat clichés that really fix the place in your mind, and make it like no other, and may even endear it to you, years later in another country far away. Let me illustrate.

A few days ago, I was reading a piece in an American magazine by Mr Cyril Connolly,[2] a writer with whom I feel a strong sympathy and never more than in this piece, which was about the widespread Americanising of Europe. What are

otherness /'ʌðənɪs/ *n.* the quality or condition of being other or different, especially if exotic or strange
attribute /'ætrɪbjuːt/ *n.* a quality or characteristic that someone or sth. has
conversely /'kɒnvɜːslɪ/ *adv.* in an opposite way
commentator /'kɒmənteɪtə/ *n.* one who writes or delivers a commentary or commentaries
take off to discontinue
demolish /dɪ'mɒlɪʃ/ *v.* to show that an idea or theory is completely wrong
refinement /rɪ'faɪnmənt/ *n.* the quality of being polite and well educated and able to judge the quality of things; the state of having the sort of manners that are considered typical of a high social class
peril /'perɪl/ *n.* serious danger
cliché /'kliːʃeɪ/ *n.* a phrase or an idea that has been used so often that it no longer has much meaning and is not interesting
off-beat /'ɔːfbiːt/ *n.* (usually before noun) different from what most people expect
Americanise /ə'merɪkənaɪz/ *v.* to make sth./sb. American in character

those influences which many Europeans think of as all America has to offer, and which they wish had stayed on this side of the Atlantic? Connolly lists them: "jazz, gangster stories, bad films, tales of violence, science fiction." I could add some others, especially the compulsion to break up the relics of London as an eighteenth-century country town and riddle them with chromium-plated fronts and dingy "American" snack bars and amusement arcades and the tattiest attempts at modern "American" architecture. Not to mention the Cockney's[3] surrender to what he imagines is American slang, the frantic imitation bebop, the transatlantic zoot-suiter.[4] The point is that these influences, picked up I suppose from the movies, are almost always bad imitations of crummy originals. What is alarming, and what the European seems unaware of, is that they are often planted firmly in a solid English background, in the sort of place they would not be found in the American background. They do not have chrome cocktail bars along the noble stretch of North Street, in Litchfield, Connecticut,[5] or snack bars at the bottom of Zion Canyon[6]. Along the new motor parkways of New York and New England, they do not even allow the petrol companies to build their own pumps. The stations, like the overpasses, must conform to a design sanctioned by the commissioner of parks or highways and be made of the local stone. And the fences that bind the parkways are the same for a hundred miles or more and are made from a pine that fits the landscape. It is an unexpected and admirable thing about the development of the automobile age in America that Americans have developed a sense of style as watchful as that of the men who gave us the urban style of eighteenth-century London and the country style of eighteenth-century New England. (The billboard lobby and the freeways are now doing their damnedest to date this compliment.)

I sometimes think that a European deploring the horror of Pittsburgh[7] and Detroit[8] and St. Louis[9] and "your Midwest cities" is not really criticising the Midwest or American cities but the nineteenth-century city anywhere. But it is also a fact that though American towns may, and do, seethe with the random horrors that are now so faithfully transplanted to British towns, it is almost easier over here to get away from them. My European visitors are always surprised to discover how much virgin forest there appears to be on the edge of town. Theoretically, there are only two big stands of the forest primeval in this country, one in the Cascade Mountains[10] and the other in the Bitterroots,[11] both far out on the north-west Pacific Coast. But I'm thinking of long-settled country. I have taken Englishmen in a car fifteen minutes from where I am talking to you and once beyond the George Washington Bridge[12] they are weaving around great rocks and little woods as dense as the New Forest.[13] A half-hour from Times Square[14] (all right, then, two hours in the rush hour) they can be in something that looks like Fenimore Cooper country,[15] and it is not hard to imagine on dark nights an Indian slipping through the trees, slinking across the six-lane divided highway and standing as aghast at the lights of Manhattan as I am when I see what the "developers" have done to Regency[16] Mayfair.[17]

For nearly two centuries now, there has

---

compulsion /kəmˈpʌlʃən/ *n.* a strong desire to do sth., especially sth. that is wrong, silly or dangerous

riddle /ˈrɪdl/ *v.* **be riddled with** (idiom) to be full of sth., especially sth. bad or unpleasant

chromium /ˈkrəʊmɪəm/ *n.* (symb Cr) a chemical element. Chromium is a hard grey metal that shines brightly when polished and is often used to cover other metals in order to prevent them from rusting.

tatty /ˈtæti/ *adj.* in a bad condition because it has been used a lot or has not been cared for well

bebop /ˈbiːbɒp/ *n.* a type of jazz with complicated rhythms

crummy /ˈkrʌmi/ *adj.* of very bad quality

seethe /siːð/ *v.* (~ **with sth.**) to be full of a lot of people or animals, especially when they are all moving around

primeval /praɪˈmiːvəl/ *adj.* from the earliest period of the history of the world, very ancient

been a continuous argument, sometimes amiable sometimes bloodthirsty, about which country was influencing the other the most. Until about fifty years ago, the example was all one way, and the way was east to west. But it has been changing
80 very fast. Every world power leaves indelible imprints even on countries that pretend to hate it. And as Europe comes to admit, which it will soon have to, that the United States is now the ranking world power, its customs and gadgets and manners and literature and ways of doing business will
85 powerfully influence the young. They may reject it later on, as Europe pulls itself around and asserts again, as I don't doubt it will want to, its own pride and independence.

But in the meantime, Britain still retains an advantage which will not pass over to America, I think for a long time to come. It is this: Americans who have not been to Europe tend to
90 imagine what is best about her, Europeans who have not been in America tend to imagine what is worst. Ask a few simple Americans what Britain means—ask a schoolgirl, a farmer, a shopkeeper, an elevator man (I have just tried it) what comes to mind when you say "Britain"— and they will say something like: "Oh, old buildings, more easygoing than us, I guess, beautiful countryside, tea in the afternoon, Shakespeare;" and as my elevator man added,
95 "And I understand they are very dignified, very strict, they tell me, in their law courts."

This may sound very naïve to you. But it picks up a flattering myth and not, like the other way round, a libellous one. My own daughter, 14 years old, swings violently between wanting to go to England and being afraid to. Why does she want to go? Because she imagines the place peopled with Mr Pickwick[18] and Romeo and Juliet[19] and Robin Hood,[20]
100 not to mention Laurence Olivier;[21] and because she is crazy about the tables that Sheraton[22] designed and the chairs and desks of Hepplewhite[23] and imagines that every little house in England would throw out anything less graceful. She has indeed heard rude things about the cooking. But I tell her that this is steadily improving. I tell her also about the parklike countryside and the fat cattle, and the sheep as big as buffaloes in Scotland, and it is due as
105 much as anything to the fact that the grass pack of English dairyland is five times as dense as the proud grass pack of Iowa. She thinks the English countryside must be heaven. (By the way, she takes entirely for granted the stupendous beauty of the Tetons[24] and the desert and Yosemite,[25] which leave Englishmen feeling that they have come face to face with their Maker.)

And why doesn't she want to go to England? Well, she explains, wriggling nervously,
110 "Everyone would expect me to be on my best behaviour, they are so polite and—everything."

This is quite a reputation the British have built up. And the other tourist countries of Europe are not far behind. We read here about the exquisite care the French take over their food, and the dedicated way they tread on their grapes, and the devotion they bring to their
115 public buildings. We do not hear about the really garish modern housing that begins to sprout in the Parisian suburbs, or about the alarming incapacity of the French for self-government. We read about the ruthlessness
120 of the Mafia[26] as it goes about its business in

> **libel** /ˈlaɪbəl/ *n.* a piece of writing which contains bad and false things about a person
> **libellous** /ˈlaɪbələs/ *adj.* containing a libel about sb.
> **stupendous** /stjuːˈpendəs/ *adj.* extremely large or impressive, especially greater or better than you expect
> **garish** /ˈgeərɪʃ/ *adj.* very brightly coloured in an unpleasant way

New York or New Orleans but not about its stranglehold on the enslaved slum of Sicily. From Italy we read rather about the preciousness of a new Roman "find" in Tuscany[27] or about the charm of the Appian Way,[28] not about the clutter of billboards that disfigures it.

> **stranglehold** /ˈstræŋɡəlhəʊld/ n. complete control over sth. that makes it impossible for it to grow or develop
> **find** /faɪnd/ n. a thing or person that has been found, especially one that is interesting, valuable or useful

It will surely be a great day when you ask an Englishman what comes to mind at the mention of the word "America" and he replies: "The white villages of New England and the eighteenth-century houses, the neighbourly warmth of the Midwesterners, the contributions of American scholarship, the buffet meals that young American housewives whip up, the style and colour of so many American homes, the outdoor life of California, the god-given glory of Bryce Canyon[29] and the man-made marvel of Hoover Dam.[30]"

Notes

1. Alistair Cooke

Alistair Cooke (1908—2004), British-American journalist and commentator. Cooke settled in New York City after studies at the University of Cambridge and at Yale and Harvard universities. From the late 1930s he provided lively and insightful interpretations of American culture and history to British audiences in newspapers and radio broadcasts. His weekly radio program *Letter from America* (1946—2004) was one of the longest-running series on radio; *One Man's America*  (1952) and *Talk about America* (1968) collect many of its texts. His television programs include *Omnibus* (1956—1961) and the BBC-produced series *America* (1972—1973). He hosted television's *Masterpiece Theatre* from the 1970s to the early 1990s. You will find more at http://news.bbc.co.uk/2/hi/programmes/letter from merica/213674.stm.

2. Cyril Connolly

Cyril Connolly (1903—1974), English critic, novelist, and man of letters, founder and editor of *Horizon*, a magazine of contemporary literature that was a major influence in Britain in its time (1939—1950). As a critic he was personal and eclectic rather than systematic, but his idiosyncratic views were perceptive and conveyed with wit and grace.

3. Cockney

It refers to the white working-class natives of London, or the dialect/slang used by such people. In the context, it refers to Londoners in general.

4. zoot suit

It is a man's suit popular during the early 1940s, characterized by full-legged, tight-cuffed trousers and a long coat with wide lapels and heavily padded, wide shoulders.

5. Connecticut

Connecticut is a state in the New England region of the United States, located in the northeastern part of the country.

6. Zion Canyon

This is a prominent feature in Zion National Park in Utah, United States, which is 24 kilometers long and up to 800 meters deep, cut through the reddish and tan-colored Navajo Sandstone by the North Fork of the Virgin River.

7. Pittsburgh

Pittsburgh is the second largest city in Pennsylvania in the northeastern part of the United States.

8. Detroit

Detroit is the largest city in southwest Michigan in the United States.

9. St. Louis

It is an independent city completely surrounded by St. Louis county on the west, and the Mississippi river on the east, in the U.S. state of Missouri. Officially known as the City of St. Louis, it is the largest metropolis in the state.

10. the Cascade Mountains

It refers to the range of mountain in British Columbia, also Canadian Cascades. It is part of the Cascade Range, a mountainous region famous for its chain of tall volcanoes called the High Cascades that run north-south along the west coast of North America from British Columbia through Washington and Oregon to the Shasta Cascade area of Northern California. The term is also sometimes used by Washington residents to refer to the Washington section of the Cascades.

11. Bitterroots

Bitterroots, or the Bitterroot Range, is a subrange of the Rocky Mountains. The Range runs along the border of Montana and Idaho in the northwestern United States. To the north is Lolo Creek, and to the south is the Salmon River, a span of over 160 kilometers.

12. George Washington Bridge

George Washington Bridge, known informally as the GW Bridge, the GWB, or the GW, is a toll suspension bridge spanning the Hudson River, connecting the Washington Heights neighborhood in the borough of Manhattan in New York City to Fort Lee in New Jersey. The bridge contains two levels, an upper level with four lanes in each direction and a lower level with three lanes in each direction, for a total of 14 lanes of travel. Additionally, the bridge houses two paths on either side of the bridge for pedestrian traffic.

13. New Forest

New Forest is an area of southern England which includes the largest remaining tracts of unenclosed pasture land, heathland and old-growth forest in the heavily-populated south east of England.

14. Times Square

It is an intersection in New York city formed by the juncture of Broadway, Seventh avenue, and 42nd street in midtown Manhattan. Long noted as a center of the city's entertainment district, it is the site of annual New Year's Eve celebrations.

15. Fenimore Cooper country
The landscape in this place looks like the terrain that is marked by ridges of from 1,000 to 2,000 feet elevation divided at regular intervals by stream valleys.

16. Regency
It refers to the period from 1811 to 1820 in the history of the United Kingdom.

17. Mayfair
Mayfair is a fashionable district in Regency London, located by Hyde Park. It was named after an annual fair held in the district until 1708. What made Mayfair unique was that it was the first London neighborhood created exclusively for the wealthy. Many buildings of the Regency style of architecture have a white painted stucco façade and an entryway to the main front door which is framed by two columns. Regency residences typically are built as terraces or crescents, with elegant wrought iron balconies and bay windows

18. Mr Pickwick
Mr Pickwick or Mr Samuel Pickwick, is the main protagonist and founder of the Pickwick Club in *The Posthumous Papers of the Pickwick Club*, better known as *The Pickwick Papers*, the first novel by Charles Dickens which was serialised from March 1836. Mr Pickwick, a kind old gentleman, is usually portrayed by illustrators as a round-faced, clean-shaved, portly gentleman wearing spectacles. Mr Pickwick travels with his friends, Mr Nathaniel Winkle, Mr Augustus Snodgrass, and Mr Tracy Tupman, and their adventures are the chief theme of the novel.

19. Romeo and Juliet
They refer to the main characters in *The Most Excellent and Lamentable Tragedy of Romeo and Juliet*, commonly referred to as *Romeo and Juliet*, a tragedy by William Shakespeare concerning the fate of two young lovers.

20. Robin Hood
He is a legendary English outlaw of the 12th century, famous for his courage, chivalry, and practice of robbing the rich to aid the poor.

21. Laurence Olivier
Laurence Olivier or Laurence Kerr Olivier, Baron Olivier of Brighton, 1907—1989, was an Academy Award, Golden Globe, BAFTA and four-time Emmy winning English actor,
director, and producer. He is regarded by many as the greatest English speaking actor of the 20th century.

22. Sheraton
Sheraton or Thomas Sheraton (1751—1806), was a furniture designer, one of the "big three" English furniture makers of the 18th century, along with Thomas Chippendale and George Heppelwhite. Sheraton style employs slender lightweight forms, using satinwood, mahogany or painted finishes.

23. Heppelwhite
Heppelwhite (died in 1786), was a cabinet and chair maker. He was one of the "big three" English furniture makers of the 18th century, along with Thomas Sheraton and Thomas Chippendale. There are no pieces of furniture made by Heppelwhite or his firm known to exist

but he gave his name to a distinctive style of light, elegant furniture that was fashionable between about 1775 and 1800.

24. the Tetons

Teton or the Tetons may refer to the Teton range, part of the Rocky Mountains in Wyoming, or Grand Teton, the tallest mountain in the Teton Range, and Grand Teton National Park, the United States National Park situated around the range.

25. Yosemite

Yosemite or Yosemite National Park, is a national park covering an area of 3081 km^2 in California, United States. Yosemite is internationally recognized for its spectacular granite cliffs, waterfalls, clear streams, Giant Sequoia groves, and biological diversity.

26. Mafia

Mafia or the Sicilian Mafia, is a criminal secret society which first developed in the mid-19th century in Sicily. An offshoot emerged on the East Coast of the United Stated during the late 19th century following waves of Sicilian emigration. Even if originally referred only to the Sicilian Mafia, the term Mafia is today used to indicate an organized crime association such as Russian Mafia, or Japanese Mafia.

27. Tuscany

It is a region of northwest Italy between the northern Apennines and the Ligurian and Tyrrhenian sea.

28. the Appian Way

It is an ancient Roman road between Rome and Capua, begun in A.D. 312 and later extended to Brindisi, with a total length of more than 563 km.

29. Bryce Canyon

Bryce Canyon, designated Bryce Canyon National Park in 1928, consists of 37,277 acres of scenic colorful rock formations and desert wonderland in southern Utah.

30. Hoover Dam

Hoover Dam, also known as Boulder Dam, constructed between 1931 and 1936, is a concrete gravity-arch dam in the Black Canyon of the Colorado River, on the border between the U.S. states of Arizona and Nevada. The dam, located 48 km (30 miles) southeast of Las Vegas, is named after Herbert Hoover, who played an instrumental role in its construction, first as Secretary of Commerce and then later as President of the United States.

Comprehension

1. Give some examples of the Americanising of Europe. Do Europeans like to be Americanized?
2. What have Europeans ignored when they talk about Americanising of Europe?
3. Did Americans have any sense of style in the automobile age according to Alistair Cooke?
4. How does Alistair Cooke defend American cities like Pittsburgh, Detroit and St. Louis, which a European finds horrible?
5. Which country has influenced the other the most, America or Britain?
6. According to the author, how does the American public imagine England or Europe? How do Europeans tend to think of America?

7. Is Alistair Cooke justified in saying that Americans who have not been to Europe tend to imagine what is best about her?
8. What is your opinion on America, positive or negative? In what ways? Explain your opinion.
9. According to Alistair Cooke, Europeans have built up quite a reputation. Can you specify the kind of reputation some European countries have won?
10. Do you think what you have seen in movies (such as murders, horror, sci-fi, fantasy, adventures, actions, violence) is mostly what American life is about?

Further Study

Find a copy of Steinbeck's last work, *America and Americans*, from which Text I is taken and in which John Steinbeck offers a wide-reaching commentary on the American 20th century. Read it and explore Steinbeck's vision of America and Americans.

Unit 10

The Short Story

Unit Goals

☞ To read English short stories by focusing on
- characterization
- innovation in plot

☞ To know different styles of short story writing

Before Reading

1. Search on the Internet or in the library for information about Katherine Mansfield, author of Text A. Report to the class what you have found out about her life, literary career, style, etc. Tell the class what you think is special about Mansfield.
2. Recall what English short stories you have read and make a list of them. Choose the one you like best and share your knowledge with others in the class.

A Glimpse into the Text

The existentialist philosopher, Jean-Paul Sartre, once declared that "Hell is other people." What he meant was that the expectations and judgments of others are often the source of our deepest sufferings—all the more so when we are isolated from family and friends, as social psychologists have discovered. Decades before Sartre's musings or the research by psychologists, Katherine Mansfield[1] was exploring this idea in her short story, "Miss Brill[2]," a tale of contentment shattered on a Sunday park walk in Les Jardins Publique.

Text A

Miss Brill
Katherine Mansfield

Although it was so brilliantly fine—the blue sky powdered with gold and great spots of light like white wine splashed over the Jardins Publiques[3]—Miss Brill was glad that she had decided on her fur. The air was motionless, but

> splash /splæʃ/ v. (of liquid) to fall noisily onto a surface

148

5 when you opened your mouth there was just a faint chill, like a chill from a glass of iced water before you sip, and now and again a leaf came drifting—from nowhere, from the sky. Miss Brill put up her hand and touched her fur. Dear little thing! It was nice to feel it again. She had taken it out of its box that afternoon, shaken out the
10 moth powder, given it a good brush, and rubbed the life back into the dim little eyes. "What has been happening to me?" said the sad little eyes. Oh, how sweet it was to see them snap at her again from the red eiderdown! ... But the nose, which was of some black composition, wasn't at all firm. It must have had a knock, somehow. Never
15 mind—a little dab of black sealing-wax when the time came— when it was absolutely necessary... Little rogue! Yes, she really felt like that about it. Little rogue biting its tail just by her left ear. She could have taken it off and laid it on her lap and stroked it. She felt a tingling in her hands and arms, but that came from walking, she supposed. And when she breathed, something light and sad—no, not sad, exactly—something
20 gentle seemed to move in her bosom.

There were a number of people out this afternoon, far more than last Sunday. And the band sounded louder and gayer. That was because the Season had begun. For although the band played all the year round on Sundays, out of season it was never the same. It was like some one playing with only the family to listen; it didn't care how it played if there weren't any strangers present. Wasn't the conductor wearing a new coat, too? She was sure it was new.
25 He scraped with his foot and flapped his arms like a rooster about to crow, and the bandsmen sitting in the green rotunda blew out their cheeks and glared at the music. Now there came a little "flutey" bit—very pretty!—a little chain of bright drops. She was sure it would be repeated. It was; she lifted her head and smiled.

Only two people shared her "special" seat: a fine old man in a velvet coat, his hands
30 clasped over a huge carved walking-stick, and a big old woman, sitting upright, with a roll of knitting on her embroidered apron.⁴ They did not speak. This was disappointing, for Miss Brill always looked forward to the conversation. She had become really quite expert, she thought, at listening as though she didn't
35 listen, at sitting in other people's lives just for a minute while they talked round her.

She glanced, sideways, at the old couple. Perhaps they would go soon. Last Sunday, too, hadn't been as interesting as usual. An
40 Englishman and his wife, he wearing a dreadful Panama hat⁵ and she button boots.⁶ And she'd gone on the whole time about how she ought to wear spectacles; she knew she needed them; but that it was no good getting
45 any; they'd be sure to break and they'd never keep on. And he'd been so patient. He'd suggested everything—gold rims, the kind

splash /splæʃ/ v. (of liquid) to fall noisily onto a surface
snap /snæp/ v. to try to bite sb./sth.
rogue /rəʊg/ n. a person who behaves badly, but in a harmless way
tingle /'tɪŋɡ əl/ v. (of a part of your body) to feel as if a lot of small sharp points are pushing into it
scrape /skreɪp/ v. a) (in the text) to draw back a foot in making a clumsy bow b) to make an unpleasant noise by rubbing against a hard surface
flap /flæp/ v. to move or to make sth. move up and down or from side to side, often making a noise
rotunda /rəʊ'tʌndə/ n. a round building or hall, esp. one with a curved roof (i.e. a dome)
velvet /'velvɪt/ n. a type of cloth made from silk, cotton or nylon, with a thick soft surface
clasp /klɑːsp/ v. to hold sth. tightly in your hand
spectacles /'spektək əl/ n. glasses

that curved round your ears, little pads inside the bridge. No, nothing would please her.
50 "They'll always be sliding down my nose!" Miss Brill had wanted to shake her.

The old people sat on a bench, still as statues. Never mind, there was always the crowd to watch. To and fro, in front of the
55 flower beds and the band rotunda, the couples and groups paraded, stopped to talk, to greet, to buy a handful of flowers from the old beggar who had his tray fixed to the railings. Little children ran among them, swooping and
60 laughing; little boys with big white silk bows under their chins, little girls, little French dolls, dressed up in velvet and lace. And sometimes a tiny staggerer came suddenly rocking into the open from under the trees, stopped, stared,
65 as suddenly sat down "flop", until its small high-stepping mother, like a young hen, rushed scolding to its rescue. Other people sat on the benches and green chairs, but they were nearly always the same, Sunday after Sunday, and—Miss Brill had often noticed—there was something funny about nearly all of them. They were odd, silent, nearly all old, and from the way they stared they looked as though they'd
70 just come from dark little rooms or even—even cupboards!

Behind the rotunda the slender trees with yellow leaves down drooping, and through them just a line of sea, and beyond the blue sky with gold-veined clouds.[7]

Tum-tum-tum tiddle-um! tiddle-um! tum tiddley-um tum ta! blew the band.

Two young girls in red came by and two young soldiers in blue met them, and they
75 laughed and paired and went off arm-in-arm. Two peasant women with funny straw hats passed, gravely, leading beautiful smoke-coloured donkeys. A cold, pale nun hurried by. A beautiful woman came along and dropped her bunch of violets, and a little boy ran after to hand them to her, and she took them and threw them away as if they'd been poisoned. Dear me! Miss Brill didn't know whether to admire that or not! And now an ermine toque[8] and a gentleman
80 in gray met just in front of her. He was tall, stiff, dignified, and she was wearing the ermine toque she'd bought when her hair was yellow. Now everything, her hair, her face, even her eyes, was the same colour as the shabby ermine, and her hand, in its cleaned glove, lifted to dab her lips, was a tiny yellowish paw. Oh, she was so pleased to see him—delighted! She rather thought they were going to meet that afternoon. She described where she'd been—
85 everywhere, here, there, along by the sea. The day was so charming—didn't he agree? And wouldn't he, perhaps? ... But he shook his head, lighted a cigarette, slowly breathed a great deep puff into her face, and even while she was still talking and laughing, flicked the match away and walked on. The ermine toque was alone; she smiled more brightly than ever. But even the band seemed to know what she was feeling and played more softly, played tenderly,
90 and the drum beat, "The Brute! The Brute!"[9] over and over. What would she do? What was going to happen now? But as Miss Brill wondered, the ermine toque turned, raised her hand as though she'd seen someone else, much nicer, just over there, and pattered away. And the

---

railings /'reɪlɪŋ/ *n.* a fence made of upright metal bars
swoop /swuːp/ *v.* (of a bird or plane) to fly quickly and suddenly downwards, especially in order to attack sb./sth.
lace /leɪs/ *n.* a delicate material made from threads of cotton, silk, etc. that are twisted into a pattern of holes
rock /rɔk/ *v.* to move gently backwards and forwards or from side to side; to make sb./sth. move in this way
droop /druːp/ *v.* to bend, hang, or move downwards, especially because of being weak or tired
violets /'vaɪlɪt/ *n.* a small wild or garden plant with purple or white flowers with a sweet smell that appear in spring
dab /dæb/ *v.* to touch sth. lightly, usually several times
puff /pʌf/ *n.* a small amount of air or smoke that is blown out; *v.* breathing in sth. such as smoke from a cigarette or drugs
flick /flɪk/ *v.* to hit sth. with a sudden quick movement, especially using your finger and thumb together, or your hand
patter /'pætə/ *v.* to walk quickly, making quiet, tapping sounds

band changed again and played more quickly, more gayly than ever, and the old couple on Miss Brill's seat got up and marched away, and such a funny old man with long whiskers hobbled along in time to the music and was nearly knocked over by four girls walking abreast.

Oh, how fascinating it was! How she enjoyed it! How she loved sitting here, watching it all! It was like a play. It was exactly like a play. Who could believe the sky at the back wasn't painted? But it wasn't till a little brown dog trotted on solemn and then slowly trotted off, like a little "theatre" dog, a little dog that had been drugged, that Miss Brill discovered what it was that made it so exciting. They were all on stage. They weren't only the audience, not only looking on; they were acting. Even she had a part and came every Sunday. No doubt somebody would have noticed if she hadn't been there; she was part of the performance after all. How strange she'd never thought of it like that before! And yet it explained why she made such a point of starting from home at just the same time each week—so as not to be late for the performance—and it also explained why she had a queer, shy feeling at telling her English pupils how she spent her Sunday afternoons. No wonder! Miss Brill nearly laughed out loud. She was on the stage. She thought of the old invalid gentleman to whom she read the newspaper four afternoons a week while he slept in the garden. She had got quite used to the frail head on the cotton pillow, the hollowed eyes,[10] the open mouth and the high pinched nose.[11] If he'd been dead she mightn't have noticed for weeks; she wouldn't have minded. But suddenly he knew he was having the paper read to him by an actress! "An actress!" The old head lifted; two points of light quivered in the old eyes. "An actress—are ye?" And Miss Brill smoothed the newspaper as though it were the manuscript of her part and said gently; "Yes, I have been an actress for a long time."

The band had been having a rest. Now they started again. And what they played was warm, sunny, yet there was just a faint chill—a something, what was it?—not sadness—no, not sadness—a something that made you want to sing. The tune lifted, lifted, the light shone; and it seemed to Miss Brill that in another moment all of them, all the whole company, would begin singing. The young ones, the laughing ones who were moving together, they would begin and the men's voices, very resolute and brave, would join them. And then she too, she too, and the others on the benches—they would come in with a kind of accompaniment—something low, that scarcely rose or fell, something so beautiful—moving.... And Miss Brill's eyes filled with tears and she looked smiling at all the other members of the company. Yes, we understand, we understand, she thought—though what they understood she didn't know.

Just at that moment a boy and a girl came and sat down where the old couple had been. They were beautifully dressed; they were in love. The hero and heroine, of course, just arrived from his father's yacht. And still soundlessly singing, still with that trembling smile, Miss Brill prepared to listen.

"No, not now," said the girl. "Not here, I can't."

> hobble /ˈhɒb əl/ v. to walk in an awkward way, usually because the feet are injured
> abreast /əˈbrest/ adv. walking or moving next to each other, side by side
> trot /trɒt/ v. to move fairly fast, taking small quick steps
> invalid /ˈɪnvælɪd/ n. a person who needs other people to take care of them, because of an illness they have had for a long time
> frail /freɪl/ adj. (especially of an old person) physically weak and thin
> quiver /ˈkwɪvə/ v. to shake slightly; to make a slight movement
> manuscript /ˈmænjʊskrɪpt/ n. a copy of a book, piece of music, etc. before it has been printed
> accompaniment /əˈkʌmpənɪmənt/ n. music that is played to support a singer or instrument

"But why? Because of that stupid old thing at the end there?" asked the boy. "Why does she come here at all—who wants her? Why doesn't she keep her silly old mug at home?"

> mug /mʌɡ/ n. (slang) a person's face
> whiting /'waɪtɪŋ/ n. a small sea fish with white flesh that is used for food
> dash /dæʃ/ v. to go somewhere very quickly

"It's her fu-fur which is so funny," giggled the girl. "It's exactly like a fried whiting."

"Ah, be off with you!" said the boy in an angry whisper. Then: "Tell me, ma petite chérie—"

"No, not here," said the girl. "Not yet."...

On her way home she usually bought a slice of honey-cake at the baker's. It was her Sunday treat. Sometimes there was an almond in her slice, sometimes not. It made a great difference. If there was an almond it was like carrying home a tiny present—a surprise—something that might very well not have been there. She hurried on the almond Sundays[12] and struck the match for the kettle in quite a dashing way.

But today she passed the baker's by, climbed the stairs, went into the little dark room—her room like a cupboard—and sat down on the red eiderdown.[13] She sat there for a long time. The box that the fur came out of was on the bed. She unclasped the necklet quickly; quickly, without looking, laid it inside. But when she put the lid on she thought she heard something crying.

More about the Text

1. Katherine Mansfield

Katherine Mansfield (1888—1923) was born in Wellington, New Zealand, and began her literary career after she moved to London in 1908. Her short stories are often compared with the stories of Anton Chekhov. Instead of striving for neat, well-made plots, Mansfield is concerned with mood and the revelation of character. Some of Mansfield's best known stories are "The Garden Party," "The Fly," and "A Cup of Tea."

2. Miss Brill

"Miss Brill" was published in Mansfield's collection of stories entitled *The Garden Party and Other Stories* in 1922. It has become one of Mansfield's most popular stories, and has been reprinted in numerous anthologies and collections. The story is typical of Mansfield's style, featuring a stream-of-consciousness narration to show the psychological complexity of everyday experience in her characters' lives.

3. Jardins Publiques

This is French for "Public Gardens."

4. embroidered apron

This is an apron that is decorated with a pattern of stitches, usually using coloured thread.

5. Panama hat

It is a man's hat made from fine woven straw.

6. button boots

They are boots with bullon design in the front.

7. gold-veined clouds

Gold-veined clouds are clouds penetrated with golden sun rays.

8. ermine toque

Ermrne toque is a woman's small brimless hat, made from the white fur of the stoat. In the text this is used as metonymy, a figure of speech in which the name of an attribute (the woman) is substituted for the thing itself (ermine toque). Common examples of metonymy are "The Crown" for the monarchy; "The Bench" for the judiciary; "The Pentagon" for the US Defense Ministry.

9. "The Brute! The Brute!"

Brute means "a large animal" literally, used in the text as an onomatopoeia, functioning as a pun.

10. hollowed eyes

Hollowed eyes mean eyes sinking deeply into the face.

11. pinched nose

Pinched nose is the nose which is pale and thin, especially because of illness, cold or worry.

12. almond Sundays

Almond Sundays are those Sundays when Miss Brill could buy a slice of honey-cake with an almond in it as a present.

13. eiderdown

Eiderdown is a thick, warm cover for a bed, filled with feathers or other soft material, and usually placed on top of a sheet and blankets.

Check Your Understanding

1. Where is the story set, England or France? Can you find details in the story that give clues as to the setting of the story?
2. How much are we told about Miss Brill? Can you find pieces of information that somehow reveal Miss Brill's age, occupation, family life, etc?
3. Where is Miss Brill when the story begins? Is she sitting in her room, walking to the park, or sitting on a park bench watching people around her?
4. What details in the story show that Miss Brill cherishes her fur neckpiece? How does the fur look to other people's eyes? How is this related to the theme of the story?
5. As Miss Brill sits on the bench, she observes people sitting beside her, playing around her and walking in front of her. Can you put yourself in the position of Miss Brill and see through her eyes? Do you think that what Miss Brill has observed has symbolic meaning?
6. Does Miss Brill judge women and men in the park differently? How does this reflect her character?
7. Do you think Miss Brill's perception of the band and the music it plays has anything to do with the revelation of her character? How?
8. Where is the climax of the story?
9. What insight into herself does Miss Brill get from the remarks of the young boy and girl at the end of the story?

10. How do you feel about Miss Brill? Do you sympathize with her or not? Why?

Paraphrasing

1. Miss Brill always looked forward to the conversation. She had become really quite expert, she thought, at listening as though she didn't listen, at sitting in other people's lives just for a minute while they talked round her.
2. And sometimes a tiny staggerer came suddenly rocking into the open from under the trees, stopped, stared, as suddenly sat down "flop," until its small high-stepping mother, like a young hen, rushed scolding to its rescue.
3. And what they played was warm, sunny, yet there was just a faint chill—a something, what was it?—not sadness—no, not sadness—a something that made you want to sing.
4. She hurried on the almond Sundays and struck the match for the kettle in quite a dashing way.

Some Information about English Style

1. Characterization

The way a writer presents a character in a story is known as **characterization**. A writer may tell you directly what a character is like. He may make direct comments revealing what he thinks about a character. (For instance, it is possible for a writer to use evaluative adjectives such as "poor," "lonely," "pitiable," etc. to describe Miss Brill.) However, it is more common for a writer to develop a character indirectly, allowing the readers to draw their own conclusions. Techniques for such indirect characterization may include:

- describing the character's physical appearance;
- stating the character's actions and/or words;
- revealing the character's thoughts;
- showing how the character is treated by others.

A writer may, of course, use both direct and indirect methods of characterization in presenting a character.

In "Miss Brill," Mansfield uses several techniques to reveal what Miss Brill is like. These include:

1) Focusing on Miss Brill's neckpiece

Mansfield chooses to focus on one item of Miss Brill's clothing—her neckpiece, a fox fur. In paragraph one, we see that the fur is a precious thing to Miss Brill, who keeps the fox fur carefully wrapped in its box, and touches it lovingly when she takes it out. In the view of others, however, the fur piece is quite worn and unattractive. At the end of the story, it is compared to a "fried whiting." The constant appearance of the neckpiece thus takes on a special significance in revealing the character.

2) Revealing what Miss Brill thinks

Most of the story lets the reader know what is going on in Miss Brill's mind. During her visit to the park, she speaks to no one; she does nothing. Her imagination, however, is active—weaving stories, sometimes critical and sometimes sympathetic, identifying herself with what is happening around her. From what Miss Brill thinks, readers can draw their own conclusions about her character.

3) **Showing how Miss Brill is treated by others**

The story takes a sharp turn when the young couple comes to sit beside Miss Brill. Before they come, Miss Brill has been engulfed in a daydream, viewing herself as an "actress" playing an indispensable role in the park scene. When she overhears the conversation between the boy and the girl, she discovers, to her agony, how others perceive her in the real world.

4) **Showing how the character behaves**

At the end of the story, Miss Brill bypasses the bakery, without buying herself a piece of honey-cake, her usual Sunday treat, and returns to her "cupboard" of a room. It is clear that she is crying as she puts away her fur. From Miss Brill's behaviour, readers may make their own judgment of her character and even make predictions about what might happen in the future.

Compare Mansfield's innovative techniques with the conventional way of "telling" the reader about a character. What difference does it make?

2. Plot and plotline

Plot is the carefully worked-out sequence of related events or actions in a story. A plot has a structure—that is, all the individual parts of the story are arranged and interrelated in order to lead to a satisfying conclusion.

In the traditional style, the plot of a story is usually developed in the following sequence:

Structural elements of plot in a traditional story

Can you find such a plotline in the story of Miss Brill? What comments can you make on Mansfield's technique(s) in organizing details?

Practice

Building word power

1. Fill in each blank with an appropriate word chosen from the list below.

hollowed	abreast	pinched	dashing
solemn	invalid	frail	resolute

(1) The prisoner took a(n) _____ vow to avenge the wrongs he had suffered.
(2) The hero of the play was a smiling _____ cavalry office.
(3) The beggar's face was _____ from hunger and cold.
(4) The cheerleaders, walking four _____, entered the stadium.
(5) The _____ eyes of the sick man followed the doctor's movements anxiously.
(6) The crystal was too _____ to be shipped and had to be carried by hand.

(7) Although she is confined to a wheelchair, the patient does not think of herself as a(an) _____.

(8) Once I make up my mind to do something, you will find me _____.

2. Below are some specific verbs that have been used in the text to describe different manners of walking or movement. Can you use them in other contexts, such as the following? (Take note of the correct form of each word when you are filling in the blank.)

| hobble | swoop | dash | patter | trot |
| rush | march | quiver | flop | droop |

(1) She _____ along (the corridor) in her bare feet.
(2) A herd of gazelles _____ off with incredible speed and grace.
(3) They _____ in the parade to the beat of the drums.
(4) He hurried off, his assistants _____ after him.
(5) When he thought there was going to be an earthquake, he _____ out into the street, still in his pajamas.
(6) Ambulance crews _____ to the scene of the accident.
(7) After a day's hard work, he went home and _____ into a chair.
(8) The leaves on the trees _____ in the breeze.
(9) The plant needs some water—it's starting to _____.
(10) Because her shoes were too tight, the woman _____ along.

Grammar and Usage

Look at these two sentence fragments from the text:
—*She had taken it out of its box that afternoon, shaken out the moth **powder**....*
—*...the blue sky **powdered** with gold and great spots of light....*

As shown, some nouns may also be used as verbs. Can you translate the following sentences by using the given nouns as verbs?

| anger | battle | book | picture | chair | flower | seat | pencil |
| pin | room | eye | | dam | oil | shoulder | storm |

(1) 你的票订好了吗?
(2) 昨天谁主持会议?
(3) 他对我们寄托了很大的希望。
(4) 这厅能坐一千人。
(5) 它描绘了大学生的生活。
(6) 他匆忙用铅笔在上面记下了时间。
(7) 我们应当负起这些责任来。
(8) 人们带着怀疑的眼光注视着他。
(9) 我希望我们能住同一个房间。
(10) 这些花开得很好,但结果不多。

(11) 我们决定筑一条拦河坝。
(12) 他忙着给自行车上油。
(13) 医生们苦战了六昼夜来抢救他的生命。
(14) 这使我们气愤至极,把他痛打了一顿。
(15) 一千多学生冲进了参议院大楼。

Writing Task

Write a report on a favorite story of yours, focusing on a prominent structural element of the story, such as characterization, plot, point-of-view, tone, or theme. (You may refer to the list of stories provided at the end of this unit, under "Further Study.")

Text B

The Gift of the Magi[1]

O. Henry[2]
(Abridged and Edited)

For many North Americans, the Christmas season would not be complete without a reading of "The Gift of the Magi." First published in 1906, the story has been a popular favorite at Christmas
5 for more than a century, rivaling Dickens' A Christmas Carol as the best-loved, non-religious, Christmas fiction. What gives the story such lasting popularity? Simply put, the answer is that O. Henry's "The Gift of the Magi" is an ingenious
10 tale that seldom fails to touch a reader's heart no matter how often—nor even whatever season—it is told.

One dollar and eighty-seven cents. That was all. And sixty cents of it was in pennies. Della finished her cry and attended to her cheeks with a powder rag. Tomorrow would be
15 Christmas Day, and she had only $1.87 with which to buy Jim a present. She had saved every day for months; but with Jim's salary only $20 per week—and what with expenses—there remained only $1.87 to buy him a present. Many a happy hour she had spent planning something nice for him. Something fine and rare and sterling—something just a little bit near to being worthy of the honor of being owned by her Jim—but, Oh! Just one dollar and
20 eighty-seven cents!

Suddenly, she turned from the window and stood before the mirror, her eyes shining brilliantly. She pulled down her hair and let it fall to its full length.

Now, there were two possessions of Jim and
25 Della in which they both took a mighty pride. One

> sterling /ˈstɜːlɪŋ/ n. the money system in Britain, based on the pound; adj. (in the text) of excellent quality

157

was Jim's gold watch that had been his father's and his grandfather's. The other was Della's hair. Had the queen of Sheba lived in the flat across the airshaft,³ Della would have let her hair hang out the window some day to dry just to depreciate Her Majesty's jewels and gifts. Had King Solomon been the janitor, with all his treasures piled up in the basement, Jim would have pulled out his watch every time he passed, just to see him pluck at his beard from envy.

So now Della's beautiful hair fell about her rippling and shining like a cascade of brown waters. It reached below her knee and made itself almost a garment for her. And then she did it up again nervously and quickly.

On went her old brown jacket; on went her old brown hat. With a whirl of skirts and with the brilliant sparkle still in her eyes, she fluttered out the door and down the stairs to the street.

Where she stopped the sign read: "Mme. Sofronie. Hair Goods of All Kinds." One flight up Della ran, and collected herself, panting. Madame, large, too white, chilly, hardly looked the "Sofronie."

"Will you buy my hair?" asked Della.

"I buy hair," said Madame. "Take yer hat off and let's have a sight at the looks of it."

Down rippled the brown cascade.

"Twenty dollars," said Madame, lifting the mass with a practiced hand.

"Give it to me quick," said Della.

Oh, and the next two hours tripped by on rosy wings. Forget the hashed metaphor. She was ransacking the stores for Jim's present.

She found it at last. It surely had been made for Jim and no one else. There was no other like it in any of the stores, and she had turned all of them inside out. It was a platinum fob-chain simple and chaste in design, properly proclaiming its value by substance alone and not by meretricious ornamentation. It was even worthy of The Watch. As soon as she saw it she knew that it must be Jim's. It was like him. Quietness and value—the description applied to both. Twenty-one dollars they took from her for it, and she hurried home with the 87 cents. With that chain on his watch, Jim might be properly anxious about the time in any company.

When Della reached home her intoxication gave way a little to prudence and reason. She got out her curling irons and lighted the gas and went to work repairing the ravages made by generosity added to love. Within forty minutes her head was covered with tiny, close-lying curls that made her look wonderfully like a truant schoolboy. She looked at her reflection in the mirror long, carefully, and critically.

---

depreciate /dɪˈpriːʃieɪt/ v. to become less valuable over a period of time
janitor /ˈdʒænɪtə/ n. caretaker
pluck /plʌk/ v. (at sth.) to hold sth. with the fingers and pull it gently, especially more than once
whirl /wɜːl/ v. to move, or to make sb./sth. move around quickly in a circle or in a particular direction
cascade /kæsˈkeɪd/ n. a small waterfall, especially one of several falling down a steep, rocky slope
flutter /ˈflʌtə/ v. to move lightly and quickly
flight /flaɪt/ n. a series of step between two floors or levels
ransack /ˈrænsæk/ v. to search a place, making it untidy and causing damage, usually because you are looking for sth.
platinum /ˈplætɪnəm/ n. a silver-grey precious metal, used in making expensive jewelry
chaste /tʃeɪst/ adj. (formal) simple and plain in style, not decorated
meretricious /ˌmerɪˈtrɪʃəs/ adj. (formal) seeming attractive, but in fact having no real value
ornamentation /ˌɔːnəmenˈteɪʃən/ n. [U] the use of objects, designs, etc. to decorate sth.
intoxication /ɪnˌtɒksɪˈkeɪʃən/ n. the state of being excited so that you can not think clearly
prudence /ˈpruːdəns/ n. (adj. prudent) being sensible and careful when making judgments and decisions
truant /ˈtruːənt/ n. a child who stays away from school without permission

"If Jim doesn't kill me," she said to herself, "before he takes a second look at me, he'll say I look like a Coney Island chorus girl.⁴ But what could I do—what could I do with a dollar and eighty-seven cents?"

At 7 o'clock the coffee was made and the frying-pan was on the back of the stove hot and ready to cook the chops.

Jim was never late. Della doubled the fob chain in her hand and sat on the corner of the table near the door that he always entered. Then she heard his step on the stair away down on the first flight, and she turned white for just a moment. She had a habit for saying little silent prayers about the simplest everyday things, and now she whispered: "Please God, make him think I am still pretty."

The door opened and Jim stepped in and closed it. He looked thin and very serious. Poor fellow, he was only twenty-two—and to be burdened with a family! He needed a new overcoat and he was without gloves.

Jim stopped inside the door, as immovable as a setter at the scent of quail. His eyes were fixed upon Della, and there was an expression in them that she could not read, and it terrified her. It was not anger, nor surprise, nor disapproval, nor horror, nor any of the sentiments that she had been prepared for. He simply stared at her fixedly with that peculiar expression on his face.

Della wriggled off the table and went for him.

"Jim, darling," she cried, "don't look at me that way. I had my hair cut off and sold because I couldn't have lived through Christmas without giving you a present. It'll grow out again—you won't mind, will you? I just had to do it. My hair grows awfully fast. Say 'Merry Christmas!' Jim, and let's be happy. You don't know what a nice—what a beautiful, nice gift I've got for you."

"You've cut off your hair?" asked Jim, laboriously, as if he had not arrived at that patent fact yet even after the hardest mental labor.

"Cut it off and sold it," said Della. "Don't you like me just as well, anyhow? I'm me without my hair, ain't I?"

Jim looked about the room curiously.

"You say your hair is gone?" he said, with an air almost of idiocy.

"You needn't look for it," said Della. "It's sold, I tell you—sold and gone, too. It's Christmas Eve, boy. Be good to me, for it went for you. Shall I put the chops on, Jim?"

Out of his trance Jim seemed quickly to wake. He enfolded his Della. For ten seconds let us regard with discreet scrutiny some inconsequential object in the other direction. Eight dollars a week or a million a year—what is the difference? A mathematician or a wit would give you the wrong answer. The magi brought valuable gifts, but that was not among them. This dark assertion will be illuminated later on.

Jim drew a package from his overcoat pocket and threw it upon the table.

---

setter /ˈsetə/ n. a large dog, with long hair, sometimes used in hunting

quail /kweɪl/ n. a small brown bird, whose meat and eggs are used for food

wriggle /ˈrɪɡəl/ v. to move somewhere by twisting and turning your body or part of it

patent /ˈpeɪtənt/ n. the official right to be the only person to make, use or sell a product or an invention; adj. (in the text) (formal) used to emphasize that sth. bad is very clear and obvious

trance /trɑːns/ n. a state in which you are thinking so much about sth. that you do not notice what is happening around you

illuminate /ɪˈljuːmɪneɪt/ v. (formal) to make sth. clearer or easier to understand

"Don't make any mistake, Dell," he said, "about me. I don't think there's anything in the way of a haircut or a shave or a shampoo that could make me like my girl any less. But if you'll unwrap that package you may see why you had me going a while at first."

White and nimble fingers tore at the string and paper. And then an ecstatic scream of joy; and then, alas! a quick feminine change to hysterical tears and wails, necessitating the immediate employment of all the comforting powers of the lord of the flat.

> necessitate /nɪˈsesɪteɪt/ v. to make sth. necessary
> tresses /ˈtresɪz/ n. [pl] (literary) a woman's long hair
> adorn /əˈdɔːn/ v. (formal) to make sth./sb. look more attractive by decorating it or them with sth.
> singe /sɪndʒ/ v. to burn the surface of sth. slightly; to be burnt in this way
> dandy /ˈdændi/ n. (old-fashioned, especially AmE) sth. very good or agreeable
> duplication /ˌdjuːplɪˈkeɪʃən/ n. one of two or more things that are the same in every detail
> sacrifice /ˈsækrɪfaɪs/ v. to give up sth. that is important or valuable to you in order to get or do sth. that seems more important for yourself or for another person

For there lay The Combs—the set of combs, side and back, that Della had worshipped long in a Broadway window. Beautiful combs, pure tortoise shell, with jeweled rims—just the shade to wear in the beautiful vanished hair. They were expensive combs, she knew, and her heart had simply craved and yearned over them without the least hope of possession. And now, they were hers, but the tresses that should have adorned the coveted adornments were gone.

But she hugged them to her bosom, and at length she was able to look up with dim eyes and a smile and say: "My hair grows so fast, Jim!"

And then Della leaped up like a little singed cat and cried, "Oh, oh!"

Jim had not yet seen his beautiful present. She held it out to him eagerly upon her open palm. The dull precious metal seemed to flash with a reflection of her bright and ardent spirit.

"Isn't it a dandy, Jim? I hunted all over town to find it. You'll have to look at the time a hundred times a day now. Give me your watch. I want to see how it looks on it."

Instead of obeying, Jim tumbled down on the couch and put his hands under the back of his head and smiled.

"Dell," said he, "let's put our Christmas presents away and keep 'em a while. They're too nice to use just at present. I sold the watch to get the money to buy your combs. And now suppose you put the chops on."

The magi, as you know, were wise men—wonderfully wise men—who brought gifts to the Babe in the manger. They invented the art of giving Christmas presents. Being wise, their gifts were no doubt wise ones, and here I have lamely related to you the uneventful chronicle of two foolish children in a flat who most unwisely sacrificed for each other the greatest treasures of their house. But in a last word to the wise of these days, let it be said that of all who give gifts these two were the wisest. Of all who give and receive gifts such as they are wisest. Everywhere they are wisest. They are the magi.

Notes

1. The Gift of the Magi

This story initially appeared in one of O. Henry's best-known collection of stories, *The Four Million*, which was published in 1906. Upon its publication, the story caught the attention of the American public as well as reviewers. It was frequently mentioned as a prime example of O. Henry's work and has appeared in several anthologies of American short stories.

2. **O. Henry**

O. Henry was the pseudonym of William Sydney Porter (1862—1910), an American short story writer, born in North Carolina. Porter had a chequered early career, which included a term in prison for embezzlement (1896). He began to write short stories in prison, based on his observations of life, and published the first of his many collections, *Cabbages and Kings*, in 1904. He was prolific, humorous, and highly ingenious, especially in his use of coincidence, and became the most famous writer of his kind at that time.

3. **airshaft**

It refers to a long, narrow, usually vertical passage in a building used as a way of allowing air in or out.

4. **a Coney Island chorus girl**

This refers to a very poorly paid entertainer in a musical chorus line in Coney Island, a New York City public beach resort.

Comprehension

1. Where does the title of this story come from? Who were the Magi?
2. Where and when (approximately) does this story take place? How do you know?
3. How does O. Henry describe Della's hair? What adjectives or other expressions have been used? Can you estimate the length of Della's hair in centimeters?
4. Why do you suppose the author chose the name Mme. Sofronie for the hair buyer?
5. "The next two hours tripped by on rosy wings." What does this sentence suggest about Della's mood after the hair transaction?
6. Why would Della buy a platinum fob-chain (watch-chain) rather than a gold one?
7. In what social class would you place Jim and Della? How have you made this judgment? Would the story work just as well if Jim and Della were of a different social class?
8. How would you classify this story? Comic? Tragic? Ironic? Romantic?
9. The author concludes that the young couple was simultaneously foolish and wise. How can that be? What was the wisdom that Della and Jim possessed that justified them foolishly sacrificing "the greatest treasures of their house?"
10. From what point of view is this story told? What comment can you make on the narrative style? Can you see the difference between Text I and Text II in terms of the angle from which the story is told?

Further Study

Below is a select list of some well-known short story writers and their best-known works. Look up in an anthology or search on the Internet for more information about them. Make a plan to read some of them in your spare time.

Washington Irving (1783—1859)
- *Rip Van Winkle*
- *The Legend of Sleepy Hollow*

Edgar Allan Poe (1809—1849)
- *The Fall of the House of Usher*
- *The Murders in the Rue Morgue*

James Joyce (1882—1941)
- *Dubliners* ("Araby" "The Dead")

James Thurber (1894—1961)
- *The Secret Life of Walter Mitty*

Kate Chopin (1850—1904)
- *The Story of an Hour*
- *A Pair of Silk Stockings*

Mark Twain (1835—1902)
- *Luck*
- *The Prince and the Pauper*
- *The Man that Corrupted Hadleyburg*

Saki (1870—1916)
- *The Mouse*
- *The Open Window*

Earnest Hemingway (1899—1961)
- *Hills Like White Elephants*
- *A Clean, Well-lighted Place*

Unit 11

Education

Unit Goals

☞ To explore the role of education
☞ To learn to develop a thesis statement
☞ To develop an argument through exemplification

Before Reading

1. In small groups, discuss the following:
   ☞ Should curriculum always be relevant to student's daily lives?
   ☞ Can all things be learnt by doing?
   ☞ Which is more important in children's education, to develop practical life skills or to acquire knowledge? Do the two contradict each other?
   ☞ Do you enjoy hands-on activities?
2. Search in an encyclopedia or on the Internet for biographical information about John Dewey and his philosophy of education.

A Glimpse into the Text

  No educator had a more profound influence on education in America than John Dewey. Before Dewey, all American public schools followed a strict routine—teachers taught facts from textbooks and maintained tight discipline; students memorized facts from textbooks and followed instructions. Dewey believed that this was too narrow a concept of education, that education should evolve to make better use of the native intelligence of children and better meet the needs of society—indeed, that the public school should become a microcosm of society, in which students prepared for their adult lives in a democratic society. Dewey's ideas remain as controversial today as they were when he wrote the following passage in 1899. Despite the controversy, however, his concept of "progressive education" has been adopted by almost every public school in America.

Text A

The School and Social Progress
John Dewey[1]

The great thing to keep in mind regarding the introduction of active occupations into the school is that through them the entire spirit of the school is renewed. The school has a chance to affiliate itself with life, to become the child's habitat, where he learns through directed living; instead of being a place to learn lessons having an abstract and remote reference to some possible living to be done in the future. The school gets a chance to be a miniature community, an embryonic society. This becomes its fundamental goal, and from this arise continuous and orderly sources of instruction.

It is this liberation from narrow utilities, this openness to the possibilities of the human spirit that makes practical activities in the school the allies of art, science, and history. In educational terms, this means that these active occupations shall not be mere practical devices for future employment—the gaining of better technical skills as cooks, seamstresses, or carpenters—but also activities to develop scientific insight into natural materials and processes, as well as points of departure whence children might be led into a realization of the historical development of man. The actual significance of this can be told better through one illustration taken from actual school work than by general discourse.

There is nothing which strikes the average intelligent visitor more oddly than to see boys, as well as girls, of ten, twelve, and thirteen years of age engaged in sewing and weaving. If we look at this from the standpoint of preparation of the children for sewing on buttons and making patches, we get a narrow and utilitarian conception—an activity that hardly justifies giving prominence to this sort of work in the school. But if we look at it from another side, we find that this work provides a point of departure from which the child can trace and follow the progress of mankind in history, getting an insight also into the materials used and the mechanical principles involved. In connection with these activities, the historical development of man is recapitulated. For example, the children are first given the raw material—the flax, the cotton plant, the wool as it comes from the back of the sheep (if we could take them to the place where the sheep are sheared, so much the better). Then a study

---

microcosm /ˈmaɪkrəʊkɒzəm/ *n.* [C, U] a small place, society or situation which has the same characteristics as sth. much larger

affiliate /əˈfɪlieɪt/ *v.* [usually passive] ~ **sb./sth. (with/to sb./sth.)** to link a group, a company, or an organization very closely with another larger one

embryonic /ˌembrɪˈɒnɪk/ *adj.* (formal) in an early stage of development

discourse /dɪsˈkɔːs/ *n.* [C, U] (formal) a long and serious treatment or discussion of a subject in speech or writing

utilitarian /ˌjuːtɪlɪˈteərɪən/ *adj.* (formal) designed to be useful and practical rather than attractive

recapitulate /ˌriːkəˈpɪtʃʊleɪt/ *v.* (formal) (also **recap**) ~ **(on sth.)** /~ **sth.** to repeat or give a summary of what has already been said, decided, etc.

flax /flæks/ *n.* [U] a plant with blue flowers, grown for its stem that is used to make thread and its seeds that are used to make linseed oil

is made of these materials from the standpoint of their adaptation to the uses to which they may be put. For instance, a comparison of the cotton fiber with wool fiber is made. I did not know until the children of such a school told me, but the reason for the late development of the cotton industry as compared with the woolen industry is that the cotton fiber is very difficult to free by hand from the seeds. The children in one school group worked thirty minutes freeing cotton fibers from the boll and seeds, and succeeded in getting out less than one ounce. They could easily believe that one person could only gin one pound of cotton a day by hand, and could understand why their ancestors wore woolen instead of cotton clothing. Among other things discovered as affecting the utility of the two fabrics was the shortness of the cotton fiber as compared with that of wool, the former being three millimeters in length, while the latter is three centimeters in length; also that the fibers of cotton are smooth and do not cling together, while the wool has a certain roughness which makes the fibers stick, thus assisting the spinning. The children worked this out for themselves with the actual material, aided by questions and suggestions from their teacher.

They then followed the processes necessary for working the fibers into cloth. They reinvented the first frame for carding wool—a couple of boards with sharp pins in them for scratching it out. They redevised the simplest process for spinning wool—a pierced stone through which the wool is passed and which, as it is twirled, draws out the fiber, while the children kept the spun wool in their hands until it was gradually drawn out and wound upon them. Then the children were introduced to the next invention in historical order—in this way passing in review the entire process up to the weaving loom. I need not speak of the science involved in this—the study of the fibers, of geographical features, the conditions under which the raw materials are grown, the great centers of manufacture and distribution, the physics involved in the machinery of production; nor, again, of the historical side—the influence which these inventions have had upon humanity. You could concentrate the history of all mankind into the evolution of flax, cotton, and wool fibers into clothing. By this, I mean that certain very real and important avenues to the consideration of the history of the race are thus opened—that the mind is introduced to much more fundamental and controlling influences than usually appear in the political and chronological records that pass for history.

Now, what is true of this one instance of fibers used in fabrics can be true of every material used in every active occupation. The occupation supplies the child with a genuine motive; it gives him first hand experience; it brings him into contact with physical realities. It does all this, but in addition it can be translated into historical and scientific value. With the growth of the child's mind in power and knowledge, these activities cease to be a pleasant occupation merely; they become more and more a medium to even greater knowledge.

When occupations in the school are conceived in this broad and generous way, I can only stand lost in wonder at objections so often heard, that such occupations are out of place in the school because they are materialistic, utilitarian, or even menial in their tendency. It sometimes seems to me that those who make these objections must live in quite another world. The world in which most of us live is one in which everyone has a calling and

---

boll /bəʊl/ *n.* the part of the cotton plant that contains the seeds

gin /dʒɪn/ *v.* to remove seeds from (cotton) with a gin (a machine for separating cotton fibers from the seeds)

conceive /kənˈsiːv/ *v.* ~ **(of) sth. (as sth.)** (formal) to form an idea, a plan, etc., in our mind; to imagine sth.

menial /ˈmiːniəl/ *adj.* (usually disapproving) (of work) not skilled or important, and often boring or badly paid

calling /ˈkɔːlɪŋ/ *n.* a strong desire or feeling of duty to do a particular job, especially one in which you help other people

occupation, something to do. Some are managers
85 and others are subordinates. But the great thing
for one, as for the other, is that each shall have
had the education which enables him to see
within his daily work all there is of large and
human significance. How many of the employed
90 are today mere appendages to the machines
which they operate! This may be due in part to
the machine itself, or to the regime which lays
so much stress upon the products of the
machine; but it is certainly due in large part to
95 the fact that the worker has had no opportunity
to develop his imagination and his sympathetic
insight into the social and scientific values to be found in his work. Until such insights are
systematically laid hold of in the years of childhood and youth, until they are trained in social
directions, enriched by historical interpretation, controlled and illuminated by scientific methods,
100 we certainly are in no position even to locate the source of our economic evils, much less to
deal with them effectively.

> **appendage** /əˈpendɪdʒ/ *n.* (formal) a smaller or less important part of sth. larger
> **afford** /əˈfɔːd/ *v.* (formal) to provide sb. with sth.
> **labored** /ˈleɪbəd/ *adj.* (of writing, speaking, etc.) not natural and seeming to take a lot of effort
> **radical** /ˈrædɪkəl/ *adj.* [usually before noun] concerning the most basic and important parts of sth.; thorough and complete
> **relegate** /ˈrelɪgeɪt/ *v.* ~ **sb./sth. (to sth.)** to give sb. a lower or less important position, rank, etc. than before
> **permeate** /ˈpɜːmieɪt/ *v.* (of an idea, an influence, a feeling, etc.) to affect every part of sth.
> **saturate** /ˈsætʃəreɪt/ *v.* [often passive] ~ **sth./sb. (with/in sth.)** to fill sth./sb. completely with sth. so that it is impossible or useless to add any more

To achieve this, a change is necessary in the attitude of the school. Our school methods,
and to a very considerable extent our curriculum, are inherited from a period when learning
and command of certain symbols, affording as they did the only access to learning, were
105 all-important. The ideals of this period are still largely in control. Our present education is
highly specialized, one-sided, and narrow. It is an education dominated almost entirely by a
mediaeval conception of learning. It is something which appeals for the most part simply to
the intellectual aspect of our natures, to accumulate information, and to get control of the
symbols of learning; not to our impulses and tendencies to make, to do, to create, to produce,
110 whether in the form of utility or of art.

But why should I make this labored presentation? The obvious fact is that our social
life has undergone a thorough and radical change. If education is to have any meaning for
life, it must pass through an equally complete transformation—a transformation that is
already in progress. Modifications which often appear (even to those most actively concerned
115 with them) to be mere changes of detail, mere improvement within the school mechanism, are
in reality signs and evidences of evolution. The introduction of active occupations into the
school, of nature study, of elementary science, of art, of history; the relegation of merely
abstract learning to a secondary position; the change in the moral school atmosphere, in the
relationships of pupils and teachers—of discipline; the introduction of more active, expressive,
120 and self-directing factors—all these are not mere accidents, they are necessities of the larger
social evolution. It remains but to organize all these factors, to appreciate them in their
fullness of meaning, and to put the ideas and the ideals they involve into complete,
uncompromising possession of our school system. To do this means to make each one of our
schools an embryonic community, active with the types of occupations that reflect the life of
125 the larger society, and permeated throughout with the spirit of art, history, and science. When
the school introduces and trains each child of society into membership within such a little
community, saturating him with a spirit of service, and providing him with the instruments of
effective self-direction, we shall have the deepest and best guaranty of a larger society which

is worthy, lovely, and harmonious.

More about the Text

1. John Dewey

John Dewey (1859—1952), American pragmatic philosopher, psychologist, and educator whose theories had a profound influence on public education in the first half of the 20th century, especially in the United States. Dewey's philosophy of education, instrumentalism (also called pragmatism), focused on learning-by-doing rather than rote learning and dogmatic instruction.

2. The School and Society

The selection is an adaptation from a small book entitled *The School and Society* (1899), which evolved from three lectures that John Dewey delivered to parents and friends of the Laboratory School that Dewey established in 1896 in an attempt to facilitate research and experimentation into new principles and methods and to allow the children to take an experimental approach to their own learning. The book soon became a sort of manifesto of the progressive school movement of the early 1900s, and is probably Dewey's most popular and most translated publication.

Check Your Understanding

1. What does the word "renew" imply to you? In what ways is the entire spirit of the school renewed through the introduction of active occupations?
2. What practical activities have you participated in at school? In what sense are practical activities in the school "the allies of art, science and history?"
3. Have you ever done any sewing or weaving? How did you like it? What perspectives may we take to look at children engaged in sewing and weaving in the school?
4. What do children learn from sewing and weaving? Explain in your own words.
5. What good are active occupations to the child, according to Dewey? Do you see any other benefits?
6. What are some objections against active occupations in the school?
7. How can education help the child better understand work and society, according to Dewey?
8. Is Dewey justified in saying that "Our present education is highly specialized, one-sided and narrow?"
9. Is Dewey pessimistic about the future prospects of education? Why or why not?
10. What does Dewey visualize the ideal school in relation to society to be? Do you think his ideal is attainable?

Paraphrasing

1. The school has a chance to affiliate itself with life, to become the child's habitat, where he learns through directed living; instead of being a place to learn lessons having an abstract and remote reference to some possible living to be done in the future.

2. It is this liberation from narrow utilities, this openness to the possibilities of the human spirit that makes practical activities in the school the allies of art, science, and history.
3. But the great thing for one, as for the other, is that each shall have had the education which enables him to see within his daily work all there is of large and human significance.
4. Until such insights are systematically laid hold of in the years of childhood and youth, until they are trained in social directions, enriched by historical interpretation, controlled and illuminated by scientific methods, we certainly are in no position even to locate the source of our economic evils, much less to deal with them effectively.
5. To do this means to make each one of our schools an embryonic community, active with the types of occupations that reflect the life of the larger society, and permeated throughout with the spirit of art, history, and science. When the school introduces and trains each child of society into membership within such a little community, saturating him with a spirit of service, and providing him with the instruments of effective self-direction, we shall have the deepest and best guaranty of a larger society which is worthy, lovely, and harmonious.

Some Information about English Style

1. Writing the thesis statement

◆ **What is a thesis statement?**

A thesis is a main point, a main idea or central message of an essay. The sentence that captures the position on this main idea is a thesis statement. In other words, a thesis statement is a single declarative sentence that states what the writer wants the reader to know, believe, or understand after having read the essay. A thesis is different from a topic. A topic names what the writer wants to say; the thesis statement condenses what he or she has to say into a single statement and gives his or her point of view about it.

The thesis statement makes an argumentative assertion about the topic, states the conclusions that the writer has reached about the topic, or indicates to the reader the scope, purpose, and direction of the paper. In addition, it identifies the relationships between the pieces of evidence that the writer is using to support his or her argument. In a word, the thesis statement must assert the point, suggest the evidence, and structure the argument, all in one.

◆ **Where is the thesis statement usually found?**

The thesis statement is usually found in the introductory paragraph(s). The advantage of putting it in the introduction is that the reader knows from the beginning what the writer is going to talk about and how he or she feels about that topic. In other words, it establishes the writer's position and gives the reader a sense of direction. It may sometimes be appropriate to present the thesis statement later in the paper after the writer has laid the groundwork for the position. The thesis statement may be as short as one sentence that summarizes the whole paper. It may be expressed in several sentences or in an entire paragraph, especially in a long paper.

◆ **What are the qualities of a good thesis statement?**
- The thesis statement should be **as specific as possible**; it should cover only what the writer will discuss in the essay and should be supported with specific evidence.
- The thesis statement should be **as clear as possible** so the reader understands exactly what the writer means.

- The thesis statement should be **original**. After making the thesis statement, the writer should be prepared to answer "So what?" about the thesis statement and to explain why the point is worthy of a paper and why the reader should read it.

◆ Is there a thesis statement in the present selection? Where is it? Is it effective? How?

2. Developing an argument through exemplification
◆ Exemplification

"Exemplification" means "the giving of an example." Expressions such as *for example, for instance, take... for example, to demonstrate/illustrate, as an illustration* ...etc., are indicators of exemplification. Examples may be specific names (people, places, products, etc.), anecdotes, personal experience, expert opinions, facts and statistics, or research findings.

The functions of examples vary. Personal-case examples, taken from one's own experience, may create intimacy and drama. Typical-case examples, based on actual events or situations, are specially convincing since they are authentic and objective in nature. Hypothetical examples, invented by the writer when actual examples are not readily available, are often used in scientific writing as a way of generalizing the qualities of a variety of specific cases. Extended examples, extending to an entire paragraph, or even an entire essay, function as concrete illustrations of ideas that are too complex to be illustrated with a single example.

Effective examples are relevant, accurate (especially when facts, figures, and statistics are cited), and non-contradictory. They are also *representative*, reflecting the majority rather than the one-in-a-million cases.

◆ **Developing an essay through exemplification**

An author may choose to use one or more well-developed examples to support his thesis in an article. Essays developed through exemplification usually start with a main idea, belief, or opinion—something abstract—(i.e. the thesis statement) and then give examples to illustrate that main point. A typical structure may go as follows:

Introduction, which states the thesis
Body, which supports the thesis in one or more of the following ways:
- Each paragraph is an argument or point supported by some examples.
- Each paragraph is a developed example that illustrates the thesis.
- Each paragraph is a separate aspect of one extended example.

Conclusion, which restates the thesis and reiterates the main idea
- What example does Dewey give to support his argument that the introduction of active occupations into the school will renew the entire spirit of education? What type of example is it? Is it effective? Explain how.

Practice

Building word power

1. Fill in each blank with an appropriate word by adding to the given word in brackets the necessary prefix or suffix or both as is required.

(1) When hot weather comes there will be a _____ of interest in swimming. (renew)

(2) The two hospitals have a close _____, sometimes sharing equipment. (affiliate)
(3) _____ is the belief that the best action or decision in a particular situation is the one which benefits the most people. (utility)
(4) He was _____ proud of his achievements. (justify)
(5) His work as a simultaneous interpreter requires strong powers of persistent _____. (concentrate)
(6) Teaching is all about _____ people to learn. (motive)
(7) He sought _____ by reading the great philosophers. (illuminate)
(8) The _____ of her plays means that she is able to reach a wide audience. (access)
(9) She's always talking in _____. (abstract)
(10) Reduction in government spending will _____ further cuts in public services. (necessity)
(11) It's nice to have an _____ audience. (appreciate)
(12) Technical innovation is _____ in improving the qualities of products. (instrument)

2. **Below are ten pairs of sentences. The blank in sentence a of each pair can be filled in with a word in its proper form as is used in the reading selection. The blank in sentence b can be filled in with the same word, but with a different meaning. After you have finished, compare your answers with a classmate.**

(1) a. The union opposed the _____ of the new technology because of the loss of jobs it would cause.
    b. The author says in his _____ that the novel is based on his own childhood.
(2) a. "Without let or hindrance" is a legal _____ which means "freely."
    b. The lease on our house is near the end of its _____.
(3) a. The project provides a good _____ of how people can work together.
    b. The magazine has _____ in black and white and in colour.
(4) a. His enthusiasm for study _____ his teacher favorably.
    b. The disease _____ the whole community, sometimes wiping out whole families.
(5) a. The building is undergoing _____ from garage to living quarters.
    b. Last year he starred in the film _____ of Bill Cronshaw's best-selling novel.
(6) a. We got so wet that our clothes _____ to us.
    b. She _____ to the hope that her husband will come back to her.
(7) a. We should explore every _____ in the search for an answer to this problem.
    b. Many people walked down the _____ through the centre of the park.
(8) a. Video is a good _____ for practising listening to a foreign language.
    b. She's slim, of _____ height, with dark hair.
(9) a. The old corrupt, totalitarian _____ was overthrown.
    b. Under the new _____ in our office no one is allowed to leave early.
(10) a. Creative work _____ to me irresistibly.
    b. The parents _____ against the school's decision not to admit the child.

3. **Fill in each blank with the best answer by choosing A, B, C or D.**
(1) He began to feel that the church was his true _____ and at the age of 30 joined a seminary.
    A. occupation   B. profession   C. career   D. vocation

(2) The school is based on the _____ principle that each child should develop its full potential.
   A. basic   B. fundamental   C. essential   D. central
(3) My computer makes a _____ low buzzing noise.
   A. continuous   B. continual   C. constant   D. on-going
(4) You can't just do it however you like—you must follow _____.
   A. process   B. procedure   C. proceeding   D. progress
(5) The taxi came from the farm and had a _____ smell of stale straw.
   A. strange   B. peculiar   C. odd   D. queer
(6) The plan, brilliant in its _____, failed because of inadequate preparation.
   A. idea   B. notion   C. concept   D. conception
(7) The invention of the computer was a(n) _____ in the history of man.
   A. progress   B. advance   C. breakthrough   D. milestone
(8) Assuring the patient that she has a _____ and not imaginary problem is the first step.
   A. real   B. actual   C. true   D. existent
(9) The merry-go-round _____ noisily.
   A. turned   B. twirled   C. whirled   D. spun
(10) _____ have been made by many people who would be affected by the proposed changes.
   A. Objections   B. Complaints   C. Protests   D. Criticisms
(11) We've got copies of all the documents, but we haven't managed to _____ the originals.
   A. find   B. track down   C. trace   D. locate
(12) The _____ of the quarrel between the two men was jealousy.
   A. reason   B. cause   C. factor   D. root

Grammar and usage

Translate the following sentences into English by using the key words in the brackets.

(1) 假日临近时，他的情绪高涨起来。(spirits)
(2) 不论年龄或年级，所有学生都必须参加这一测试。(reference to)
(3) 如果我们需要再雇用员工，会与你取得联系的。(arise)
(4) 如果你想要这个项目成功，你就需要征求支持者的意见。(ally)
(5) 她开始谈论该城市的起源。(discourse)
(6) 我没有时间闲聊。(engage in)
(7) 考试作弊是没有任何正当理由的。(justify)
(8) 某些特点适用于所有的语言。(true of)
(9) 我们如果当选，就能把我们的思想变为行动。(translate)
(10) 历史给我们提供了值得注意的经验教训。(afford)
(11) 他随心所欲，想干什么就干什么。(impulse)
(12) 因为被降级去做案头工作，她辞职了。(relegate)
(13) 宴会洋溢着友谊的气氛。(permeate)
(14) 那种画充斥了市场。(saturate)
(15) 人们慷慨赞助高尚的事业。(worthy)

📖 Improving your understanding of the exemplification essay and the thesis statement

1. Fill in the following box to show the structure of the reading selection.

	Paragraph number	Function
Introduction		states the thesis that
Body		supports the thesis by
Conclusion		reiterates the main idea that

2. The following are some draft thesis statements that are too general or vague. Rewrite to make each of them specific and clear.
   (1) Aerobic exercise is good for you.
   (2) My difficulties in English are unbelievable, but I am doing very well in mathematics.
   (3) There are advantages and disadvantages to using statistics.
   (4) There are serious objections to today's horror movies.
   (5) We must save the whales.
   (6) World hunger has many causes and effects.
   (7) In this essay, I will discuss the effects of pesticides on fish populations.
   (8) The feminist movement protects women's rights.
   (9) In this paper, I will discuss the relationship between fairy tales and early childhood.
   (10) Our thoughts are influenced by the media.

📖 Writing task

Frost says that metaphor is the whole of thinking. Look around you and see if you can find the use of metaphors in everyday life, when naming an object, describing a person, or conducting research in your field of study. Write an essay to support Frost's assertion, using exemplification as a means of exposition.

Text B

Education by Poetry[1]

Robert Frost[2]
(Abridged)

5   Robert Frost (1874—1963) was undoubtedly the most revered American poet of the 20th Century. His poems such as "Stopping by Woods on a Snowy Evening," "Fire and Ice," and "The Road Not Taken" successfully wove complex philosophical themes into seemingly uncomplicated natural scenes, thereby earning

> revered /rɪˈvɪəd/ *adj.* greatly respected and admired
> thereby /ˌðeəˈbaɪ/ *adv.* (formal or old-fashioned) as a result of this action

Frost a critical and popular acclaim likely to endure through the 21st Century. In this speech, which he delivered at Amherst College in 1930, the poet laments the sorry state of poetry at colleges in America, and proposes a rationale for its revival.

I know whole colleges where all American poetry is barred—whole colleges. I know whole colleges where all contemporary poetry is barred.

It comes pretty hard on poetry, I sometimes think, — what it has to bear in the teaching process. I know whole colleges where, though they let in older poetry, they manage to bar all that is poetical in it by treating it as something other than poetry. That is the best general way of settling the problem; treat all poetry as if it were something else than poetry, as if it were syntax, language, science. Then you can even come down into the American and contemporary poetry without any special risk.

One other way to rid the curriculum of the poetry nuisance has been considered. More merciful than the others it would neither abolish nor denature the poetry, but only turn it out to disport itself, with the plays and games—in no wise discredited, though given no credit for. Any one who liked to teach poetically could take his subject, whether English, Latin, Greek or French, out into the nowhere along with the poetry. One side of a sharp line would be left to the rigorous and righteous; the other side would be assigned to the flowery where they would know what could be expected of them.

They are having night schools now, you know, for college graduates. Why? Because they have not been educated enough to find their way around in contemporary literature. They don't know what they may safely like in the libraries and galleries. They don't know how to judge an editorial when they see one. They don't know how to judge a political campaign. They don't know when they are being fooled by a metaphor, an analogy, a parable. And metaphor is, of course, what we are talking about. Education by poetry is education by metaphor.

I would be willing to throw away everything else but that: enthusiasm tamed by metaphor. I do not think anybody ever knows the discreet use of metaphor, his own and other people's, the discreet handling of metaphor, unless he has been properly educated in poetry.

Poetry begins in trivial metaphors, pretty metaphors, "grace" metaphors, and goes on to the profoundest thinking that we have. Poetry provides the one permissible way of saying one thing and meaning another. People say, "Why don't you say what you mean?" We never do

---

acclaim /əˈkleɪm/ n. [U] public approval and praise

rationale /ˌræʃəˈnɑːl/ n. [C, U] (formal) the reasons or intentions for a particular set of thoughts or actions

revival /rɪˈvaɪvəl/ n. [C, U] when sth. becomes more active or popular again

bar /bɑː/ v. to forbid or prevent sb. from doing sth.

rid /rɪd/ v. (written) to remove sth. that is causing a problem from a place, group, etc.

disport /dɪˈspɔːt/ v. (old-fashioned or humorous) to enjoy yourself by doing sth. active

wise /waɪz/ n. way

discredit /dɪsˈkredɪt/ v. to make people stop respecting sb./sth.

righteous /ˈraɪtʃəs/ adj. morally correct

flowery /ˈflaʊəri/ adj. (usually disapproving) too complicated; not expressed in a clear and simple way

parable /ˈpærəbəl/ n. a short story that teaches moral or spiritual lesson, especially one of those told by Jesus as recorded in the Bible

discreet /dɪˈskriːt/ adj. careful in what you say or do, in order to keep sth. secret or to avoid causing embarrassment or difficulty for sb.

permissible /pəˈmɪsəbəl/ adj. (formal) acceptable according to the law or a particular set of rules

that, do we, being all of us too much poets. We like to talk in parables and in hints and in indirections—whether from diffidence or some other instinct.

I have wanted in late years to go further and further in making metaphor the whole of thinking. I find some one now and then to agree with me that all thinking, except mathematical thinking, is metaphorical, or all thinking except scientific thinking. The mathematical might be difficult for me to bring in, but the scientific is easy enough.

Once on a time all the Greeks were busy telling each other what the All was—or was like unto. All was three elements, air, earth, and water (we once thought it was ninety elements; now we think it is only one). All was substance, said another. All was change, said a third. But best and most fruitful was Pythagoras'[3] comparison of the universe with number. Number of what? Number of feet, pounds, and seconds was the answer, and we had science and all that has followed in science. The metaphor has held and held, breaking down only when it came to the spiritual and psychological or the out of the way places of the physical.

Let's take two or three more of the metaphors now in use to live by. Everything is an event now. Another metaphor. A thing, they say, is all event. Do you believe it is? Not quite. I believe it is almost an event. But I like the comparison of a thing with an event.

I notice another from the same quarter. "In the neighborhood of matter space is something like curved." Isn't that a good one! It seems to me that that is simply and utterly charming—to say that space is something like curved in the neighborhood of matter. "Something like."

Another metaphor that has interested us in our time and has done all our thinking for us is the metaphor of evolution. Never mind going into the Latin word. The metaphor is simply the metaphor of the growing plant or of the growing thing. And somebody very brilliantly, quite a while ago, said that the whole universe, the whole of everything, was like unto a growing thing. That is all.

What I am pointing out is that unless you are at home in the metaphor, unless you have had your proper poetical education in the metaphor, you are not safe anywhere. Because you are not at ease with figurative values: you don't know the metaphor in its strength and its weakness. You don't know how far you may expect to ride it and when it may break down with you. You are not safe in science; you are not safe in history.

Take the way we have been led into our present position morally. It is by a sort of metaphorical gradient. There is a kind of thinking—to speak metaphorically—there is a kind of thinking you might say was endemic. It was always there. And every now and then in some mysterious way it becomes epidemic in the world. It uses honesty, first,—frankness, sincerity—those words; picks them up, uses them. "In the name of honesty, let us see what we are." You know. And then it picks up the word joy. "Let us in the name of joy, which is the enemy of our ancestors, the Puritans[4].... Let us in the name of joy, which is the enemy of the kill-joy Puritan...." You see. "Let us," and so on.

Let me ask you to watch a metaphor breaking down here before you.

Somebody said to me a little while ago, "It

---

indirection /ˌɪndɪˈrekʃən/ n. the act of avoiding clearly mentioning or saying sth.

diffidence /ˈdɪfɪdəns/ n. the condition of being shy or not confident of one's abilities

quarter /ˈkwɔːtə/ n. aspect

ride /raɪd/ vt. to try to control someone and force them to work

gradient /ˈɡreɪdiənt/ n. the rate at which temperature, pressure, etc. changes, or increases and decreases, between one region and another

in the name of sth. (said or done) in order to help a particular thing succeed

kill-joy /ˈkɪldʒɔɪ/ n. (disapproving) a person who likes to spoil other people's enjoyment

is easy enough for me to think of the universe as a machine, as a mechanism."

I said, "You mean the universe is like a machine?"

He said, "No. I think it is one.... Well, it is like...."

"I think you mean the universe is like a machine."

"All right. Let it go at that."

I asked him, "Did you ever see a machine without a pedal for the foot, or a lever for the hand, or a button for the finger?"

He said, "No—no."

I said, "All right. Is the universe like that?"

And he said, "No. I mean it is like a machine, only...."

"... it is different from a machine," I said.

He wanted to go just that far with that metaphor and no further. And so do we all. All metaphor breaks down somewhere. That is the beauty of it. It is touch and go with the metaphor, and until you have lived with it long enough you don't know when it is going. You don't know how much you can get out of it and when it will cease to yield. It is a very living thing. It is as life itself.

I have heard this ever since I can remember, and ever since I have taught: the teacher must teach the pupil to think. I saw a teacher once going around in a great school and snapping pupils' heads with thumb and finger and saying, "Think." That was when thinking was becoming the fashion. The fashion hasn't yet quite gone out. We still ask boys in college to think, as in the nineties, but we seldom tell them what thinking means; we seldom tell them it is just putting this and that together; it is just saying one thing in terms of another. To tell them is to set their feet on the first rung of a ladder the top of which sticks through the sky.

We ask people to think, and we don't show them what thinking is. Somebody says we don't need to show them how to think; by and by they will think. We will give them the forms of sentences and, if they have any ideas, then they will know how to write them. But that is preposterous. All there is to writing is having ideas. To learn to have ideas is to learn to use metaphors.

I remember a boy saying, "He is the kind of person that wounds with his shield."[5] That may be a slender one, of course. It goes a good way in character description. It has poetic grace. "He is the kind that wounds with his shield." But these are slighter metaphors than the ones we live by. They have their charm, their passing charm. They are as it were the first steps toward the great thoughts, grave thoughts, thoughts lasting to the end.

The metaphor whose manage we are best taught in poetry—that is all there is of thinking. It may not seem far for the mind to go but it is the mind's furthest. The richest accumulation of all the ages, the richest education of the ages, is the noble metaphors we have rolled up into poetry.[6]

---

touch and go [not usually before noun](informal) used to say that the result of a situation is uncertain and that there is a possibility that sth. bad or unpleasant will happen

rung /rʌŋ/ n. one of the bars that forms a step in a ladder

shield /ʃiːld/ n. sth. or someone used as protection or providing protection

manage /ˈmænɪdʒ/ n. (in the context) use (of metaphor)

Notes

1. Education by Poetry

The present selection is excerpted from *Education by Poetry: A Meditative Monologue* (1930), an address given by Frost to the Amherst Alumni Council in November of 1930.

2. Robert Frost

Robert Lee Frost (1874—1963). American poet who was much admired for his depictions of the rural life of New England, his command of American colloquial speech, and his realistic verse portraying ordinary people in everyday situations. Frost published his first books in Great Britain in the 1910s, but he soon became in his own country the most read and constantly anthologized poet. He was awarded the Pulitzer Prize for poetry in 1924, 1931, 1937, and 1943. Among Frost's volumes of poetry are *New Hampshire* (1923), *West-running Brook* (1928), *Collected Poems* (1930), *A Further Range* (1936), *A Witness Tree* (1942), *Steeple Bush* (1947), and *In the Clearing* (1962). *A Masque of Reason* (1945) and *A Masque of Mercy* (1947) were blank verse plays.

3. Pythagoras

Pythagoras (circa 582 BC—circa 507 BC), Greek philosopher and mathematician, founder of the mathematical, mystic, religious, and scientific society called Pythagoreans. He is best known for the Pythagorean theorem and is considered the first true mathematician.

4. Puritan

Puritan, a member of a group of English Protestants who in the 16th and 17th centuries advocated strict religious discipline along with simplification of the ceremonies and creeds of the Church of England. A Puritan may also refer to one who lives in accordance with Protestant precepts, especially one who regards pleasure or luxury as sinful.

5. He is the kind of person that wounds with his shield.

Most people wound others with their weapon, but he is the kind of person who wounds others by defending himself with his shield. In other words, he doesn't strike out at others; he is strong by using his shield and letting those wronging him bounce off his shield.

6. metaphor ...rolled up into poetry

The use of metaphor is best taught in poetry, and poetry is all thought. A metaphor doesn't seem that great, but it takes the mind further than any other figure of speech (it accomplishes more). The best of mankind and education grows out of the metaphors we find in poetry.

Comprehension

1. What are the ways some colleges have dealt with poetry?
2. What do you make of Frost's observation that "Education by poetry is education by metaphor?"
3. What does metaphor mean to you? What, specially, does Frost say metaphor is?
4. Do you like poetry? Has poetry taught you anything? How does poetry teach, according to

Frost?
5. Do you use metaphor in your life and in what situations? What are our motives for using metaphor according to Frost?
6. What metaphors from science does Frost use in his speech?
7. What example(s) does Frost offer to show the limits of metaphor?
8. What does thinking mean according to Frost? Based on your experience of being a student, have you ever been taught to "think?" Would you rather be taught to think, or to be crammed with knowledge? Why?
9. Can you find a thesis statement in this selection? What is the message that Frost wants to get across to the reader?
10. How does Frost organize this article? Can you see how the different parts are linked?

Further Study

 Find out more about

- John Dewey
- Robert Frost

Unit 12

Treasury of Fantasy

Unit Goals

☞ To read fantasy as a literary genre
☞ To use colloquialism at an appropriate level

Before Reading

1. Search on the Internet or in the library for brief biographical information about Kurt Vonnegut Jr., his style, his major works and the way they are related to the genre of fantasy.
2. What does "shaggy dog" mean in the title of Vonnegut's story? Does it only refer to a dog with shaggy hair and an untidy look? Have you heard of the phrase "shaggy dog story?" What type of story is that? What, in your opinion, does "Tom Edison's Shaggy Dog" really mean?

A Glimpse into the Text

A "shaggy dog story" is one that stretches the truth beyond mere exaggeration in order to achieve a comic effect. This shaggy-dog story was published by Kurt Vonnegut, Jr. in 1953—one of his earliest publications. By the early 1970s, Kurt Vonnegut, Jr. had become the most popular science fiction writer in America by successfully fusing science fiction with black humour in novels such as The Sirens of Titan, Cat's Cradle, Mother Night, God Bless You Mr. Rosewater, and Slaughterhouse Five. In the present selection, a clever shaggydog story about a very clever shaggy dog, the elements of a style that would eventually make the author famous world-wide are already evident.

Text A

Tom Edison's Shaggy Dog

Kurt Vonnegut Jr.[1]
(Edited and Abridged)

Two old men sat on a park bench one morning in the sunshine of Tampa, Florida[2]—one trying to read a book he was plainly enjoying while the other,

> **shaggy** /ˈʃægi/ *adj.* having long untidy hair, fur, etc.

named Bullard, told him the story of his life in the
5 loud tones of a public address system. At their feet
lay Bullard's dog, similarly tormenting the book
reader by probing his ankles with a large, wet nose.
　　"Pardon me," said the man with the book,
"but do you suppose you could move your dog
10 somewhere else? He keeps—"
　　"Him?" said Bullard, heartily. "Friendliest
dog in the world. Don't need to be afraid of him."
　　"I'm not afraid of him," said the book reader.
"It's just that he drives me crazy, sniffing at my ankles. His nose is wet... Scat, boy!"
15　　"His wet nose shows he's healthy," said Bullard.
　　"Sorry," said the other man, evenly. He slammed his book shut, stood and jerked his
ankle away from the dog. "I've got to be on my way. Good day, sir."
　　He stalked across the park, found another bench, sat down with a sigh, and began once
more to read. His respiration had just returned to normal when he once again felt the wet
20 sponge of the dog's nose on his ankles.
　　"Oh—it's you!" said Bullard, sitting beside him for a second time. "Don't blame you for
moving on. It was stuffy back there. No shade to speak of and not a sign of a breeze." The dog
continued to sniff annoyingly at the stranger's ankles as Bullard continued his chatter. "Sa-ay,
I've been blowing off all about my life and haven't asked about yours. What's your line?"
25　　"My line?" said the stranger crisply, laying down his book. "Sorry—I've never had a
line. I've been a drifter since the age of nine, since Edison set up his laboratory next to my
home, and showed me the intelligence analyzer."
　　"Edison?" said Bullard. "Thomas Edison, the inventor?"
　　"If you want to call him that, go ahead," said the stranger.
30　　"If I want to call him that"—Bullard guffawed— "I guess I will! Father of the light bulb
and I don't know what."
　　"If you want to think he invented the light bulb, go ahead. No harm in it." The stranger resumed his reading.
35　　"Say what is this?" said Bullard, suspiciously. "You pulling my leg? What this about an intelligence analyzer? I never heard of that."
　　"Of course you haven't," said the
40 stranger. "Mr. Edison and I promised to keep it a secret. I've never told anyone. Mr. Edison broke his promise and told Henry Ford,³ but Ford made him promise not to tell anybody else—for the good of humanity."
45　　Bullard was entranced. "Uh, this intelligence analyzer," he said. "It analyzed intelligence, did it?"
　　"Maybe I can tell you," said the stranger.

torment /ˈtɔːment/ v.	to annoy a person or an animal in a cruel way because you think it is amusing
probe /prəʊb/ v.	to touch, examine or look for sth., especially with a long thin instrument
scat /skæt/ v.	(usu imperative) (informal) go away; leave
jerk /dʒɜːk/ v.	to move or to make sth. move with a sudden short sharp movement
sniff /snɪf/ v. ~ (at) (sth.)	to breathe air in through the nose in order to discover or enjoy the smell of sth.
blow off	to relieve or release (pressure); let off
guffaw /gəˈfɔː/ v.	to laugh noisily
resume /rɪˈzjuːm/ v.	(formal) to begin again or continue after an interruption
pull sb's leg	(informal) to play a joke on sb., usually by making them believe sth. that is not true
entrance /ˈentrəns/ v.	[usually passive] (written) to make sb. feel great pleasure and admiration so that they give sb./sth. all their attention

"It's a terrible thing to keep this bottled up year in and year out. But how can I be sure that it won't go any further?"

"My word as a gentleman," Bullard assured him.

"I don't suppose I could find a stronger guarantee than that, could I?"

"There is no stronger guarantee," agreed Bullard proudly. "Cross my heart and hope to die!"

"Very well." The stranger closed his eyes, seeming to travel backward through time. He was silent for a full minute, during which Bullard watched with awe and respect.

"It was back in the fall of 1879," he said at last, softly. "Back in the village of Menlo Park, New Jersey. I was a boy of nine. A young man we all thought was a wizard had set up a laboratory next door to my home, and there were flashes and crashes inside, and all sorts of scary goings on. The neighborhood children were warned to keep away, not to make any noise that would bother the wizard.

"I didn't get to know Edison right off, but his dog Sparky and I got to be steady pals. A dog a whole lot like yours, Sparky was, and we used to wrestle all over the neighborhood. Yes, sir, your dog is the image of Sparky."

"Is that so?" said Bullard, flattered.

"Gospel," replied the stranger. "Well, one day Sparky and I were wrestling around, and we wrestled right up to the door of Edison's laboratory. The next thing I knew, Sparky had pushed me in through the door, and bam! I was sitting on the laboratory floor, looking up at Mr. Edison himself."

"Bet he was sore," said Bullard, delighted.

"You can bet I was scared," said the stranger. "I thought I was face to face with Satan himself. Edison had wires hooked to his ears and running down to a little black box in his lap! I started to scoot, but he caught me by my collar and made me sit down."

"'Boy,' said Edison, 'it's always darkest before the dawn. I want you to remember that.'"

"'Yes, sir.' I said."

"'For over a year, my boy,' Edison said to me, 'I've been trying to find a filament that will last in an incandescent lamp. Hair, string, splinters—nothing works. Then while I was trying to think of something else to try, I started tinkering with another idea, just letting off steam, and put this together,' he said, showing me the little black box. 'I thought maybe intelligence was just a certain kind of electricity, so I made this intelligence analyzer here. It works! You're the first to know. Why shouldn't you be. It will be your generation that will grow up in the glorious new era when people will be as easily graded as oranges.'"

"I don't believe it!" said Bullard.

"May I be struck by lightning! And it did work, too. Edison had tried out the

---

bottle sth. up to not allow other people to see that you are unhappy, angry, etc. especially when this happens over along period of time

year in, year out every year

cross my heart (**and hope to die**) (informal) used to emphasize that you are telling the truth or will do what you promise

gospel /ˈɡɒspəl/ n. (**also gospel truth**) (informal) the complete truth

sore /sɔː/ adj. (informal, especially AmE) upset and angry especially because you have been treated unfairly

scoot /skuːt/ v. (informal) to go or leave somewhere in a hurry

filament /ˈfɪləmənt/ n. a thin wire in a light bulb that produces light when electricity is passed through it

incandescent /ˌɪnkænˈdesənt/ adj. (technical) giving out light when heated

splinter /ˈsplɪntə/ n. a small thin sharp piece of wood, metal, glass, etc. that has broken off a larger piece

analyzer on the men in his shop without telling them what he was up to. The smarter a man was, by gosh, the farther the needle on the little black box swung to the right. I let him try it on me, and the needle just lay where it was and trembled. But dumb as I was, then is when I made my one and only contribution to the world. As I say, I haven't lifted a finger since."

"Whadja do?" said Bullard, eagerly.

"I said, 'Mr. Edison, let's try it on the dog.' And I wish you could have seen the show that dog put on when I said it! Old Sparky barked and howled and scratched to get out. But we cornered him, and Edison held him down while I touched the wires to his ears. And would you believe it, that needle sailed clear across the dial; way past a little red pencil mark on the dial face!"

"The dog busted it," said Bullard.

"'Mr. Edison, sir,' I said, 'what's that red mark mean?'"

"'My boy,' said Edison, 'it means the instrument is broken, because that red mark is me.'"

"I'll say it was broken," said Bullard.

"But it wasn't broken. No, sir! Edison checked the thing, and it was in apple-pie order.[4] It was then that Sparky, crazy to get out, gave himself away."

"How?" said Bullard suspiciously.

"We really had him locked in, see? There were three locks on the door—a hook and eye,[5] a bolt, and a regular knob and latch. That dog stood up, unhooked the hook, pushed the bolt back, and had the knob in his teeth when Edison stopped him."

"No!" said Bullard.

"Yes!" said the other, his eyes shining. "And then is when Edison showed me what a great scientist he was. He was willing to face the truth, no matter how unpleasant it might be."

"'So!' said Edison to Sparky. 'Man's best friend, huh? Dumb animal, huh?'"

"That Sparky was a caution. He pretended not to hear. He scratched himself and bit fleas and went around growling at ratholes—anything to get out of looking Edison in the eye."

"'Pretty soft, isn't it, Sparky?' said Edison. 'Let somebody else worry about getting food, building shelters and keeping warm, while you sleep in front of a fire or go chasing after girls or raise hell with the boys. No mortgages, no politics, no work, no worry. Just wag the old tail or lick a hand, and you're all taken care of.'"

"'Mr. Edison,' I said, 'do you mean to tell me dogs are smarter than people?'"

"'Smarter?' said Edison. 'I'll tell the world! And what have I been doing for the past year? Slaving to invent a light bulb so dogs can play at night!'"

"'Look, Mr. Edison,' said Sparky, 'why not—'"

"Hold on!" roared Bullard.

"Silence!" said the stranger, triumphantly. "'Look, Mr. Edison,' said Sparky, 'why not keep quiet about this? It's been working out to everybody's satisfaction for hundreds of thousands of years. Let sleeping dogs lie.[6]

gosh /gɔʃ/ (interjection, old-fashioned, informal) expressing surprise
scratch /skrætʃ/ v. to make an irritating nose by rubbing sth. with sth. sharp
bust /bʌst/ v. (informal) to break sth.
caution /ˈkɔːʃən/ n. [spoken] an amusing or surprising person or thing
growl /graʊl/ v. ~ (at sb./sth.) (of animals, especially dogs) to make a low sound in the throat, usually as a sign of anger
raise hell (informal) to indulge in wild celebration; to create an uproar; to object violently

You forget all about it, destroy the intelligence analyzer, and I'll tell you what to use for a lamp filament.'"

"Hogwash!" said Bullard, his face purple.

The stranger stood. "You have my solemn word as a gentleman. That dog rewarded me for my silence with a stock-market tip that made me independently wealthy for the rest of my days. And the last words that Sparky ever spoke were to Thomas Edison. "'Try a piece of carbonized cotton thread,' he said. Later, he was torn to bits by a pack of dogs that had gathered outside the door, listening."

The stranger reached down and patted Bullard's dog. "A small token of my esteem, sir, for an ancestor of yours who talked himself to death. Good day." He tucked his book under his arm and walked away, his step brisk and spry as though the Florida sunshine were already working its magic.

> **hogwash** /ˈhɒɡwɒʃ/ *n.* (informal, especially AmE) an idea, argument, etc. that you think is stupid
> **token** /ˈtəʊkən/ *n.* something that is a symbol of a feeling, a fact, an event, etc.
> **spry** /spraɪ/ *adj.* = SPRIGHTLY (especially of older people) full of life and energy

More about the Text

1. Kurt Vonnegut Jr.

Kurt Vonnegut Jr., born in 1922, American novelist and short-story writer, is best known for his irreverent satires of social and political trends and for his vision of life as an absurd, apocalyptic comedy. Vonnegut's fable-like tales often use science-fiction or fantasy techniques, presenting fictional worlds that mirror reality in grotesque or exaggerated ways. Vonnegut insists that humans have no choice but to view modern civilization with a mixture of sadness and humor and that the cruelty of life must be countered with a genuine charity for human weakness.

Vonnegut's novels often mix contrasting literary styles, intertwining philosophical speculation with homespun advice or incorporating his own crude line drawings into the narrative. Among his most consistent themes are the destructive powers of technology and the dehumanizing impersonality of modern society. Many of the same characters reappear in a number of Vonnegut's works. The present story is included in a collection of his short stories entitled *Welcome to the Monkey House* (1968). Though it can mainly be read as a fun story without suggesting the grave themes mentioned above, it still savors of a touch of irony on the vulnerability of human intelligence and man's ability to keep a secret.

2. Tampa, Florida

It is a coastal city in western Florida on Tampa Bay of the Gulf of Mexico.

3. Henry Ford

Henry Ford (1863—1947) is a U.S. automobile manufacturer who did not invent the car, but rather the assembly method for mass production of cars, specifically the Ford Motor Car.

4. apple-pie order

It refers to a state of ideal orderliness.

5. **hook and eye**
   It is a small metal hook and ring used for fastening clothes. Here it refers to a kind of lock with the similar shape. 锁扣铰链
6. **Let sleeping dogs (a sleeping dog) lie. (Also: Don't wake a sleeping dog.)**
   It refers to leaving an existing situation alone rather than risk provoking something worse.

Check Your Understanding

1. Where does this story take place? Why do you think the author chose that particular location as the setting for the story?
2. How would you describe the character named Bullard?
3. Why do you think the other main character is left nameless by the author?
4. The question "What's your line?" is an idiom in English. Based upon its context in the story, what do you suppose it means?
5. What do you know of Edison's accomplishments? Besides the electric light bulb, what else did he invent?
6. When does Sparky start to talk in human language and why?
7. Does the stranger trust Bullard not to repeat the story he is about to hear? How do you know?
8. Why do you think the author has chosen the name "Sparky" for Edison's dog?
9. Why do the dogs outside the door attack Sparky and kill him?
10. Why do you think the stranger has told Bullard this shaggy-dog story?

Paraphrasing

1. His respiration had just returned to normal when he once again felt the wet sponge of the dog's nose on his ankles.
2. I've been blowing off all about my life and haven't asked about yours. What's your line?
3. You pulling my leg? What this about an intelligence analyzer?
4. It's a terrible thing to keep this bottled up year in and year out.
5. That Sparky was a caution.
6. You have my solemn word as a gentleman. That dog rewarded me for my silence with a stock-market tip that made me independently wealthy for the rest of my days.

Some Information about English Style

1. Fantasy

The dictionary meaning of "fantasy" may refer to the creative power of the imagination, an image or dream created by the imagination, an unrealistic and impractical idea, or in psychology, the creation of exaggerated mental images in response to an ungratified need. In relation to all these semantic references, fantasy as a genre of fiction has become a term for a type of fiction featuring imaginary worlds and magical or supernatural events. The genre of fantasy does not merely belong to the literature written for or about children or teenagers, often with clear-cut moral lines between good and evil, truth and lies. Many modern writers, such as Kurt Vonnegut, also write fantasy stories to present to the adult world a much more complex and perplexing aspect of their life. Both types of fantasy share the general attribute that they often combine traditional tales with supernatural or surreal details.

In "Edison's Shaggy Dog," the fantastic nature of the story is revealed and developed when the stranger begins to tell his boyhood story as Edison's young neighbor. It reaches its climax when Edison's dog, Sparky, starts to speak English and demonstrates human sophistication.

Can you locate the surreal details in the text and see how they contribute to the humor and irony of the story?

2. Colloquialism

Most dictionaries use *colloq.* as a usage label for certain words and phrases. *Colloquial* means informal, or characteristic of a conversational style, as opposed to a formal, literary style. A colloquial expression, or a colloquialism, is an informal word or phrase that is more common in conversation than in formal speech or writing. What is important to remember is that, when you use colloquialisms, you should use them correctly in appropriate situations. Vonnegut's "Edison's Shaggy Dog" is illustrative of how informal and colloquial expressions can be used in a way that can not only serve but also create an overall tone of fun in a story.

Examples of colloquial expressions in the text include:
- **words,** such as "*pals, sore, scoot, scat...*"
- **phrasal verbs,** such as "*blow off...*"
- **idiomatic expressions,** such as "*to pull one's leg...*"

How do these colloquialisms function to create the mood of the story?

Practice

Building word power

1. The underlined colloquial expressions in the following sentences are all taken from Vonnegut's text in the present unit. Please change them into more formal expressions and briefly explain the difference resulting from the change.

(1) Bullard continued his chatter. "Sa-ay, I've been <u>blowing off</u> all about my life and haven't asked about yours. What's your line?"

(2) "<u>You pulling my leg</u>? What this about an intelligence analyzer? I never heard of that."

(3) His dog Sparky and I got to be <u>steady pals</u>.

(4) "There is no stronger guarantee," agreed Bullard proudly. "<u>Cross my heart and hope to die</u>!"

(5) "Bet he was <u>sore</u>," said Bullard, delighted.

(6) I started to <u>scoot</u>, but he caught me by my collar and made me sit down.

(7) "Is that so?" said Bullard, flattered. "<u>Gospel</u>," replied the stranger.

(8) "<u>That Sparky was a caution</u>. He pretended not to hear."

(9) "But it wasn't broken. No, sir! Edison checked the thing, and it was in apple-pie order."

(10) "Let somebody else worry about getting food... while you sleep in front of a fire or go chasing after girls or raise hell with the boys."

2. Lewis Carroll's children's classic *Alice's Adventures in Wonderland* has been a favorite of young readers since it was first published in 1865. The following excerpt depicts a scene at the Mad Hatter's tea party, which is one of the most famous of Alice's fantastic experiences in Wonderland. Can you fill in each blank with the appropriate form of a word or phrase chosen from the list below?

crowd	indignant	nothing	civil	without
encourage	remark	room	a great many	asleep
curiosity	rude	set out	make	rest

There was a table _____ (1) under a tree in front of the house, and the March Hare and the Mad Hatter were having tea at it: a Dormouse was sitting between them, fast _____ (2), and the other two were using it as a cushion, _____ (3) their elbows on it, and talking over its head. "Very uncomfortable for the Dormouse," thought Alice, "only as it's asleep, I suppose it doesn't mind."

The table was a large one, but the three were all _____ (4) together at one corner of it. "No room! No room!" they cried out when they saw Alice coming. "There's plenty of _____ (5)!" said Alice _____ (6), and she sat down in a large arm-chair at one end of the table.

"Have some wine," the March Hare said in an _____ (7) tone.

Alice looked all round the table, but there was _____ (8) on it but tea. "I don't see any wine," she _____ (9).

"There isn't any," said the March Hare.

"Then it wasn't very _____ (10) of you to offer it," said Alice angrily.

"It wasn't very civil of you to sit down _____ (11) being invited," said the March Hare.

"I didn't know it was your table," said Alice, "it's laid for _____ (12) more than three."

"Your hair wants cutting," said the Hatter. He had been looking at Alice for some time with great _____ (13), and this was his first speech.

"You should learn not to _____ (14) personal remarks," Alice said with some severity, "it's very _____."

3. The following is the Chinese translation of the last part of the Mad Hatter's tea party scene in *Alice's Adventures in Wonderland*. Can you translate it back to English and then compare your work with Lewis Carroll's original version? Tell what difference you find and what you learn from such comparison.

这份粗鲁爱丽思实在忍无可忍了:她愤愤然起身就走。惰儿鼠(Dormouse)立马又睡着了,另外两位(三月兔 March Hare 和疯狂制帽人 Mad Hatter)则对爱丽思的离去毫不在乎;她还掉头看了一两眼,暗中希望他俩还会叫她回去。但她最后一次看到他们的时候,他俩正在往茶壶里塞惰儿鼠呢。

"不管怎样,我决不再上那儿去了!"爱丽思嘟囔着,一边小心翼翼地在林中择路而行,"这是我这辈子参加的最恶心的茶会!"

说话间,她忽然注意到一棵树上有一扇门,这门一直通到树里头去。"这可真奇怪!"她心想,"不过,今天什么东西都很奇怪。我想我不如这会儿就进去瞧瞧。"说着她就走进去了。

她见自己又来到那间长长的大厅,挨着那张小小的玻璃桌。"呵,这回我可知道怎么对付了,"她自言自语道,先动手拿起那把小小的金钥匙,打开通往花园的门,再一口一口嚼起那朵蘑菇(她还留了一片在口袋里),一直嚼到身体变成大约一英尺高,然后才沿着小小的通道一步步往下走。哈!她终于到那片美丽的花园,四周是一畦畦灿烂的鲜花,还有清凉的喷泉。

Improving your writing style

1. Readers have found humor—sometimes black humor—one of the most appealing elements in Vonnegut's fantasy fiction. The present story owes much of its humor to various rhetorical devices typical of a shaggy dog story. Can you find examples from the text to illustrate the humor created by such devices?

2. As the story develops and with the change of the two men's roles in their interaction, the fantastic nature of the tale becomes more and more evident. Point out these fantastic elements and analyze their effect on the reader.

Writing task

Vonnegut's shaggy dog story in this present unit seems to have no serious significance as many of the author's other writings, yet it is one of Vonnegut's most anthologized stories. What do you think is the reason for its popularity? What literary value does it possess to deserve our attention and appreciation?

Text B

Harry Potter and the Philosopher's Stone
J. K. Rowling[1]
(Extract from Chapter 17)

The Harry Potter series of fantasy novels is a global, pop-culture phenomenon. Beginning in 1997 with Harry Potter and the Philosopher's Stone the stories about a seemingly ordinary boy, Harry Potter, who discovers he is a wizard, has captured the imagination of tens of millions of children, adolescents, and adults alike. By the

end of 1999, the top three positions on the New York Times list of bestsellers were held by the first three books of the series. By the publication of the fourth book in 2000, parents and children were standing in long lineups at bookstores all around the world waiting for its release—and they did so again for the fifth and sixth books, the latest one published in 2005. This extract is taken from the initial book of the series and offers a taste of what the excitement was all about.

Quirrell[2] snapped his fingers. Ropes sprang out of thin air and wrapped themselves tightly around Harry.

"You're too nosy to live, Potter. Scurrying around the school on Halloween like that, for all I knew you'd seen me coming to look at what was guarding the Stone."

"You let the troll in?"

"Certainly. I have a special gift with trolls—you must have seen what I did to the one in the chamber back there? Unfortunately, while everyone else was running around looking for it, Snape,[3] who already suspected me, went straight to the third floor to head me off—and not only did my troll fail to beat you to death, that three-headed dog didn't even manage to bite Snape's leg off properly."

"Now, wait quietly, Potter. I need to examine this interesting mirror."

It was only then that Harry realised what was standing behind Quirrell. It was the Mirror of Erised.[4]

"This mirror is the key to finding the Stone," Quirrell murmured, tapping his way around the frame. "Trust Dumbledore[5] to come up with something like this... but he's in London.... I'll be far away by the time he gets back...."

All Harry could think of doing was to keep Quirrell talking and stop him from concentrating on the mirror.

"I saw you and Snape in the forest—" he blurted out.

"Yes," said Quirrell idly, walking around the mirror to look at the back. "He was on to me by that time, trying to find out how far I'd got. He suspected me all along. Tried to frighten me—as though he could, when I had Lord Voldemort[6] on my side..."

Quirrell came back out from behind the mirror and stared hungrily into it.

"I see the Stone.... I'm presenting it to my master... but where is it?"

Harry struggled against the ropes binding him, but they didn't give. He had to keep Quirrell from giving his whole attention to the mirror.

"But Snape always seemed to hate me so much."

"Oh, he does," said Quirrell casually, "heavens, yes. He was at Hogwarts[7] with your father, didn't you know? They loathed each other. But he never wanted you dead."

"But I heard you a few days ago, sobbing—I thought Snape was threatening you...."

For the first time, a spasm of fear flitted across Quirrell's face.

"Sometimes," he said, "I find it hard

scurry /ˈskʌri/ *v.* to run with quick short steps

troll /trəʊl/ *n.* (in Scandinavian stories) a creature that looks like an ugly person

head sb off to get in front of sb. in order to make them turn back or change direction

give /gɪv/ *v.* to bend or stretch under pressure

flit /flɪt/ *v.* to move lightly and quickly from one place or thing to another

to follow my master's instructions—he is a great wizard and I am weak—"

"You mean he was there in the classroom with you?" Harry gasped.

"He is with me wherever I go," said Quirrell quietly. "I met him when I travelled around the world. A foolish young man I was then, full of ridiculous ideas about good and evil. Lord Voldemort showed me how wrong I was. There is no good and evil, there is only power, and those too weak to seek it.... Since then, I have served him faithfully, although I have let him down many times. He has had to be very hard on me." Quirrell shivered suddenly. "He does not forgive mistakes easily. When I failed to steal the stone from Gringotts, he was most displeased. He punished me... decided he would have to keep a closer watch on me...."

Quirrell's voice trailed away. Harry was remembering his trip to Diagon Alley—how could he have been so stupid? He'd seen Quirrell there that very day, shaken hands with him in the Leaky Cauldron.

Quirrell cursed under his breath.

"I don't understand... is the Stone inside the mirror? Should I break it?"

Harry's mind was racing.

What I want more than anything else in the world at the moment, he thought, is to find the Stone before Quirrell does. So if I look in the mirror, I should see myself finding it—which means I'll see where it's hidden! But how can I look without Quirrell realising what I'm up to?

He tried to edge to the left, to get in front of the glass without Quirrell noticing, but the ropes around his ankles were too tight: he tripped and fell over. Quirrell ignored him. He was still talking to himself. "What does this mirror do? How does it work? Help me, Master!"

And to Harry's horror, a voice answered, and the voice seemed to come from Quirrell himself.

"Use the boy.... Use the boy...."

Quirrell rounded on Harry.

"Yes-Potter-come here."

He clapped his hands once, and the ropes binding Harry fell off. Harry got slowly to his feet.

"Come here," Quirrell repeated. "Look in the mirror and tell me what you see."

Harry walked towards him.

"I must lie," he thought desperately. "I must look and lie about what I see, that's all."

Quirrell moved close behind him. Harry breathed in the funny smell that seemed to come from Quirrell's turban. He closed his eyes, stepped in front of the mirror, and opened them again.

He saw his reflection, pale and scared-looking at first. But a moment later, the reflection smiled at him. It put its hand into its pocket and pulled out a blood-red stone. It winked and put the Stone back in its pocket—and as it did so, Harry felt

---

gasp /gɑːsp/ v. to take a quick deep breath with open mouth, especially when surprised or in pain

trail away (of sb's speech) to become gradually quieter and then stop

say sth., speak, etc. under your breath to say sth. quietly so that people cannot hear

up to sth. (spoken) doing sth., especially sth. bad

edge /edʒ/ v. to move or to move sth. slowly and carefully in a particular direction

trip /trɪp/ v. to catch your foot on sth. and fall or almost fall

round on sb. to suddenly speak angrily to sb. and criticize or attack them

turban /ˈtɜːbən/ n. a long piece of fabric wound tightly around the head, worn especially by Sikh, Muslim and Hindu men

95   something heavy drop into his real pocket. Somehow—incredibly—he'd got the Stone.

     "Well?" said Quirrell impatiently. "What do you see?"

     Harry screwed up his courage.

     "I see myself shaking hands with Dumbledore," he invented. "I—I've won the house cup for Gryffindor."

100   Quirrell cursed again.

     "Get out of the way," he said. As Harry moved aside, he felt the Philosopher's Stone against his leg. Dare he make a break for it?

     But he hadn't walked five paces before a high voice spoke, though Quirrell wasn't moving his lips.

105   "He lies... He lies..."

     "Potter, come back here!" Quirrell shouted. "Tell me the truth! What did you just see?"

     The high voice spoke again.

     "Let me speak to him... face-to-face..."

     "Master, you are not strong enough!"

110   "I have strength enough... for this..."

     Harry felt as if Devil's Snare was rooting him to the spot. He couldn't move a muscle. Petrified, he watched as Quirrell reached up and began to unwrap his turban. What was going on? The turban fell away. Quirrell's head looked strangely small without it. Then he turned slowly on the spot.

115   Harry would have screamed, but he couldn't make a sound. Where there should have been a back to Quirrell's head, there was a face, the most terrible face Harry had ever seen. It was chalk white with glaring red eyes and slits for nostrils, like a snake.

     "Harry Potter...." it whispered.

     Harry tried to take a step backward but his legs wouldn't move.

120   "See what I have become?" the face said. "Mere shadow and vapour.... I have form only when I can share another's body... but there have always been those willing to let me into their hearts and minds... Unicorn blood has strengthened me, these past weeks... you saw faithful Quirrell drinking it for me in the forest... and once I have the Elixir of Life,[8] I will be able to create a body of my own... Now... why don't you give me that Stone in your pocket?"

125   So he knew. The feeling suddenly surged back into Harry's legs. He stumbled backward.

     "Don't be a fool," snarled the face. "Better save your own life and join me... or you'll meet the same end as your parents... They died begging me for mercy..."

     "LIAR!" Harry shouted suddenly.

130   Quirrell was walking backward at him, so that Voldemort could still see him. The evil face was now smiling.

     "How touching..." it hissed. "I always value bravery... Yes, boy, your parents

135 were brave... I killed your father first; and he put up a courageous fight... but your mother needn't have died... she was trying to protect you... Now give me the Stone,

---

screw up your courage to force oneself to be brave enough to do sth.

make a break for sth./for it to run towards sth. in order to try and escape

root sb. to sth. to make sb. unable to move because of fear, shock, etc.

petrified /ˈpetrɪfaɪd/ *adj.* extremely frightened

slit /slɪt/ *n.* a long narrow cut or opening

elixir /ɪˈlɪksə/ *n.* (literary) a magic liquid that is believed to cure illnesses or to make people live for ever

surge /sɜːdʒ/ *v.* to fill sb. with a strong feeling

snarl /snɑːl/ *v.* ~(sth.) (at sb.) to speak in an angry or bad tempered way

unless you want her to have died in vain."

140 　"NEVER!"

Harry sprang toward the flame door, but Voldemort screamed "SEIZE HIM!" and the next second, Harry felt Quirrell's hand close on his wrist. At once, a needle-
145 sharp pain seared across Harry's scar; his head felt as though it was about to split in two; he yelled, struggling with all his might, and to his surprise, Quirrell let go of him. The pain in his head lessened—he looked
150 around wildly to see where Quirrell had gone, and saw him hunched in pain, looking at his fingers—they were blistering before his eyes.

> sear /sɪə/ v. (written) to cause sb. to feel sudden and great pain
> blister /'blɪstə/ n. a swelling on the surface of the skin that is filled with liquid and is caused, for example, by rubbing or burning v. to form blisters; to make sth. form blisters
> lunge /lʌndʒ/ v. ~ (at/towards/for sb./sth.) to make a sudden powerful forward movement in order to attack sb.
> pin /pɪn/ v. to make sb. unable to move by holding them or pressing them against sth.
> screech /skriːtʃ/ v. to make a loud high unpleasant sound; to say sth. using this sound
> wrench /rentʃ/ v. to pull or twist sth./sb./yourself suddenly and violently

"Seize him! SEIZE HIM!" shrieked Voldemort again, and Quirrell lunged, knocking Harry clean off his feet landing on top of him, both hands around Harry's neck—Harry's scar
155 was almost blinding him with pain, yet he could see Quirrell howling in agony.

"Master, I cannot hold him—my hands—my hands!"

And Quirrell, though pinning Harry to the ground with his knees, let go of his neck and stared, bewildered, at his own palms—Harry could see they looked burned, raw, red, and shiny.

160 　"Then kill him, fool, and be done!" screeched Voldemort.

Quirrell raised his hand to perform a deadly curse, but Harry, by instinct, reached up and grabbed Quirrell's face—

"AAAARGH!"

Quirrell rolled off him, his face blistering, too, and then Harry knew: Quirrell couldn't
165 touch his bare skin, not without suffering terrible pain—his only chance was to keep hold of Quirrell, keep him in enough pain to stop him from doing a curse.

Harry jumped to his feet, caught Quirrell by the arm, and hung on as tight as he could. Quirrell screamed and tried to throw Harry off—the pain in Harry's head was building—he couldn't see—he could only hear Quirrell's terrible shrieks and Voldemort's yells of, "KILL
170 HIM! KILL HIM!" and other voices, maybe in Harry's own head, crying, "Harry! Harry!"

He felt Quirrell's arm wrenched from his grasp, knew all was lost, and fell into blackness, down... down... down...

Notes

1. J. K. Rowling

J. K. Rowling, born in 1965 in Chipping Sodbury, England, is the author of the 1997 book *Harry Potter and the Sorcerer's Stone* (also titled *Harry Potter and the Philosopher's Stone*), which tells about the magical adventures of a boy wizard named Harry Potter. The Harry Potter books dominated bestseller lists in the late 1990s and early 2000s, attracting fans worldwide among children and adults alike. The book was

a sensational hit, and by the end of 1999 the top three slots on the *New York Times* list of bestsellers were taken by the first three books in the Harry Potter series. By the 2000 release of the fourth book in the series, Harry Potter and the Goblet of Fire, Harry Potter had become a global pop culture phenomenon, with parents and children standing in line at bookstores waiting for the book's release, and Rowling had become one of the world's best-known authors. After the 2003 release of the fifth Harry Potter book, The Order of the Phoenix, the BBC reported that Rowling's books had been translated into 60 languages (including ancient Greek) and had sold over 250 million copies worldwide. The sixth book in the series, Harry Potter and the Half-Blood Prince was released in 2005. Rowling announced late in 2006 that the title of the seventh and final book in the series woud be Harry Potter and the Deathly Hallows.

From the beginning Rowling planned the Harry Potter series as a seven-book sequence, one book for each year of Harry's secondary school career at Hogwarts. The Harry Potter books combine two powerful genres—the school story and magical fantasy—but Rowling's treatment of these is almost entirely original. She does not avoid serious issues, such as self-sacrifice and death, and the series has successfully crossed the boundary between adults' and children's books.

In a body of work as big as the Harry Potter series, it is difficult to take one small part as representative of the whole. The extract given here—recommended by a student who is a Harry Potter fan—comes from the end of the first book in the series, *Harry Potter and the Philosopher's Stone*, which tells the following story: Harry Potter thinks he is an ordinary boy—until he is rescued by a beetle eyed giant of a man, enrolls at Hogwarts School of Witchcraft and Wizardry, learns to play Quidditch and does battle in a deadly duel. All because Harry Potter is a wizard! In the present excerpt, for the first time since he was attacked as a baby, Harry comes face to face with Lord Voldemort.

Copies available in China and on line title this book "Harry Potter and the Sorcerer's Stone," which is also the title of the book for the American market. This is a matter of copyright, as British and American editions come under separate copyright regulations and are required to have different titles. "Philosopher's Stone" is the correct title, as that was the name given by alchemists and philosophers of the Middle Ages and later to the legendary stone that had the power to change all base metals into gold and confer eternal life. The book mentions Nicholas Flamel and his wife Perenelle. Flamel was a 14th Century alchemist, the only one to have discovered the philosopher's stone according to legend. Alchemy and the search for the philosopher's stone was the foundation on which the science of chemistry was built in the West.

2. Quirrell

He is a stuttering and seemingly harmless man, and a professor of Defense against the Dark Arts at Hogwarts. Quirrel appears as nervous and squirelly as his name suggests for most of the story. It turns out later, however, that Quirrel has faked his withdrawing meekness and is actually a cold-blooded conniver.

3. Snape

Snape is a professor of Potions at Hogwarts. Sevens Snape dislikes Harry and appears to be an evil man for most of the story. His name associates him not only with unfair snap judgments of others but also with his violent intentions to snap the bones of his enemies.

4. **Mirror of Erised**

   The Mirror of Erised (Desire) plays an important role in the Harry's growing understanding of his internal conflict. The inscription around the top of the mirror translates: "I show not your face but your heart's desire."

5. **Dumbledore**

   He is the kind, wise head of Hogwarts. Though he is a famous wizard, Dumbledore is as humble and adorable as his name suggests. He appears to have an almost superhuman level of wisdom, knowledge, and personal understanding, and it seems that he may have set up the whole quest for the Sorcerer's Stone so that Harry could prove himself.

6. **Voldemort**

   He is a great wizard gone bad. When he killed Harry's parents, Voldemort gave Harry a lightning-shaped scar. Voldemort has thus shaped Harry's life so that Harry's ultimate destruction of him appears as a kind of vengeance. Voldemort, whose name in French means either "flight of death" or "theft of death," is associated both with high-flying magic and with deceit throughout the story. He is determined to escape death by finding the Sorcerer's Stone. Voldemort's weak point is that he cannot understand love, and thus cannot touch Harry's body, which still bears the traces of Harry's mother's love for her son.

7. **Hogwarts**

   Hogwarts is a school of Witchcraft and Wizardry.

8. **the Elixir of Life**

   It is a potion produced by the Philosopher's Stone that will make the drinker immortal.

Comprehension

1. What is a "philosopher's stone?"
2. Magic mirrors often appear in fantasy tales. Can you name another story containing a magic mirror?
3. Why is Harry Potter trying to divert Quirrell's attention from concentrating on the mirror?
4. Why does Quirrell wear a turban?
5. "There is no good and evil, there is only power, and those too weak to seek it," says Quirrell. What German philosopher of the 19th Century is the author, J.K. Rowling, paraphrasing with this sentence? How do you interpret this statement? Do you agree with it? Why or why not?
6. What qualities does this passage possess that would make it particularly suitable for adaptation into a movie?
7. How does Harry get the Sorcerer's Stone?
8. Why can't Quirrell seize Harry even at Voldemort's desperate command to do so? Has Harry defeated Quirrell with ease?
9. If you possessed a "philosopher's stone" and could either turn base metals into gold or extend life indefinitely (but not both) which would you choose to do? Why?
10. Based upon what you have read in this passage, do you think the Harry Potter series deserves the fame it has gathered?

Further Study

- Lewis Carroll: *Alice's Adventures in Wonderland*
- C.S.Lewis: *The Narnia Chronicles*
- J.R.R.Tolkein: *The Lord of the Rings*
- Kurt Vonnegut: *Slaughterhouse-Five; Galapagos*
- Read the following passage and answer the comprehension questions that follow.

Harry Potter and the Sad Grown-ups

Walking through my train yesterday, staggering from my seat to the buffet and back, I counted five people reading *Harry Potter* novels. Not children—these were real grown-ups reading children's books. It was as if I had wandered into a John Wyndham scenario where the adults' brains have been addled by a plague and they have returned to childishness, avidly hunting out their toys and colouring-in books.

Maybe that would have been understandable. If these people had jumped whole-heartedly into a second childhood it would have made more sense. But they were card-carrying grown-ups with laptops and spreadsheets returning from sales meetings and seminars. Yet they chose to read a children's book.

I don't imagine you'll find this headcount exceptional. You can no longer get on the London Tube and not see a Harry Potter book, and I presume the same is true on the Glasgow Metro or the Manchester trams, or the beaches of Ibiza or clubs of Ayia Napa. Who told these adults they should read a kids' book? Do we see them ploughing through Tom's Midnight Garden? Of course not; if you suggested it they would rightly stare, bemused, and say: Isn't that a kids' book? Why would I want to read that? I'm 37...42...63.

Nor is it just the film; these throwback readers were out there in droves long before the movie campaign opened. Warner Brothers knows it can't hope to recoup one hundred million dollars costs through ticket sales to children alone. But the adult desire to tangle with Harry, Hermione and Voldemort existed long before the director Chris Columbus got his hands on the story.

So who are these adult readers who have made JK Rowling the second-biggest female earner in Britain (after Madonna)? As I have tramped along streets knee-deep in Harry Potter paperbacks, I've mentally slotted them into three groups.

First come the Never-Readers, whom Harry has enticed into opening a book. Is this a bad thing? Probably not. Ever since the invention of moving pictures, writing has many advantages over film, but it can never compete with its magnetic punch. If these books can re-establish the novel as a thrilling experience for some people, then this can only be for the better. If it takes obsession-level hype to lure them into a bookshop, that's fine by me. But will they go on to read anything else? Again, we can only hope. It has certainly worked at schools, especially for boys, whose reading has clearly taken an upward swing—for this alone, Rowling deserves her rewards.

The second groups are the Occasional Readers. These people claim that tiredness, work and children allow them to read only a few books a year. Yet now to be part of the crowd, to say they've read it—they put Harry Potter on their oh-so-select reading list. It's infuriating, it's maddening, it sends me ballistic. Yes, I'm a writer myself, writing difficult, unreadable, hopefully unsettling novels, but there are so many other good books out there, so much rewarding, enlightening, enlarging works of fiction for adults; and yet these sad cases are swept along by the hype, the faddism, into reading a children's book. Put like that, it's worse than maddening, it's pathetic. When I rule the world, all editions will carry a heavy-print warning: "This Is A Children's Book, Designed For Under Elevens. It May Seriously Damage Your Credibility." I can dream, can't I?

The third group are the Regular Readers, for whom Harry is sandwiched between McEwan and Balzac, Roth and Dickens. This is the real baffler—what on earth do they get out of reading it? Why bother? But if they can rattle through it in a week just to say they've been there—like going to Longleat or the Eiffel Tower—the worst they're doing is encouraging others.

By now you're asking: "What's he got against these books, they're just a bit of escapism, just a great fantasy?" First, let me make it clear, I'm not here to criticize or praise the quality of JK's prose or inventiveness. They may indeed be the best children's novels ever written. But I'm sure JK would be the first to agree that they are children's books, that they are successful precisely because they appeal so directly to the childish imagination, address problems and questions different from those that mesmerize us in adult life. A child is free to wonder about magic, to believe in the clear purity of the struggle between good and evil, to bask in simple, unquestioning friendships. As adults, we deal with the constantly muddled nature of good and evil, we carry a responsibility for the safety of others, we crave success and fear failure, we confront the reality instead of dreams.

And this is why different books are written for these two tribes. When I read a novel, I look to it to tell me some truths about human life—the truths that non-fiction cannot reach. These might be moral, sexual, political or psychological truths and I expect my life to be enlarged, however slightly by the experience of reading something fictional. I cannot hope to come closer to any of these truths through a children's novel, where nice clean white lines are painted between the good guys and the evil ones, where magic exists, and where there are adults on hand to delineate rules. Adult fiction is about a world without rules.

1. From the passage, we know that *Harry Potter* is _____.
   A. written for people of different ages
   B. popular in all the countries of the world
   C. originally written for kids
   D. more popular with adults than children

2. The author mentioned Tom's Midnight Garden in the third paragraph most likely to _____.
   A. compare it with *Harry Potter*
   B. demonstrate that adults don't like kid's book
   C. argue that the adults like *Harry Potter* not because they like kid's book
   D. prove that not all kid's books are popular with adults

3. In the author's opinion, the Never-Readers who read *Harry Potter* _____.
   A. will enjoy reading book from then on
   B. will read many other books
   C. are mostly boys
   D. are more likely to be movie fans

4. All of the following can be concluded from the passage except _____.
   A. the author thinks that the book should be published for certain readers
   B. the only reason that the *Harry Potter* book sells well is the film
   C. some people read the book just because somebody else has read it
   D. the author doesn't think *Harry Potter* is a wonderful book
5. The attitude of the author to the adults who fall in love with the novel *Harry Potter* is ___.
   A. indifferent
   B. praiseful
   C. critical
   D. neutral

Unit 13

Human Folly

Unit Goals

- To discuss human folly
- To appreciate informal classical prose
- To use synonymous expressions to avoid monotony
- To use parallelism & amplification for rhetorical purposes

Before Reading

1. Check a literary encyclopedia or search the Internet for information about Joseph Addison (nationality, historical context, literary career, etc.). Make a note of important information.
2. Compare your findings with your partner and discuss what you expect from the author in the present text.
3. Discuss within a group of four some action of folly from your own experience or others.
4. Do you agree with the quote from Addison "It is only imperfection that complains of what is imperfect. The more perfect we are, the more gentle and quiet we become towards the defects of others."? Why or why not?

A Glimpse into the Text

That the grass always seems greener on the other side of the fence is generally acknowledged to be true by most people, although few actually climb over a fence to confirm it. In this eighteenth century essay, Joseph Addison explores the old saying with an allegory in which people give up their own "lot" for another, only to discover that not only is the grass no greener there, but far less attractive than ever they imagined.

Text A

The Folly of Discontent with One's Own Lot

Joseph Addison[1]
(Abridged and Edited)

It is a celebrated thought of Socrates,[2] that if all the misfortunes of mankind were cast into a public stock, in order to be equally distributed among

> celebrated /ˈselɪbreɪtɪd/ *adj.* famous for having good qualities
> cast into throw sth. somewhere

Joseph Addison (1672—1719)

the whole species, those who now think themselves the most unhappy, would prefer the share they are already possessed of before that which would befall them by such a division. Horace³ has carried this thought a great deal farther in his first satire, which implies that the hardships and misfortunes we lie under are more easily borne by us than those of any other person's would be if we could change conditions with him.

As I was ruminating on these two remarks, and seated in my elbow chair, I insensibly fell asleep; when, in a sudden, methought there was a proclamation made by Jupiter⁴ that every mortal should bring in his grief and calamities, and throw them together in a heap. There was a large plain appointed for this purpose. I took my stand in the center of it, and saw the whole human species marching one after another and throwing down their several loads, which immediately grew up into a prodigious mountain.

There was a certain lady of a thin airy shape, who was very active in this solemnity. She carried a magnifying glass in one of her hands, and was clothed in a loose flowing robe embroidered with several figures of fiends and specters. There was something wild and distracted in her looks. Her name was Fancy. She led every mortal to the appointed place after having assisted him in making up his pack and laying it upon his shoulders. My heart melted within me to see my fellow-creatures groaning under their respective burdens, and to consider that prodigious bulk of human calamities which lay before me.

There were, however, several persons who gave me great diversion upon this occasion. I observed one bringing in a parcel very carefully concealed, which I discovered to be Poverty. Another, after a great deal of puffing, threw down his luggage, which upon examining I found to be his wife.

There were multitudes of lovers addled with burdens composed of darts and flames; but what was very odd, though they sighed as if their hearts would break under these calamities, they could not persuade themselves to cast them into the heap when they came up to it, but after a few efforts shook their heads and marched away as heavy laden as they came. I saw multitudes of old women throw down their wrinkles, and several young ones who stripped themselves of a tawny skin. There were very great heaps of red noses, large lips, and rusty teeth; the truth of it is, I was surprised to see the greatest part of the mountain made up of bodily deformities.

befall /bɪˈfɔːl/ v. (used only in the third person of sth. unpleasant) to happen to sb.
satire /ˈsætərə/ n. [C] a type of writing that criticizes with humor
ruminate on think deeply about sth.
remark /rɪˈmɑːk/ n. [C] sth. that you say or write which expresses an opinion, thought, etc. about sth.
insensibly /ɪnˈsensəbli/ adv. unawares
methought /mɪˈθɔːt/ v. past tense of "methinks," an old or humorous use, equal to "I think"
proclamation /ˌprɒkləˈmeɪʃən/ n. [C, U] an official statement about sth. important which is made to the public
solemnity /səˈlemnɪti/ n. [U] the state of being solemn
be embroidered with to decorate fabric with a pattern of stitches usually using coloured thread
specter /ˈspektə/ n. (literary) a ghost
bulk /bʌlk/ n. [U] the (large) size or quantity of sth.
puff /pʌf/ v. (informal) to breathe loudly and quickly, especially after you have been running
addled /ˈædld/ adj. confused, unable to think clearly
laden /ˈleɪdn/ adj. heavily loaded with sth.
multitudes of an extremely large number of things or people
deformity /dɪˈfɔːmɪti/ n. [C, U] a condition in which a part of the body is not the normal shape because of injury, illness or because it has grown wrongly

Observing one advancing toward the heap with a larger cargo than ordinary upon his back, I found upon his near approach that it was only a natural hump, which he disposed of with great joy among this collection of human miseries. There were likewise distempers of all sorts; though I could not but observe there were many more imaginary than real. One little packet I could not but take notice of was a complication of all the diseases incidental to human nature, and that was in the hand of a great many people. But what most of all surprised me, there was not a single vice or folly thrown onto the whole heap; at which I was very much astonished, having concluded within myself, that every one would take this opportunity to get rid of his passions, prejudices, and frailties.

I took notice in particular of a very profligate fellow, who came laden with his crimes; but upon searching in his bundle I found that instead of throwing his guilt away, he had only laid down his memory. He was followed by another worthless rogue, who flung away his modesty instead of his ignorance.

When the whole race of mankind had thus cast their burdens, the phantom, seeing me an idle spectator of what had passed, approached me. I grew uneasy at her presence, when all of a sudden she held her magnifying glass before my eyes. I no sooner saw my face in it but was startled at the shortness of it, which now appeared to me in its utmost aggravation. The immoderate breadth of my features made me very much out humor with my own countenance, upon which I threw it from me like a mask. It happened very luckily that one who stood by me had just before thrown down his visage, which it seems was too long for him. It was indeed extended to a most shameful length; I believe his chin was, modestly speaking, as long as my whole face.

As I was regarding very attentively this confusion of miseries, Jupiter issued out a second proclamation: that every one was now to exchange his affliction with any such other bundle as should be delivered to him. Upon this Fancy began again to bestir, parceling out the whole heap with incredible activity, and recommending to every one his particular packet. The hurry and confusion at this time could not be expressed.

A venerable, gray-headed man, who had laid down his colic, and who wanted an heir to his estate, snatched up an undutiful son that had been thrown into the heap by an angry father. The graceless youth pulled the old gentleman by the beard, and had like to have knocked his brains out; so that meeting the true father, who came towards him with a fit of the gripes, he begged him to take his son again, and give him back his colic; but they were incapable either of them to recede from the choice they had made. A poor galley slave, who had thrown down his chains, took up the gout in their stead, but made such wry faces, that one might easily perceive he was no great gainer by the bargain. It was pleasant enough to see the several exchanges that were made, for

---

hump /hʌmp/ *n.* a large lump on the back of a person, caused by an unusual curve in the spine

distemper /dɪˈstempə/ *n.* [U] an infectious disease of animals, especially cats and dogs, that causes fever and coughing

complication /ˌkɒmplɪˈkeɪʃən/ *n.* [C, usually pl.] a new problem or illness that makes treatment of a previous one more complicated or difficult

incidental to happening as a natural result of sth.

profligate /ˈprɒflɪgɪt/ *adj.* using money, time, materials, etc. in a careless way

phantom /ˈfæntəm/ *n.* a ghost; a thing that exists only in your imagination

countenance /ˈkaʊntɪnəns/ *n.* a person's face or their expression

visage /ˈvɪzɪdʒ/ *n.* (literary) a person's face

parcel sth. out to divide sth. into parts or between several people

recede from to withdraw or retreat from a previous decision

sickness against poverty, hunger against want of appetite, and care against pain.

The female world were very busy among themselves in bartering for features; one was trucking a lock of gray hairs for a carbuncle; another was making over a short waist for a pair of round shoulders, a third exchanging a bad face for a lost reputation; but on all these occasions there was not one of them who did not think the new blemish more much disagreeable than the old one. I made the same observation on every other misfortune or calamity which everyone brought upon himself in lieu of what he had parted with, whether it be that all the evils which befall us are in some measure suited and proportioned to our strength, or that every evil becomes more supportable by our being accustomed to it, I shall not determine.

I could not from my heart forbear pitying the poor humpbacked gentleman, who went off a very well-shaped person with a stone in his bladder; nor the fine gentleman who had struck up this bargain with him, that limped through a whole assembly of ladies, who used to admire him, with a pair of shoulders peeping over his head.

I must not omit my own particular adventure. My friend with the long visage had no sooner taken upon him my short face but he made such a grotesque figure in it that I could not forbear laughing. On the other hand, I found that I myself had no great reason to triumph; for as I went to touch my forehead, I missed and clapped my finger upon my upper lip. I saw two other gentlemen by me in the same ridiculous circumstances. These had made a foolish swap between a couple of thick bandy legs and two long trap-sticks that had no calves to them. One of these looked like a man walking upon stilts, and was so lifted up into the air above his ordinary height that his head turned round with it; while the other made such awkward circles as he attempted to walk, that he scarcely knew how to move upon his new supporters.

The heap was at last distributed among the two sexes, who made a most piteous sight as they wandered up and down under the pressure of their new burdens. The whole plain was filled with murmurs and complaints, groans and lamentations. Jupiter, at length, taking compassion on the poor mortals, ordered them a second time to lay down their loads, with a design to give every one his own again. They discharged themselves with a great deal of pleasure; after which, the phantom which had led them into such gross delusions was commanded to disappear. There was sent in her stead a goddess of quite a different figure; her motions were steady and composed, her aspect serious but cheerful. Her name was Patience. She afterwards returned every man his own proper calamity and, teaching him how to bear it in the most commodious manner; he marched off with it contentedly, being very well pleased that he had not been left to his own choice.

Besides the several pieces of morality to be drawn out of this vision, I learned from it never to repine at my own misfortunes or

barter for sth. to exchange goods, property, services, etc. for other goods, etc. without using money

making over sth. for sth. else to give sth. for sth. else

calamity /kəˈlæmɪti/ *n.* [C, U] an event that causes great harm or damage

in lieu of sth. in stead of sth.

swap /swɒp/ *n.* [usually sing.] an act of exchanging one thing or person for another

trap-stick /ˈtræp stɪk/ *n.* a stick used in playing the game of trapball; hence, fig., a slender leg

stilt /stɪlt/ *n.* [usually pl.] one of two long pieces of wood that have a step on the side that you can stand on, so that you can walk above the ground

lamentation /ˌlæmənˈteɪʃən/ *n.* [C, U] (formal) an expression of great sadness or disappointment

delusion /dɪˈluːʒən/ *n.* [C] a false belief or opinion about yourself or your situation

repine at to complain about

to envy the happiness of another, since it is impossible for any man to form a right judgment of his neighbor's sufferings; for which reason too, I have determined never to think too lightly of another's complaints, but to regard the sorrows of my fellow-creatures with sentiments of humanity and compassion.

More about the Text

1. Joseph Addison

Joseph Addison (1672—1719) is an English essayist, poet, and dramatist. He was a leading contributor to and guiding spirit of the earliest modern English periodicals *The Tatler* (1709—1711) and *The Spectator* (1711—1712, 1714). One of the most admired masters of English prose, Addison brought to perfection the periodical essay. The present essay is taken from the collection of *The Spectator*. Aiming to "enliven morality with wit, and to temper wit with morality," *The Spectator* presented a fictional club whose imaginary members expressed the writers' ideas about society. It made serious discussion of letters and politics a normal pastime of the leisured class, set the pattern and established the vogue for the periodical in the 18th century, and helped create a receptive public for novelists.

2. Socrates

Socrates (469—399 BC) is a Greek philosopher of Athens. Famous for his view of philosophy as a pursuit proper and necessary to all intelligent men, he is one of the great examples of a man who lived by his principles even though they ultimately cost him his life.

3. Horace

Horace (65—8 BC) is a leading lyric poet in Latin. His works include Odes, Epodes, Satires, and letters.

4. Jupiter

Jupiter is the Roman God of Greek God Zeus, the most authoritative among the Greco-Roman mythology.

Check Your Understanding

1. Why does the author give the name "Fancy" to the "lady of a thin airy shape"?
2. Why would young women wish to rid themselves of a tawny skin?
3. Why do you suppose the people that the author dreams of never throw away their vices?
4. What are the burdens observed by the author that people wants so desperately to discard?
5. According to the author, what is the result of exchanging one burden for another?
6. How do you compare "Fancy" and "Patience?"
7. What does "I" feel about the burdened human race?
8. What is the moral of the story?

Paraphrasing

1. It is a celebrated thought of Socrates, that if all the misfortunes of mankind were cast into a public stock, in order to be equally distributed among the whole species, those who now think themselves the most unhappy, would prefer the share they are already possessed of before that which would befall them by such a division.
2. Horace has carried this thought a great deal farther in his first satire, which implies that the hardships and misfortunes we lie under are more easily borne by us than those of any other person's would be if we could change conditions with him.
3. My heart melted within me to see my fellow-creatures groaning under their respective burdens, and to consider that prodigious bulk of human calamities which lay before me.
4. The heap was at last distributed among the two sexes, who made a most piteous sight as they wandered up and down under the pressure of their new burdens.
5. I have determined never to think too lightly of another's complaints, but to regard the sorrows of my fellow-creatures with sentiments of humanity and compassion.

Some Information about English Style

1. Informal classical prose

Informal prose is also known as "familiar essay," "personal essay," or "periodical essay," when printed in a newspaper or magazine. In the eighteenth century, British periodicals underwent significant developments. Appealing to an educated middle-class audience, the periodical essay as perfected by Addison was not scholarly, but casual in tone, in a more relaxed and conversational manner and adaptable to a number of subjects, including daily life, ethics, religion, science, economics, and social and political issues.

Addison's style of informal prose has been widely praised. Dr. Samuel Johnson once said that *"His (Addison's) prose is the model of the middle style; on grave subjects not formal, on light occasions not groveling; pure without scrupulosity; and exact without apparent elaboration; always equable, and always easy, without glowing words or pointed sentences."* Johnson also maintained that *"Whoever wishes to attain an English style, familiar but not coarse, and elegant but not ostentatious, must give his days and nights to the volumes of Addison."*

2. The use of synonymous expressions to avoid monotony

When we look closely at this essay, typical of Addison's style, we can not but be impressed by his skill of plain writing without being tedious and boring. A technique employed by Addison is using synonymous words, phrases, or sentence structures to achieve variety. For example:

 (1) Addison uses the following synonyms for the word "burden":
  pack/load/parcel/packet/bundle/luggage/cargo/heap/stock/bulk
 (2) When Addison describes the state or the action of people under their respective burdens, he uses different grammatical structures, such as:
  lie under / be possessed of / befall
 (3) Addison also uses different sentence structures to express people's emotion or

compassion, such as:

- *My heart melted within me to see my fellow-creatures groaning under their respective burdens, and to consider that prodigious bulk of human calamities which lay before me. (Para.3)*
- *I could not from my heart forbear pitying the poor humpbacked gentleman, who went off a very well-shaped person with a stone in his bladder. (Para.11)*

3. Parallelism and amplification

Both parallelism and amplification are rhetorical devices often used in oratory and prose to attain a particular effect. As has been illustrated in Unit 2 (The Inaugural Address of Bill Clinton), parallelism involves balancing the structural elements within a sentence or between sentences. Here are further examples of parallelism in the present selection:

- The whole plain was filled with *murmurs and complaints, groans and lamentation*. (two noun phrases in parallel)
- Her *motions were steady and composed, her aspect serious but cheerful*. (two adjective phrases in parallel)
- Besides the several pieces of morality to be drawn out of this vision, I <u>learned</u> from it <u>never to</u> repine at my own misfortunes or to envy the happiness of another, since it is impossible for any man to form a right judgment of his neighbor's sufferings; for which reason too, I have <u>determined never to</u> think too lightly of another's complaints, but to regard the sorrows of my fellow-creatures with sentiments of humanity and compassion. (two clauses in parallel)

Amplification involves repeating a word or expression while adding more detail to it, in order to emphasize what might otherwise be passed over. Amplification allows you to call attention to and emphasize or expand an idea, so that the reader realizes its importance or centrality in the discussion. Examples of amplification from Text B:

- He felt a wild longing for the unstained purity of his boyhood—his rose-white boyhood, as Lord Henry had once called it. (expanding "boyhood")
- It was his beauty that had ruined him, his beauty and the youth that he had prayed for. (emphasizing and expanding "beauty")
- What was youth at best? A green, an unripe time, a time of shallow moods, and sickly thoughts. (expanding the notion of "youth")
- For it was an unjust mirror, this mirror of his soul that he was looking at. (emphasizing "mirror")

Practice

Building word power

1. Complete each of the following sentences with the appropriate form of the word provided.

(1) celebration

He _____ the surrounding mountains for their beauty.
Venice is _____ for its exquisite buildings.
It is not easy to acquire immediate _____ in a field.

(2) sense
   He showed total _____ to the animal's fate.
   _____ and _____ is one of Jane Austin's famous novels.
(3) form
   Her face was _____ by anger.
   Lord Byron was very attractive in spite of his slight _____.
(4) support
   Her _____ family saw her through tough career crises.
   The movie featured Robert Lindsay in a _____ role.
   Labour became more _____ when the midwife allowed her husband to come near her.
(5) complicate
   An experienced doctor can always foresee _____.
   The car ran out of petrol, and as a further _____, I had no money!

2. **Select an appropriate suffix for each of the following words.**

   -laden,   -mania,   -ware,   -craft

   (1) fashion- _____
   (2) calorie- _____ cream cakes
   (3) brass _____
   (4) car- _____
   (5) ego- _____
   (6) stage- _____
   (7) silver _____
   (8) earthen _____
   (9) bush _____
   (10) glass _____
   (11) house _____
   (12) state _____

Grammar and Usage

Translate the following sentences into English.
(1) 作为医生,你必须承担责任与风险。(incidental to)
(2) 人不能食言。(recede from)
(3) 一个偶然的机缘使我们在大学的校园相遇。(throw sb./sth. together)
(4) 如果我是你,我会果断行动,证明给老板看。(change conditions with sb.)
(5) 这个项目由于缺乏财政资助而告吹。(for want of)

Improving your writing style

1. **Work in a group of four to find as many synonymous expressions as possible from the text to replace the following underlined parts. Then reorder**

the following sentences to retell the story. (A change of structure may be required in some sentences.)

(1) People are happy to throw down their physical imperfections.
(2) The narrator saw people coming in large numbers to ....
(3) The narrator was surprised to see the bulk of human miseries
(4) The narrator saw many deformities were lain down as personal burdens.
(5) He was surprised that a great number of burden were more imaginary than real.
(6) Jupiter made a proclamation that....
(7) Men complain and lament their misfortunes even more.
(8) A father threw away his worthless son for some physical pain.
(9) Women bartered health for youth and beauty.
(10) Later many discovered that they are no great gainer by the exchange.
(11) One should have compassion on his neighbour.

2. Fill in the blanks with one word at a time to complete the following essay, then comment on how synonyms are used to avoid monotony and to achieve vividness.

Hey, What's Your Sino-sign?

Like Western astrology, the Chinese Zodiac provides speculations about the personalities of the people born in the various years starting with the Year of Rat.

Rat people are said to be those who use every means to succeed. They are strong-willed and perfectionists. Dragon, Monkey or Ox people make ideal partners for Rats, but not Horses or Rabbits.

The Ox is honest, realizable and sociable. He is also creative, acquisitive and needs security. The best _____ (1) for Ox people are Snakes or Roosters. The Sheep and the Dog are animals for them to _____ (2).

The Tiger is confident, somewhat conceited and loves to be admired, but he is also warm and courageous. As for lifelong _____ (3), Tigers should _____ (4) _____ (5) Horses, Dogs and Pigs, while Monkeys and Snakes are to be _____ (6).

The Rabbit is kind, affectionate and likes to make friends. Rabbit relationships tend to be long-lasting. They are advised to _____ (7) the Sheep, Dog or Pig. The Rooster and Rat may _____ (8) _____ (9).

Being a natural leader, the Dragon person is alert, strong, inventive, intellectual, and full of energy. As for _____ (10) _____ (11), the Rat, Monkey or Rooster are ideal _____ (12). But marriages between the Dog and the Dragon may be _____ (13).

The Snake is devoted, serious, stubborn, introspective, and controls his emotions well most of the time. Snakes should _____ (14) the Ox or the Rooster. But they are advised to be _____ (15) of the Pig or the Tiger.

The Horse is popular, cheerful, energetic, gregarious and likes to indulge in practical jokes, and gossip. Horses are told to try to find Tigers, Sheep, or Dogs as their _____ (16), but not Rats or other Horses.

The Sheep is ambitious, realistic, hard-working, seldom reveals any emotion, yet tries hard to serve the community. The Horse, Rabbit and Pig are their _____ (17) mates, but, they are asked to _____ (18) of the ox and the dog, because dissension will tend to divide them.

The Monkey is agile, versatile, persuasive and undaunted by failure. The Monkey uses humour and strength to get by most of the time. For partners, they are asked to _____ (19) Rats and Dragons, but they are told not to _____ (20) around with Tigers or Rabbits.

Those born in the year of the Rooster are supposed to be romantic, outgoing, energetic, profound, enterprising and forceful. Personal setbacks don't deter the Rooster. They are advised to marry the Ox, Dragon or Snake, and, if they do, the marriage is said to be able to "endure 100 generations." But Roosters should _____ (21) distance from Rabbits or other Roosters.

The Dog is regarded as very thorough and skilful at word. It is said that Dogs are found to be reliable, unassuming, quiet, loyal and friendly. Their other _____ (22) are to be found in Tigers, Rabbits or Horses. But they are told to _____ (23) away from Dragons and Sheep.

The Pig is said to be witty, loyal, truthful, idealistic, but sensual. Their best mates are said to be people born in the year of the Sheep, Rabbit, and Tiger. Their worst mates are other Pigs or Snakes.

3. Revise the following sentences, using parallel structures.
   (1) She is lovely, kind-hearted, and has a quick mind.
   (2) To chew carefully and eating slowly are necessary for good digestion.
   (3) On the train I met with a girl from my hometown and who just graduated from Tianjin University with a MA degree.
   (4) I was knocked down by a motorcycle, but it was not serious.

4. Use your imagination and fill in each blank to form amplification.
   (1) He showed a remarkable taste, a taste for _____, _____, _____.
   (2) Nora felt a great longing for freedom, _____.
   (3) Dorian Grey had long been fooling himself in regard to redemption, _____.
   (4) Winston Churchill showed determination, _____ to fight against the phantom of Hitler.

Writing task

Write an essay on human folly based on your discussion (Before Reading Task 3).

Text B

The Picture of Dorian Gray
Oscar Wilde[1]
(Abridged and Edited)

The Picture of Dorian Gray by Ivan Albright, 1943, oil on canvas

Oscar Wilde is best known for his theatrical comedy, The Importance of Being Earnest, and his novel, The Picture of Dorian Gray. The play is satirical and wickedly witty; the novel is eloquent, ingenious, and ultimately tragic. Together, the two
5 works paint a remarkably true portrait of the character of Oscar Wilde himself and—again as with Wilde's actual life—reflect the perils of losing your identity and damaging one's integral image.

10   It was a lovely night, so warm that he threw his coat over his arm and did not even put his silk scarf round his throat. As he strolled home, smoking his cigarette, two young men in evening dress passed him. He heard one of them whisper to the other, "That is Dorian Gray." He remembered how pleased he used to be when he
15 was pointed out, or stared at, or talked about. He was tired of hearing his own name now. Half the charm of the little village where he had been so often lately was that no one knew who he was. He had often told the girl whom he had lured to love him that he was poor, and she had believed him. He had told her once that he was wicked, and she had laughed at him and answered that wicked people were always very old and very ugly. What a laugh she had!—
20 just like a *thrush* singing. And how pretty she had been in her cotton dresses and her large hats! She knew nothing, but she had everything that he had lost.

When he reached home, he threw himself down on the sofa in the library, and began to think over some of the things that Lord Henry[2] had said to him.

Was it really true that one could never change? He felt a wild longing for the unstained
25 purity of his boyhood—his rose-white boyhood, as Lord Henry had once called it. But was it all *irretrievable*? Was there no hope for him?

Ah! In what a monstrous moment of pride and passion he had prayed that the portrait should bear the burden of his days, and he keep the *unsullied* splendour of eternal
30 youth! All his failure had been due to that. Better for him that each sin of his life had brought its sure swift *penalty* along with it. There was purification in punishment. Not "Forgive us our sins" but "*Smite* us for our
35 *iniquities*" should be the prayer of man to a most just God.

Once, some one who had terribly loved him had written to him a mad letter,

---

thrush /θrʌʃ/ *n.* [C] a bird with a brown back and brown spots on its chest
irretrievable /ˌɪrɪˈtriːvəbl/ *adj.* (formal) of a situation that you can never make right or get back
unsullied /ʌnˈsʌlɪd/ *adj.* (literary) not spoiled by anything; still pure or in the original state
penalty /ˈpenlti/ *n.* [C] a punishment for breaking a law, rule or contract
smite /smaɪt/ *v.* (old use or literary) to punish sb.
iniquity /ɪˈnɪkwɪti/ *n.* [C, U] (formal) the fact of being very unfair or wrong

ending with these idolatrous words: "The world is changed because you are made of ivory and gold. The curves of your lips rewrite history." The phrases came back to his memory, and he repeated them over and over to himself. Then he loathed his own beauty. It was his beauty that had ruined him, his beauty and the youth that he had prayed for. But for those two things, his life might have been free from stain. His beauty had been to him but a mask, his youth but a mockery. What was youth at best? A green, an unripe time, a time of shallow moods, and sickly thoughts. Why had he worn its livery? Youth had spoiled him.

It was better not to think of the past. Nothing could alter that. It was of himself, and of his own future, that he had to think. James Vane[3] was hidden in a nameless grave in Selby churchyard. Alan Campbell[4] had shot himself one night in his laboratory, but had not revealed the secret that he had been forced to know. The excitement, such as it was, over Basil Hallward's[5] disappearance would soon pass away. It was already waning. He was perfectly safe there. Nor, indeed, was it the death of Basil Hallward that weighed most upon his mind. It was the living death of his own soul that troubled him. Basil had painted the portrait that had marred his life. He could not forgive him that. It was the portrait that had done everything. Basil had said things to him that were unbearable, and that he had yet borne with patience. The murder had been simply the madness of a moment. As for Alan Campbell, his suicide had been his own act. He had chosen to do it. It was nothing to him.

A new life! That was what he wanted. That was what he was waiting for. Surely he had begun it already. He would be good.

As he thought of Hetty Merton,[6] he began to wonder if the portrait in the locked room had changed. Surely it was not still so horrible as it had been? Perhaps if his life became pure, he would be able to expel every sign of evil passion from the face. Perhaps the signs of evil had already gone away. He would go and look.

He took the lamp from the table and crept upstairs. As he unbarred the door, a smile of joy flitted across his strangely young-looking face and lingered for a moment about his lips. Yes, he would be good, and the hideous thing that he had hidden away would no longer be a terror to him. He felt as if the load had been lifted from him already.

He went in quietly, locking the door behind him, as was his custom, and dragged the purple hanging from the portrait. A cry of pain and indignation broke from him. He could see no change, save that in the eyes there was a look of cunning and in the mouth the curved wrinkle of the hypocrite. The thing was still loathsome—more loathsome, if possible, than before—and the scarlet dew that spotted the hand seemed brighter, and more like blood newly spilled. Then he trembled. Had it been merely vanity that had made him do his one good deed? Or the desire for a new sensation, as Lord Henry had hinted, with his mocking laugh? Or that passion to act a part that sometimes makes us do things finer than we are ourselves? Or, perhaps, all these? And why was the red stain larger than it had been? It seemed to have crept like a horrible disease over the wrinkled fingers. There was blood on the painted feet, as though the thing had dripped—blood even on the hand that had not held

---

idolatrous /aɪˈdɒlətrəs/ *adj.* showing too much love or admiration for sb./sth.

loathe /ləʊð/ *v.* (not used in the progressive tenses) to dislike sb./sth. very much

wane /weɪn/ *v.* (written) to become gradually weaker or less important

mar /mɑː/ *v.* to damage or spoil sth. good

flit /flɪt/ *v.* [usually +*adv./prep.*] ~ (**from A to B**) to move lightly and quickly from one place or thing to another

linger /ˈlɪŋgə/ *v.* to continue to exist for longer than expected

the knife. Confess? Did it mean that he was to confess? To give himself up and be put to
85 death? He laughed. He felt that the idea was monstrous. Besides, even if he did confess, who
would believe him? There was no trace of the murdered man anywhere. Everything belonging
to him had been destroyed. He himself had burned what had been below-stairs. The world
would simply say that he was mad.

They would shut him up if he persisted in his story... Yet it was his duty to confess, to suffer
90 public shame, and to make public atonement. There was a God who called upon men to tell
their sins to earth as well as to heaven. Nothing that he could do would cleanse him till he had
told his own sin. His sin? He shrugged his shoulders. The death of Basil Hallward seemed
very little to him. He was thinking of Hetty Merton. For it was an unjust mirror, this mirror of
his soul that he was looking at. Vanity? Curiosity? Hypocrisy? Had there been nothing more
95 in his renunciation than that? There had been something more. At least he thought so. But
who could tell?... No. There had been nothing more. Through vanity he had spared her. In
hypocrisy he had worn the mask of goodness. For curiosity's sake he had tried the denial of
self. He recognized that now.

But this murder—was it to dog him all his life? Was he always to be burdened by his
100 past? Was he really to confess? Never. There was only one bit of evidence left against him.
The picture itself—that was evidence. He would destroy it. Why had he kept it so long? Once
it had given him pleasure to watch it changing and growing old. Of late he had felt no such
pleasure. It had kept him awake at night. When he had been away, he had been filled with
terror lest other eyes should look upon it. It had brought melancholy across his passions.
105 Its mere memory had marred many moments of joy. It had been like conscience to him. Yes,
it had been concience. He would destroy it.

He looked round and saw the knife that had stabbed Basil Hallward. He had cleaned it
many times, till there was no stain left upon it. It was bright, and glistened. As it had killed the
painter, so it would kill the painter's work, and all that that meant. It would kill the past, and
110 when that was dead, he would be free. It would kill this monstrous soul-life, and without its
hideous warnings, he would be at peace. He seized the thing, and stabbed the picture with it.

There was a cry heard, and a crash. The cry was so horrible in its agony that the frightened
servants woke and crept out of their rooms.

After about a quarter of an hour, a policeman got the coachman and one of the footmen and
115 crept upstairs. They knocked, but there was no reply. They called out. Everything was still.
Finally, after vainly trying to force the door, they got on the roof and dropped down on to
the balcony. The windows yielded easily
—their bolts were old.

When they entered, they found hanging
120 upon the wall a splendid portrait of their
master as they had last seen him, in all the
wonder of his exquisite youth and beauty.
Lying on the floor was a dead man, in
evening dress, with a knife in his heart. He
125 was withered, wrinkled, and loathsome of
visage. It was not till they had examined
the rings that they recognized who it was.

atonement /əˈtəʊnmənt/ *n.* [U] actions showing you are sorry for doing sth. wrong in the past
cleanse /klenz/ *v.* ~ **sb. (of /from sth.)** (literary) to make sb. free from guilt or sin
renunciation /rɪˌnʌnsiˈeɪʃən/ *n.* [U] (formal) an act of stating publicly that you no longer believe sth. or that you are giving sth. up
dog /dɒg/ *v.* (of a problem or bad luck) to cause you trouble for a long time
glisten /ˈglɪsən/ *v.* to shine
yield /jiːld/ *v.* to move, bend or break because of pressure

Notes

1. Oscar Wilde

Oscar Wilde (1854—1900) was an Irish poet and dramatist, whose reputation rests upon his comic masterpieces Lady Windermere's Fan (1892) and The Importance of Being Earnest (1895). Among Wilde's other best-known works are his only novel *The Picture of Dorian Gray* (1891) and his fairy tales, especially *The Happy Prince*.

Enthralled by his own exquisite portrait, Dorian Gray exchanges his soul for eternal youth and beauty. Influenced by his friend Lord Henry Wotton, he is drawn into a corrupt double life; indulging his desires in secret while remaining a gentleman in the eyes of polite society. Only his portrait bears the traces of his decadence.

2. Lord Henry

He is a nobleman and a close friend of Basil Hallward. His pleasure-seeking philosophy of "new Hedonism," which espouses garnering experiences that stimulate the senses without regard for conventional morality, plays a vital role in Dorian's development.

3. James Vane

James Vane is brother of Sibyl, Dorian's love. Vane tracks Dorian down, intending to kill him because he has wronged her but Vane is accidentally shot and killed when he intrudes on a hunting party.

4. Alan Campbell

A stuttering and seemingly harmless man, and a professor of Defense against the Dark Arts at Hogwarts. Quirrel appears as nervous and squirelly as his name suggests for most of the story. It turns out later, however, that Quirrel has faked his withdrawing meekness and is actually a cold-blooded conniver.

5. Basil Hallward

Basil Hallward is an artist, and a friend of Lord Henry. Basil becomes obsessed with Dorian after meeting him at a party. He claims that Dorian possesses a beauty so rare that it has helped him realize a new kind of art; through Dorian, he finds "the lines of a fresh school." Dorian also helps Basil realize his artistic potential, as the portrait of Dorian that Basil paints proves to be his masterpiece.

6. Hetty Merton

Hetty Merton is a simple village girl (mentioned in paragraph one), he started to fall in love with when Dorian was staying alone at a small inn in the country.

Comprehension

1. What can you tell about Dorian Grey from the opening of this story?
2. What might the girl mentioned have possessed that Dorian Gray had lost?
3. What was happening to the portrait of Dorian Gray that he kept hidden in his attic?
4. Why had Dorian's one good deed not changed the portrait for the better?
5. What was the outcome of stabbing the portrait of Dorian Gray?

6. What is the moral of this story?

Further Study

📖 For those who want to read more of Joseph Addison's essays, here are some of his most famous works. You can find them in the *Norton Anthology of English Literature.*

- Thoughts in Westminster Abbey
- Sir Roger

You can also refer to *Life of Addison* from *Lives of the Poets* by Samuel Johnson to learn more about Addison's biography and criticism of his works.

📖 To read more on Oscar Wilde at http://www.victorianweb.org/authors/wilde/wildeov.html.

Unit 14

Human Quest

Unit Goals

- To learn to put the world's disparities in perspective
- To learn how to introduce subject matter in writing
- To use impersonal nouns as the subject of the sentence
- To practice non-rhetorical devices for emphasis

Before Reading

1. Work in a group of four to speculate what guns, germs and steel represent in Jared Diamond's book *Guns, Germs and Steel: The Fates of Human Societies* (1997) and then compare your answers with reviews of the book on the Internet.
2. Listen to the video clip in which Diamond explains his motivation for writing the book at http://www.ucla.edu/spotlight/archive/html_2004_2005/fac0505_jared_diamond.html#.

A Glimpse into the Text

Jared Diamond is a physiologist and evolutionary biologist. He was awarded the 1998 Pulitzer Prize for nonfiction for his *Guns, Germs, and Steel: The Fates of Human Societies* (1997). The following essay was taken from the prologue of this eminent book. It asks the question "Why are there inequalities between different cultures of the world?", then proceeds to answer that question from a biogeological perspective.

Geographer and biologist Jared Diamond gets a lesson in bow-and-arrow hunting in Papua New Guinea.

Text A

Yali's Question

Jared Diamond[1]
(Abridged and Edited)

We all know that history has proceeded very differently for peoples from different parts of the globe. In the 13,000 years since the end of the last Ice Age,[2] some parts of the world developed literate industrial societies with metal tools, other parts developed only non-literate farming societies, and others retained societies of hunter-gatherers with stone tools. Those historical inequalities have cast long shadows on the modern world, because the literate societies with metal tools have conquered or exterminated the other societies. While those differences constitute the most basic fact of world history, the reasons for them remain uncertain and controversial. This puzzling question of their origins was posed to me 25 years ago in a simple, personal form.

In July 1972 I was walking along a beach on the tropical island of New Guinea,[3] where as a biologist I studied bird evolution. I had already heard about a remarkable local politician named Yali, who was touring the district then. By chance, Yali and I were walking in the same direction on that day, and he overtook me. We walked together for an hour, talking during the whole time.

Yali radiated charisma and energy. His eyes flashed in a mesmerising way. He talked confidently about himself, but he also asked lots of probing questions and listened intently. Our conversation began with a subject then on every New Guinean's mind—the rapid pace of political developments. Papua New Guinea, as Yali's nation is now called, was at that time still administered by Australia as a mandate of the United Nations, but independence was in the air. Yali explained to me his role in getting local people to prepare for self-government.

After a while, Yali turned the conversation and began to quiz me. He had never been outside New Guinea and had not been educated beyond high school, but his curiosity was insatiable. First, he wanted to know about my work on New Guinea birds (including how much I got paid for it). I explained to him how different groups of birds had colonised New Guinea over the course of millions of years. He then asked how the ancestors of his own people had reached New Guinea over the last tens of thousands of years, and how white Europeans had colonised New Guinea within the last 200 years.

The conversation remained friendly, even though the tension between the two societies that Yali and I represented was familiar to both of us. Two centuries ago, all New Guineans were still "living in the Stone Age." That is, they still used stone tools similar to those superseded in Europe by metal tools thousands of years ago, and they dwelt in villages not organised under any centralised political authority. Whites had arrived, imposed centralised government, and brought material goods whose value New Guineans instantly recognised, ranging from steel axes, matches, and medicines to clothing, soft drinks and umbrellas. In New Guinea, all these goods were referred to collectively as "cargo."

Many of the white colonialists openly despised New Guineans as "primitive." Even the least able of New Guinea's white "masters," as they were still called in 1972, enjoyed a far higher standard of living than New Guineans, higher even than charismatic politicians like Yali. Yet Yali had quizzed lots of whites as he was then quizzing me,

---

tropical /ˈtrɒpɪkəl/ adj. coming from, found in or typical of the tropics (one of the two imaginary lines drawn around the 23° 7′ north or south of the equator)
overtake /ˌəʊvəˈteɪk/ v. (especially BrE) to go past a moving vehicle or person ahead of you because you are going faster than they are
charisma /kəˈrɪzmə/ n. [U] the powerful personal quality that some people have to attract and impress other people
flash /flæʃ/ v. to shine very brightly for a short time
mesmerising /ˈmezməraɪzɪŋ/ adj. enchanting, charming
probing /ˈprəʊbɪŋ/ adj. intended to discover the truth
mandate /ˈmændeɪt/ n. the power given to a country to govern another country or region, especially in the past
insatiable /ɪnˈseɪʃəbəl/ adj. always wanting more of sth.
supersede /ˌsuːpəˈsiːd/ v. [often passive] to take the place of sth./sb. that is considered to be old-fashioned or no longer the best available
charismatic /ˌkærɪzˈmætɪk/ adj. having charisma

and I had quizzed lots of New Guineans. He and I both knew perfectly well that New Guineas are on the average at least as smart as Europeans. All those things must have been on Yali's mind when, with yet another penetrating glance of his flashing eyes, he asked me, "Why is it that you white people developed so much cargo and brought it to New Guinea, but we black people had little cargo of our own?"

It was a simple question that went to the heart of life as Yali experienced it. Yes, there still is a huge difference between the lifestyle of the average New Guinean and that of the average European or American. Comparable differences separate the lifestyles of other peoples of the world as well. Those huge disparities must have potent causes that one might think would be obvious.

Yet Yali's apparently simple question is a difficult one to answer. I didn't have an answer then. Professional historians still disagree about the solution; most are no longer even asking the question.

Although Yali's question concerned only the contrasting lifestyles of New Guineans and of European whites, it can be extended to a larger set of contrasts within the modern world. Peoples of Eurasian origin, especially those still living in Europe and eastern Asia, plus those transplanted to North America, dominate the modern world in wealth and power. Other peoples, including most Africans, have thrown off European colonial domination but remain far behind in wealth and power. Still other peoples, such as the aboriginal inhabitants of Australia, the Americas, and southernmost Africa, are no longer even masters of their own lands but have been decimated, subjugated, and in some cases even exterminated by European colonialists.

Thus, questions about inequality in the modern world can be reformulated as follows. Why did wealth and power become distributed as they now are, rather than in some other way? For instance, why weren't Native Americans, Africans, and Aboriginal Australians the ones who decimated, subjugated, or exterminated Europeans and Asians?

We can easily push the question back one step. As of the year A.D. 1500, when Europe's worldwide colonial expansion was just beginning, peoples on different continents already differed greatly in technology and political organisation. Much of Europe, Asia and North Africa was the site of metal-equipped states or empires, some of them on the threshold of industrialisation. Two Native American peoples, the Aztecs[4] and the Incas,[5] ruled over empires with stone tools. Parts of sub-Saharan Africa were divided among small states or chiefdoms with iron tools. Most other peoples—including all those of Australia and New Guinea, many Pacific islands, much of the Americas, and small parts of sub-Saharan Africa—lived as farming tribes or even still as hunter-gatherer bands using stone tools.

Of course, those technological and political differences as of A.D. 1500 were the immediate cause of the modern world's inequalities. Empires with steel weapons were able to conquer or exterminate tribes with weapons of stone and wood. How, though, did the world get to be the way it was in A.D. 1500?

Once again, we can easily push this question back one step further, by drawing

potent /'pəʊtənt/ adj. having a strong effect on your body or mind
transplant /træns'plɑːnt/ v. to move sb./sth. to a different place or environment
aboriginal /ˌæbə'rɪdʒənəl/ adj. relating to the original people living in Australia
decimate /'desɪmeɪt/ v. [usually passive] to kill large numbers of animals, plants or people in a particular area
subjugate /'sʌbdʒʊgeɪt/ v. [usually passive] (formal) to defeat sb./sth.; to gain control over sb./sth.

on written histories and archaeological discoveries. Until the end of the last Ice Age, around 11,000 B.C., all peoples on all continents were still hunter-gatherers. Different rates of development on different continents, from 11,000 B.C. to A.D. 1500, were what led to the technological and political inequalities of A.D. 1500. While Aboriginal Australians and many Native Americans remained hunter-gatherers, most of Eurasia and much of the Americas and sub-Saharan Africa gradually developed agriculture, herding, metallurgy, and complex political organisation. Parts of Eurasia, and one area of the Americas, independently developed writing as well. However, each of these new developments appeared earlier in Eurasia than elsewhere. For instance, the mass production of bronze tools, which was just beginning in the South American Andes[6] in the centuries before A.D. 1500, was already established in parts of Eurasia 4,000 years earlier. The stone technology of the Tasmanians,[7] when first encountered by European explorers in A.D. 1642, was simpler than what was prevalent in parts of Upper Paleolithic Europe tens of thousands of years earlier.

> metallurgy /me'tælədʒɪ/ n. [u] the scientific study of metals and their uses
> prevalent /'prevələnt/ adj. common at a particular time or in a particular place
> paleolithic /,pælɪəʊ'lɪθɪk/ adj. from or connected with the early part of the Stone Age
> disparate /'dɪspərɪt/ adj. (of two or more things) so different from each other that they cannot be compared or cannot work together

Thus we can finally rephrase the question about the modern world's inequalities as follows: why did human development proceed at such different rates on different continents? Those disparate rates constitute history's broadest pattern and my book's subject.

More about the Text

1. Jared Diamond

Jared Diamond (1937—) is an American evolutionary biologist, physiologist, bio-geographer and nonfiction author. He is best known for the Pulitzer Prize-winning book, *Guns, Germs, and Steel* (1997). He also received the National Medal of Science in 1999.

Jared Diamond won the Pulitzer Prize for his *Guns, Germs, and Steel* (1997) in which he maintains that the people of Europe and Asia were able to conquer the indigenous peoples of America, Africa, and Australia not from any innate superiority but through an accident of geography, which allowed them to develop advanced weaponry, immunity to certain diseases, and complex social structures.

2. Ice Age

Ice Age is the most recent glacial period, which occurred during the Pleistocene epoch.

3. New Guinea

It is an island in the southwest Pacific Ocean north of Australia. The western half is part of Indonesia, and the eastern half forms the major portion of Papua New Guinea.

4. **Aztecs**

It is a member of a people of central Mexico whose civilization was at its height at the time of the Spanish conquest in the early 16th century.

5. **Incas**

It is a member of the group of Quechuan peoples of highland Peru who established an empire from northern Ecuador to central Chile before the Spanish conquest.

6. **South American Andes**

It is a mountain system of western South America extending more than 8,045 km along the Pacific coast from Venezuela to Tierra del Fuego.

7. **Tasmanians**

It is the inhabitants of an island off the southeastern coast of Australia.

Check Your Understanding

1. Simply stated, what is the historical question that the author will address in this work?
2. How does the author describe Yali? What is the author's opinion of Yali and his compatriots?
3. Why is Yali's apparently simple question difficult for the author to answer? How does the author interpret Yali's question? Where in the text does the author reformulate Yali's question?
4. According to the author, how many years ago were all societies at the same level of development?
5. What has resulted from the historical inequalities since the end of the last Ice Age?
6. What factor does the author outright dismiss as an explanation for different rates of technological development around the world?
7. In which region of the world did technological advancement begin first? What did such advancement lead to?
8. What elements are considered important as the author evaluates the developments of a society?
9. What perception would you make of Yali, as a politician, and the author, as a biologist?

Paraphrasing

1. Those historical inequalities have cast long shadows on the modern world, because the literate societies with metal tools have conquered or exterminated the other societies.
2. It was a simple question that went to the heart of life as Yali experienced it.
3. Those huge disparities must have potent causes that one might think would be obvious.
4. Much of Europe, Asia and North Africa was the site of metal-equipped states or empires, some of them on the threshold of industrialisation.
5. Different rates of development on different continents, from 11,000 B.C. to A.D. 1500, were what led to the technological and political inequalities of A.D. 1500.

Some Information about English Style

1. Introducing the subject matter

There are different ways for a writer to introduce the subject matter in expository writing. In the present selection, the author takes Yali's simple question as a starting point to discuss the issue of concern, which is his inquiries into the inequalities of the world.

The author first tells of meeting with Yali and introduces Yali's question "Why is it that you white people developed so much cargo and brought it to New Guinea, but we black people had little cargo of our own?" The question is reformulated as "Why did wealth and power become distributed as they now are, rather than in some other way? For instance, why weren't Native Americans, Africans, and Aboriginal Australians the ones who decimated, subjugated, or exterminated Europeans and Asians?" At the end of the selection, the question is further rephrased as "Why did human development proceed at such different rates on different continents?" Finally the author concludes that "Those disparate rates constitute history's broadest pattern and my book's subject." Thus, the reader is led, step by step, to the author's dissertation. The author's singular pursuit of Yali's question as a device to introduce the subject of the book is fresh and illuminating.

Using questions to introduce the subject matter is an effective device in essay writing. Examples:

(1) Have you ever lingered before a stall packed with different brands of soap? Almost every American is faced with the dilemma of which kind of soap to buy.

(2) Do you favor living in a big city or in the countryside? Convenience or tranquility? This choice is always the first to enter the mind of anyone who tries to find his den.

2. Impersonal nouns as subject

Look at the following pairs of examples. Sentence A is taken from the text.
Pair 1:
A: *The **conversation** remained friendly, even though the **tension** between the two societies that Yali and I represented was familiar to both of us.*
B: *Yali and I had a friendly conversation throughout even though we felt the tension between the two societies we represented.*
Pair 2:
A: ***All those things** must have been on Yali's mind when, with yet another penetrating glance of his flashing eyes, he asked me....*
B: *He must have been pondering on all those things when... Yali asked me....*
Pair 3:
A: *As of the year A.D. 1500, when Europe's worldwide **colonial expansion** was just beginning, peoples on different continents already differed greatly in technology and political organisation.*
B: *As of the year A.D. 1500, when Europe was just beginning to expand its power throughout the world, peoples on different continents....*

While the two sentences in each pair express the same meaning, Sentence A, which takes an impersonal subject either in the form of an action noun or noun phrase, is more formal in style.

There are three common kinds of impersonal nouns used as subjects:

A. nouns expressing emotions, e.g.
—*Alarm* began to take entire possession of him.
—A great *elation* came over them.

B. nouns describing actions, e.g.
—Our *conversation* began with a subject then on every New Guinean's mind—the rapid pace of political developments (Text A).
—Another hour's *ride* will bring us to the foot of the hill.

C. Nouns denoting natural phenomena
—Dense *fog* prevented us from setting out on time.
—*Snow slides* drove the mountaineers into the campsite.

3. Non-rhetorical devices for emphasis

Rhetorical devices such as repetition, parallelism, hyperbole, and antithesis are often used for the purpose of emphasis. There are, however, other means to achieve the same effect. Look at these sentences from the text:

(1) *How, **though**, did the world get to be the way it was in A.D. 1500?*
(2) ***Even** the least able of New Guinea's white "masters," as they were **still** called in 1972, enjoyed a **far** higher standard of living than New Guineans, higher **even than** charismatic politicians like Yali.*

Words such as *ever, even, though, what / how on earth*, etc. are lexical devices to achieve the effect of emphasis.

Look at further examples from the text and note how the author creates emphasis:

(1) *This puzzling question of their origins **was posed** to me 25 years ago in a simple, personal form.* (Passive voice)
(2) ***It was** a simple question **that** went to the heart of life as Yali experienced it.* (It is... that....)
(3) *Still other peoples, such as the aboriginal inhabitants of Australia, the Americas, and southernmost Africa, are **no longer even** masters of their own lands **but** have been decimated, subjugated, and in some cases even exterminated by European colonialists.* (no longer...but)
(4) ***Why is it that** you white people developed so much cargo and brought it to New Guinea, but we black people had little cargo of our own?* (Why is it that....)

The use of passive voice and structures such as "It is... that...." "no longer... but" "Why is it that...." are syntactic devices for emphatic purposes.

Here are further examples of syntactic emphasis:
—***Do** tell me the reason, please.* (do + verb)
—***What** a pretty house you've got!* (What/How...!)
—***Extremely** sorry I am for my mistakes.* (Inversion)

It is possible to resort to other measures for emphasis, such as:
(1) Using "**all + noun**" phrases, e.g.
—*The students are **all ears** to his talk.*
—*She is **all beauty**.*
(2) Using "**adj. + and + adj.**" structure, e.g.
—*He rose **bright and early**.* (very early)
—*His father is a man who **forgives and forgets**.*

Practice

Building word power

1. Complete each of the sentences with an appropriate form of the words provided.

(1) **remain**
   A. It _____ true that sport is about competing well, not winning.
   B. I kept some of his books and gave away the _____.
   C. She fed the _____ of her lunch to the dog.

(2) **radiate**
   A. He _____ self-confidence and optimism.
   B. The bride looks _____.
   C. Over exposure to ultraviolet _____ is very harmful to the skin.

(3) **collect**
   A. What day do they _____ the rubbish?
   B. She always stays cool, calm and _____ in a crisis.
   C. A nation seems to inherit a _____ consciousness.

(4) **compare**
   A. Inflation is now at a rate _____ with that in other European countries.
   B. She was then living in _____ comfort.
   C. In terms of price there's no _____.
   D. It is a diamond beyond _____.

(5) **prevail**
   A. The _____ view seems to be that they will find her guilty.
   B. These prejudices are particularly _____ among people living in the North.
   C. The speaker talked about the _____ of violence on TV.

2. Complete the idioms and collocations.

(1) Independence was in the air (air)
   A. There is romance _____. (air)
   B. Even when he became a star he didn't have any _____. (air)
   C. We will be back _____ tomorrow morning at 7. (air)
   D. Our travel plans are still _____. (air)

(2) soft drinks; hard liquor (soft, hard)
   A. _____ wood; _____ wood
   B. _____ sell; _____ sell
   C. _____ ware; _____ ware
   D. _____-hearted; _____ hearted

(3) **flash**
   A. That brilliant poem he wrote long ago was just _____; he has produced nothing since.
   B. I will be back _____.
   C. He's always _____ money _____.
   D. I came to that point with _____.

(4) dog
   A. The man _____ after he started drinking.
   B. The Smiths settled down, bought a house and _____.
   C. Love me, _____.
   D. It is hot today, but then, what can you expect in _____?

3. **Complete the sentences with an appropriate word from the box. Note their differences.**

discrepant	disparity	incongruous
contrast	inconsistent	inequality

   (1) English weather is very _____; one moment it's raining and the next it's sunny.
   (2) The two witnesses gave widely _____ testimony.
   (3) Income _____ have narrowed sharply.
   (4) Glaring _____ exists between the rich and poor.
   (5) Boots look _____ with evening dress.
   (6) Let's have the two together to show the _____.
   (7) _____ in wealth cause social unrest.

Grammar and Usage

   (1) 护士探查伤口以确定其大小。(probe)
   (2) 那次轰炸之后，我们的房子荡然无存。(remain)
   (3) 政府着手缓和两国的紧张关系。(tension)
   (4) 世界强国时常对他国实施经济制裁。(impose)
   (5) 红十字会赈济水灾灾民。(administer)

Improving your writing style

1. **Develop a question (or questions) to introduce the following topic sentences.**

   (1) _____
   _____?
   DNA is responsible for the tremendous physical variety within the human race.

   (2) _____
   _____?
   Many of the 20th century fantasies will magically turn into reality in the new century, with the development of new technology.

   (3) _____
   _____?
   It always seems difficult to decide what kind of company you want to join when you graduate afresh from college.

   (4) _____
   _____?
   With the steady improvement of the people's living standard, a great many city dwellers take up the hobby of keeping pets.

2. Rewrite the following sentences with impersonal subjects.
  (1) The old man was suffering from disappointment and grief for days after receiving his daughter's letter from Dover.
  (2) Rebecca was seized with an inexpressible pang of envy witnessing the happiness of the young girls around her.
  (3) We took a few steps along the pebble path and saw a splendid hall before us.
  (4) Peeping through the door, Ms. Hays was horrified to see a dead woman in the sofa bed.
  (5) He is in town because there is some business for him to tend to.
  (6) I am not able to get such a good opportunity.
  (7) I suddenly thought of an idea.

3. Rewrite the following sentences to emphasize the italicized part.
  (1) *You look nice* today.
  (2) *Who* can it be?
  (3) *Why* didn't you say so?
  (4) *Where* did he find this old car?
  (5) He arrived in Beijing *a month later*.
  (6) We had *a good time* last night.
  (7) *Wonderful!*
  (8) The plane landed *safely*.
  (9) I was *very eager* to see you.
  (10) Her son was *wise*, but her daughter was *silly*.

Writing task

Fill in the following grid with appropriate terms for historical societies and their symbols. Write an essay to compare and contrast two societies you choose from the grid.

society	technology	agriculture	literacy
Societies of hunter-gatherers			
Non-literate farming societies			
Literate farming societies			
Industrial societies			
Information societies			

Text B

The Wanderer from *Thus Spoke Zarathustra*

Friedrich Nietzsche[1]

(Abridged)

Friedrich Nietzsche (1844—1900) ranks among the most influential of modern

Western philosophers. In Thus Spoke Zarathustra, the reader finds an expression of what Nietzsche named "the will to power." Living creatively, overcoming obstacles, mastering oneself, and successfully exerting one's will to power—although an act that could entail danger, pain, lies, deceptions, and masks—would result in enduring satisfaction and pleasure. Nietzsche's character, Zarathustra, embraces the will to power, and through a powerful metaphorical account of his adventures, Nietzsche attempts to persuade us all to do the same.

It was around midnight when Zarathustra made his way over the ridge of the island, that he might reach the other shore by early morning: for there he wanted to board a ship. On that shore there was a good roadstead at which foreign ships too liked to drop anchor; and these would take on board people who wanted to leave the Isles of the Blest² and cross the sea. As Zarathustra was climbing the mountain, he thought on the way of the many lonely wanderings he had undertaken since his youth, and of how many mountains and ridges and summits he had already climbed.

I am a wanderer and a mountain-climber, he said to his heart. I do not love the plains, and it seems that I cannot sit still for long.

And now whatever may come to me yet as fate and experience—a wandering will be in it and a climbing of mountains: in the end one experiences only oneself.

The time has flowed past when accidents could still befall me; and what could still fall to me now that would not already be my own!

It simply comes back, it finally comes home to me—my own self, and what of myself has long been abroad and scattered among all things and accidents.

And one more thing do I know: I stand now before my last summit and before that which has been saved up for me for the longest time. Ah, on my hardest way I must set out! Ah, I have begun my loneliest wandering!

But whoever is of my kind does not avoid such an hour, the hour that says to him: Only now are you going your way of greatness! Summit and abyss—they are now joined in one!

You are going your way of greatness: now what had hitherto been your ultimate danger has become your ultimate refuge!

You are going your way of greatness: this must now be your best courage, that there is no longer any way behind you!

You are going your way of greatness; here no one shall creep after you! Your own foot has effaced the way behind you, over which is written: Impossibility.

And if you now lack all ladders, you

---

ridge /rɪdʒ/ n. a narrow area of high land along the top of a line of hills

roadstead /ˈrəʊdsted/ n. a sheltered offshore anchorage area for ships

anchor /ˈæŋkə/ n. a heavy metal object that is attached to a rope or chain and dropped over the side of a ship or boat to keep it in one place

summit /ˈsʌmɪt/ n. the highest point of sth., especially the top of a mountain

abyss /əˈbɪs/ n. [usually sing.] (formal or literary) a very deep wide space or hole that seems to have no bottom

hitherto /ˌhɪðəˈtuː/ adv. (formal) until now

ultimate /ˈʌltɪmət/ adj. [only before noun] happening at the end of a long process

refuge /ˈrefjuːdʒ/ n. ~ (from sb. or sth.) a place, person or thing that provides shelter or protection for sb./sth.

efface /ɪˈfeɪs/ v. (formal) to make sth. disappear; to remove sth.

must learn how to climb on your own head: how else could you want to climb upward?

On your own head and away beyond your own heart! Now what was mildest in you must yet become what is hardest.

50 Whoever has constantly protected himself will at last become sickly from so much protection. Praised be what makes hard! I do not praise the land where butter and honey—flow!

One must learn to look away from oneself in order to see much:—this hardness is necessary for every climber of mountains.

But whoever tries with an importunate eye to understand, how should he see more
55 than the foregrounds of all things!

But you, O Zarathustra, wanted to see the grounds of all things and their backgrounds: so you must now climb over yourself—onward, upward, until you have even your stars beneath you!

Yes! To look down upon myself and even upon my stars: that alone would I call my
60 summit; that is still left for me as my ultimate summit!—

Thus spoke Zarathustra to himself as he climbed, consoling his heart with hard sayings: for he was sore at heart as never before. And when he came to the top of the mountain-ridge, behold, there lay the other sea spread out before him; and he stood still and was silent for a long time. And the night was cold at this height, and clear and bright with stars.

65 I recognize my lot, he said at last in sorrow. Well then! I am prepared. My ultimate solitude has just begun.

Ah, this black and sorrowful sea beneath me! Ah, this pregnant night-like moroseness! Ah, fate and sea! To you must I now climb down!

Before my highest mountain I stand and before my longest wandering: therefore I must
70 first descend deeper than I have ever done before:

—deeper into pain than I have ever descended, even into its blackest flood! Thus my fate wills it. Well then! I am prepared.

Where do the highest mountains come from? I once asked. Then I learned that they come from out of the sea.

75 The evidence is inscribed in their stone and in the walls of their summits. It is from the deepest that the highest must come to its height.—

Thus spoke Zarathustra on the peak of the mountain, where it was cold; but when he drew near to the sea and stood at last alone beneath the cliff, he had grown weary on the way and fuller of yearning than ever before.

80 Everything is still asleep now, he said. Even the sea is asleep. Drunk with sleep and strangely its eye regards me.

But its breath is warm; that I feel. And I also feel that it is dreaming. In its dreams
85 it writhes upon hard pillows.

Hark! Hark! How it groans from evil memories! Or from evil expectations?

Ah, I am sad along with you, you dark monster, and even angry at myself for your
90 sake.

---

importunate /ɪmˈpɔːtʃʊnɪt/ *adj.* (formal) asking for things many times in a way that is annoying

moroseness /məˈrəʊsnɪs/ *n.* the state of being unhappy, bad-tempered and not talking very much

inscribe /ɪnˈskraɪb/ *v.* ~ A (on/in B) to write or cut words, your name, etc. onto sth.

cliff /klɪf/ *n.* a high area of rock with a very steep side, often at the edge of the sea or ocean

yearning /ˈjɜːnɪŋ/ *n.* [C,U] ~ (for sb./sth.) (written) a strong and emotional desire

writhe /raɪð/ *v.* ~ (about/around) (in/with sth.) to twist or move your body without stopping, often because you are in great pain

hark /hɑːk/ *v.* (old use) listen

Alas, that my hand has insufficient strength! Verily, I would dearly like to redeem you from your evil dreams!

And as Zarathustra spoke thus, he
95 laughed at himself with bitterness and a heavy heart. What, Zarathustra! he said. Would you even sing consolation to the sea?

alas /əˈlæs/ *exclamation* (old use or literary) used to show you are sad or sorry	
verily /ˈverɪli/ *adv.* (old use) really; truly	
redeem /rɪˈdiːm/ *v.* to save sb. from evil	
blissful /ˈblɪsfəl/ *adj.* extremely happy; showing happiness	
caress /kəˈres/ *v.* to touch sb./sth. gently, especially in a sexual way or in a way that shows affection	

Ah, you loving fool, Zarathustra, over-blissful in your trusting! But thus have you always
100 been: you have always approached trustingly all that is terrible.

You have always wanted to caress every monster. A puff of warm breath, a soft tuft on the paw—and at once you were ready to love and to lure it.

For *love* is the danger of the loneliest, love of anything *if only it is alive*! Laughable, verily, are my folly and my modesty in love!

105 Thus spoke Zarathustra and laughed at himself a second time: but then he thought of the friends he had left behind—and as if he had wronged them with his thoughts, he was angry at what he had thought. And it soon happened that the laugher wept:—from wrath and yearning Zarathustra wept bitterly.

Notes

1. Friedrich Nietzsche

Friedrich Nietzsche (1844—1900) is a German philosopher who reasoned that Christianity's emphasis on the afterlife makes its believers less able to cope with earthly life. He argued that the ideal human, the Übermensch (Superhuman), would be able to channel passions creatively instead of suppressing them. His written works include *Beyond Good and Evil* (1886) and *Thus Spoke Zarathustra* (1883—1892).

Thus Spoke Zarathustra relates the sayings and doings of Zarathustra in a style reminiscent of the Gospels in the Bible and it is laden with biblical allusions, but it also harshly condemns Christianity and mocks the idea of a holy scripture or a holy person. Zarathustra, brimming with wisdom and love, wants to teach humanity about the overman. The overman is someone who is free from all the prejudices and moralities of human society, and who creates his own values and purpose. The present essay is taken from Part III of the book.

Friedrich Nietzsche

2. the Isles of the Blest

In the **Fortunate Isles**, also called the **Isles** (or **Islands**) **of the Blessed**, heroes and other favored mortals in Greek mythology and Celtic mythology were received by the gods into a blissful paradise. These islands were thought to lie in the Western Ocean near the encircling River Oceanus; the Madeira and the Canary Islands have sometimes been cited as possible matches.

Comprehension

1. *Thus Spoke Zarathustra* operates wholly on the level of metaphor. What is the foremost metaphor in this selection from the book?
2. Why does Zarathustra not like to travel over the plains?
3. What does the climb to the "last mountain top" signify to Zarathustra?
4. "One must learn to look away from oneself in order to see much." What can Zarathustra mean by this?
5. Why does Zarathustra experience sorrow at the top of the mountain?
6. In paragraph 31, Zarathustra comments on himself: "you have always approached trustingly all that is terrible." Could you find examples to support his judgment?
7. In the text there are quite a few instances of antonyms such as "summit" and "abyss." Can you find more pairs?
8. Why was Zarathustra angry at the end of the text?

Further Study

The web page http://www.paulagordon.com/shows/diamond/ provides information on Diamond on the Paula Gordon show (radio live conversation, Atlanta, Georgia, USA.) on the issue of inequality of human development. An excerpt of their talk in audio form can be accessed.

The web page http://www.pbs.org/gunsgermssteel/index.html tells you about the threepart TV series of *Guns, Germs and Steel* based on the book of the same title. You can also find further readings and other useful links on Jared Diamond.

The web page http://www.ucla.edu/spotlight/archive/html_2004_2005/fac0505_jared_diamond.html# provides video clips about Jared Diamond.

Vocabulary

生词总表

A

ablution	n.	Unit 6—B
abolish	v.	Unit 1—B
abolitionist	n.	Unit 8—B
aboriginal	adj.	Unit 14—A
abreast	adv.	Unit 10—A
abstainer	n.	Unit 5—B
absurdity	n.	Unit 6—A
abyss	n.	Unit 14—B
acclaim	n.	Unit 11—B
accompaniment	n.	Unit 10—A
activism	n.	Unit 8—B
addled	adj.	Unit 13—A
adorn	v.	Unit 10—B
advocate	v.	Unit 6—A
affiliate	v.	Unit 11—A
afford	v.	Unit 11—A
affront	n.	Unit 3—A
aggressive	adj.	Unit 3—A
alas		Unit 14—B
alien	adj.	Unit 8—A
allergic	adj.	Unit 6—B
ambivalent	adj.	Unit 6—B
ambush	n.	Unit 4—B
Americanise	v.	Unit 9—B
ample	adj.	Unit 3—B
anarchism	n.	Unit 8—B
anatomy	n.	Unit 2—B
anchor	n.	Unit 14—B
anomaly	n.	Unit 8—B
apology	n.	Unit 7—A
appendage	n.	Unit 11—A
appraisal	n.	Unit 3—A
archaism	n.	Unit 6—A
arena	n.	Unit 8—B
armload	n.	Unit 7—B
arrant	adj.	Unit 9—A
as it were		Unit 2—A
assiduous	adj.	Unit 4—B
assiduously	adv.	Unit 4—B
astute	adj.	Unit 6—B
asunder	adv.	Unit 8—A

atonement	n.	Unit 13—B
attribute	n.	Unit 9—B

B

bar	v.	Unit 11—B
barker	n.	Unit 7—A
barter for sth		Unit 13—A
be embroidered with		Unit 13—A
beachhead	n.	Unit 1—B
beagle	n.	Unit 5—A
beat a (hasty) retreat		Unit 5—A
bebop	n.	Unit 9—B
befall	v.	Unit 13—A
belabor	v.	Unit 1—B
berserk	adj.	Unit 7—A
beveled	adj.	Unit 5—B
bewitching	adj.	Unit 4—A
blissful	adj.	Unit 14—B
blister	n./v.	Unit 12—B
blow off		Unit 12—A
blur	v.	Unit 6—A
boll	n.	Unit 11—A
booby	n.	Unit 2—B
book	v.	Unit 4—B
bottle sth up		Unit 12—A
boudoir	n.	Unit 7—A
brass	n.	Unit 7—A
brazen	adj.	Unit 4—A
bridle	v.	Unit 9—A
brisk	adj.	Unit 5—B
buck	v.	Unit 9—A
budge	v.	Unit 4—B
bulk	n.	Unit 13—A
bureau	n.	Unit 7—B
bust	v.	Unit 12—A
by all accounts		Unit 4—B

C

cackle	v.	Unit 7—A
cadence	n.	Unit 5—A
calamity	n.	Unit 13—A

225

calling	n.	Unit 11—A	cosmology	n.	Unit 7—B
canary-colored	adj.	Unit 4—A	countenance	n.	Unit 13—A
capacious	adj.	Unit 8—A	countess	n.	Unit 8—A
caress	v.	Unit 14—B	cover	v.	Unit 3—A
carnage	n.	Unit 7—A	cramped	adj.	Unit 8—A
cascade	n.	Unit 10—B	crib	n.	Unit 2—A
cassock	n.	Unit 5—B	cross my heart		Unit 12—A
cast into		Unit 13—A	crummy	adj.	Unit 9—B
catechism	n.	Unit 6—B	Crusade	n.	Unit 8—A
caucus	n.	Unit 8—B	current	n.	Unit 8—B
caution	n.	Unit 12—A			
cavity	n.	Unit 2—A	**D**		
celebrated	adj.	Unit 13—A			
celluloid	n.	Unit 7—A	dab	v.	Unit 10—A
chagrined	adj.	Unit 3—B	dandy	n.	Unit 10—B
chaos	n.	Unit 6—A	dash	v.	Unit 10—B
charisma	n.	Unit 14—A	deadlock	n.	Unit 1—A
charismatic	adj.	Unit 14—A	debar	v.	Unit 2—B
chauffeur	n.	Unit 3—B	decadence	n.	Unit 6—A
chivalry	n.	Unit 7—B	decay	n.	Unit 6—A
chloroform	v.	Unit 7—A	decimate	v.	Unit 14—A
christening	n.	Unit 5—B	decorum	n.	Unit 3—B
chromium	n.	Unit 9—B	decree	v.	Unit 2—B
chubby	adj.	Unit 2—B	deformity	n.	Unit 13—A
churchwarden	n.	Unit 5—B	delicate	adj.	Unit 3—B
churn	v.	Unit 7—B	delicatessen (also deli)	n.	Unit 9—A
circumlocutory	adj.	Unit 6—B	deliver	v.	Unit 1—B
civility	n.	Unit 1—B	delusion	n.	Unit 13—A
clan	n.	Unit 7—B	demolish	v.	Unit 9—B
clanspeople	n.	Unit 7—B	derail	v.	Unit 3—A
clasp	v.	Unit 10—A	despairing	adj.	Unit 4—A
cleanse	v.	Unit 13—B	devastate	v.	Unit 1—A
cliché	n.	Unit 6—B	deviation	n.	Unit 8—A
cliff	n.	Unit 14—B	diffidence	n.	Unit 11—B
colony	n.	Unit 3—A	dignity	n.	Unit 5—B
commentator	n.	Unit 9—B	disarming	adj.	Unit 5—B
commerce	n.	Unit 1—B	discard	v.	Unit 6—B
commit	v.	Unit 1—B	discourse	n.	Unit 11—A
compatriot	n.	Unit 9—A	discredit	v.	Unit 11—B
complacent	adj.	Unit 9—A	discreet	adj.	Unit 11—B
complication	n.	Unit 13—A	discrepancy	n.	Unit 3—B
composite	adj.	Unit 7—A	disparate	adj.	Unit 14—A
con	v.	Unit 2—B	disport	v.	Unit 11—B
conceive	v.	Unit 11—A	dissect	v.	Unit 2—B
confound	v.	Unit 2—A	distemper	n.	Unit 13—A
connoisseur	n.	Unit 6—B	do sb in		Unit 7—A
connote	v.	Unit 8—B	documentation	n.	Unit 3—B
conscience	n.	Unit 1—A	dog	v.	Unit 13—B
contract	v.	Unit 6—B	dolt	n.	Unit 7—A
conversely	adv.	Unit 9—B	drift	v.	Unit 1—A
conviction	n.	Unit 1—A			

226

drone	n.	Unit 4—A
droop	v.	Unit 10—A
duchess	n.	Unit 8—A
dynamic	n.	Unit 8—B
dysfunction	n.	Unit 2—B

E

edge	v.	Unit 12—B
efface	v.	Unit 14—B
egalitarian	adj.	Unit 8—B
elixir	n.	Unit 12—B
elude	v.	Unit 3—B
embattled	adj.	Unit 1—B
embrace	v.	Unit 1—A
embryonic	adj.	Unit 11—A
endeavor	n.	Unit 1—B
engender	v.	Unit 4—B
engrave	v.	Unit 2—A
engulf	v.	Unit 1—A
enlist	v.	Unit 7—A
entrance	v.	Unit 12—A
entrancing	adj.	Unit 4—A
eradicate	v.	Unit 1—B
erode	v.	Unit 1—A
erupt	v.	Unit 3—A
etch	v.	Unit 7—A
etiology	n.	Unit 3—A
evaporate	v.	Unit 3—B
exasperat	v.	Unit 6—B
extravagance	n.	Unit 6—B

F

faction	n.	Unit 8—A
fag	n.	Unit 5—B
far-fetched	adj.	Unit 6—B
fawn	v.	Unit 8—A
fearsome	adj.	Unit 1—A
feature	v.	Unit 7—B
feminist	n.	Unit 8—B
fetch sb a blow		Unit 5—A
filament	n.	Unit 12—A
find	n.	Unit 9—B
flap	v.	Unit 10—A
flash	v.	Unit 14—A
flax	n.	Unit 11—A
flick	v.	Unit 10—A
flight	n.	Unit 10—B
fling	n.	Unit 7—B
fling	v.	Unit 5—A

flit	v.	Unit 12—B
flowery	adj.	Unit 11—B
flutter	v.	Unit 10—B
flyblown	adj.	Unit 6—A
foe	n.	Unit 1—B
folio	n.	Unit 8—A
fondle	v.	Unit 7—A
font	n.	Unit 5—B
forebear	n.	Unit 1—B
formulate	v.	Unit 1—B
fracture	v.	Unit 1—A
fragrance	n.	Unit 2—A
frai	adj.	Unit 10—A
fresh as a daisy		Unit 5—A
frightfully	adv.	Unit 4—A
frigid	adj.	Unit 1—B
frigidity	n.	Unit 9—A
frivolous	adj.	Unit 6—A
froth	v.	Unit 5—A
fumbling	adj.	Unit 7—A

G

gallop	v.	Unit 7—B
gape	v.	Unit 7—A
garbled	adj.	Unit 2—B
garish	adj.	Unit 9—B
gasp	v.	Unit 12—B
gender	n.	Unit 8—B
generality	n.	Unit 9—A
generosity	n.	Unit 1—B
gin	v.	Unit 11—A
glaring	adj.	Unit 8—B
glisten	v.	Unit 13—B
gosh		Unit 12—A
gospel	n.	Unit 12—A
governance	n.	Unit 9—A
gradient	n.	Unit 11—B
ground rules	n.	Unit 9—A
grouse	v.	Unit 3—A
growl	v.	Unit 12—A
gruff	adj.	Unit 5—A
guardian	n.	Unit 8—B
guffaw	v.	Unit 12—A
gush	v.	Unit 2—A

H

hackneyed	adj.	Unit 6—A
hard-headed	adj.	Unit 9—A
harebrained	adj.	Unit 8—A

hark	v.	Unit 14—B	inscribe	v.	Unit 14—B
harr	v.	Unit 7—A	insensibly	adv.	Unit 13—A
haunt	v.	Unit 9—A	insidious	adj.	Unit 2—B
hazard	v.	Unit 6—B	instantaneously	adv.	Unit 1—A
head sb off		Unit 12—B	insurmountable	adj.	Unit 3—B
heart-rending	adj.	Unit 4—A	intemperate	adj.	Unit 9—A
hearth	n.	Unit 2—A	intrigue	n.	Unit 1—A
heave	v.	Unit 5—A	invalid	n.	Unit 10—A
hedge	v.	Unit 6—B	invidious	adj.	Unit 3—A
heed	v.	Unit 1—B	invoke	v.	Unit 1—B
heir	n.	Unit 1—B	iren	n.	Unit 6—B
herd	v.	Unit 7—A	irredeemable	adj.	Unit 4—B
heritage	n.	Unit 1—B	irretrievable	adj.	Unit 13—B
highbrow	adj.	Unit 9—A			
hiss	v.	Unit 5—A	**J**		
hitherto	adv.	Unit 14—B			
hobble	v.	Unit 10—A	janitor	n.	Unit 10—B
hogwash	n.	Unit 12—A	jeer	n.	Unit 6—A
holster	n.	Unit 5—A	jerk	v.	Unit 12—A
honeysuckle	n.	Unit 2—A	jockey	v.	Unit 4—A
hullabaloo	n.	Unit 5—A	jubilant	adj.	Unit 3—B
humbug	n.	Unit 6—A	jubilation	n.	Unit 3—B
hump	n.	Unit 13—A			
hunk	n.	Unit 7—A	**K**		
hurdle	n.	Unit 3—B			
hurtle	v.	Unit 7—A	kill-joy	n.	Unit 11—B
			kindling	n.	Unit 7—B
I			knot	v.	Unit 4—A
idiosyncrasy	n.	Unit 2—B	**L**		
idolatrous	adj.	Unit 13—B			
illuminate	v.	Unit 10—B	labored	adj.	Unit 11—A
illustration	n.	Unit 7—B	lace	n.	Unit 10—A
imminent	adj.	Unit 7—B	laden	adj.	Unit 13—A
imperishable	adj.	Unit 9—A	lamentation	n.	Unit 13—A
importunate	adj.	Unit 14—B	lap	n.	Unit 2—A
impotence	n.	Unit 9—A	lard sth with sth		Unit 7—A
in a row		Unit 7—A	lard	v.	Unit 7—A
in lieu of sth		Unit 13—A	lassitude	n.	Unit 4—B
in the wink of an eye		Unit 7—B	latitude	n.	Unit 5—B
inadvertently	adv.	Unit 6—A	law-abiding	adj.	Unit 1—A
inarticulate	adj.	Unit 4—B	leggings	n.	Unit 7—B
incandescent	adj.	Unit 12—A	liaison	n.	Unit 7—B
incidental to		Unit 13—A	libellous	adj.	Unit 9—B
incongruous	adj.	Unit 8—A	lily-livered	adj.	Unit 5—A
indirection	n.	Unit 11—B	linger	v.	Unit 13—B
indolent	adj.	Unit 3—A	loathe	v.	Unit 13—B
indulge	v.	Unit 9—A	long-winded	adj.	Unit 6—B
infuse	v.	Unit 1—A	lowdown	n.	Unit 5—A
iniquity	n.	Unit 13—B	lug	v.	Unit 7—A
insatiable	adj.	Unit 14—A	lunge	v.	Unit 12—B

M

mainstream	n.	Unit 8—B
make a break for sth/for it		Unit 12—B
manage	n.	Unit 11—B
mandate	n.	Unit 14—A
maneuver	v.	Unit 1—A
manicured	adj.	Unit 7—A
manuscript	n.	Unit 10—A
mar	v.	Unit 13—B
mariner	n.	Unit 4—A
measure	n.	Unit 8—B
memento	n.	Unit 4—B
memoir	n.	Unit 8—A
menial	adj.	Unit 11—A
meretricious	adj.	Unit 10—B
mesmerising	adj.	Unit 14—A
metallurgy	n.	Unit 14—A
methought	v.	Unit 13—A
microcosm	n.	Unit 11—A
milieu	n.	Unit 3—A
modernity	n.	Unit 8—B
morbid	adj.	Unit 6—B
morocco	n.	Unit 4—A
moroseness	n.	Unit 14—B
mortal	n.	Unit 1—B
mote	n.	Unit 4—B
motion	v.	Unit 7—B
muddle	v.	Unit 2—B
mug	n.	Unit 10—A
multitudes of		Unit 13—A
muster	v.	Unit 1—A
mutate	v.	Unit 9—A
myriad	adj.	Unit 1—A

N

neat	adj.	Unit 7—A
necessitate	v.	Unit 10—B
ne'er		Unit 8—A

O

observe	v.	Unit 1—B
obsolete	adj.	Unit 6—A
off-beat	n.	Unit 9—B
orient	v.	Unit 3—A
ornamentation	n.	Unit 10—B
orthodoxy	n.	Unit 6—A
otherness	n.	Unit 9—B
ouch and go	adj.	Unit 11—B
outrageous	adj.	Unit 3—B
outright	adj.	Unit 3—A
outweigh	v.	Unit 8—A
outwit	v.	Unit 7—B
overbearing	adj.	Unit 9—A
overtake	v.	Unit 14—A

P

paddock	n.	Unit 4—A
paleolithic	adj.	Unit 14—A
pall (on sb)	v.	Unit 9—A
pamper	v.	Unit 3—A
parable	n.	Unit 11—B
paradox	n.	Unit 9—A
parcel sth out		Unit 13—A
parlour	adj.	Unit 4—A
passionate	adj.	Unit 2—A
patent	n.	Unit 10—B
pathos	n.	Unit 7—A
patrolman	n.	Unit 5—A
patter	v.	Unit 10—A
paw	n.	Unit 5—A
peer	v.	Unit 7—B
penalty	n.	Unit 13—B
perception	n.	Unit 2—A
peril	n.	Unit 9—B
permeate	v.	Unit 11—A
permissible	adj.	Unit 11—B
perverse	adj.	Unit 2—B
petrified	adj.	Unit 12—B
phantom	n.	Unit 13—A
pillar	n.	Unit 1—A
pin	v.	Unit 12—B
plague	n.	Unit 1—A
platinum	n.	Unit 10—B
plebeian	adj.	Unit 8—A
plod	v.	Unit 4—A
ploy	n.	Unit 3—B
pluck	v.	Unit 10—B
pointed	adj.	Unit 3—B
pool	n.	Unit 5—A
posterity	n.	Unit 1—A
potent	adj.	Unit 14—A
precipitate	v.	Unit 3—A
prefabricated	adj.	Unit 6—A
premonition	n.	Unit 9—A
presence of mind		Unit 7—B

229

pretentiousness	n.	Unit 6—A	repentance	n.	Unit 2—A
pretext	n.	Unit 6—A	repertoire	n.	Unit 6—B
prevalent	adj.	Unit 14—A	repine at		Unit 13—A
primeval	adj.	Unit 9—B	reproachful	adj.	Unit 3—B
probe	v.	Unit 12—A	rest	v.	Unit 1—A
probing	adj.	Unit 14—A	resume	v.	Unit 12—A
proclamation	n.	Unit 13—A	reveal	v.	Unit 2—A
profligate	n.	Unit 9—A	reverberate	v.	Unit 6—B
profligate	adj.	Unit 13—A	revered	adj.	Unit 11—B
prop	n.	Unit 3—A	reversible	adj.	Unit 6—A
prosaic	adj.	Unit 7—A	revitalize	v.	Unit 1—A
prudence	n.	Unit 10—B	revival	n.	Unit 11—B
puberty	n.	Unit 9—A	rid	v.	Unit 11—B
puff	v.	Unit 13—A	riddle	v.	Unit 9—B
puff	n.	Unit 10—A	ride	vt.	Unit 11—B
pull sb's leg		Unit 12—A	ridge	n.	Unit 14—B
purge	v.	Unit 6—B	rif	n.	Unit 2—B
			righteous	adj.	Unit 11—B
Q			road-hog	n.	Unit 4—A
			roadstead	n.	Unit 14—A
quail	n.	Unit 10—B	rock	v.	Unit 10—A
quarter	n.	Unit 11—B	rogue	n.	Unit 10—A
quietism	n.	Unit 6—A	root sb to sth		Unit 12—B
quirk	n.	Unit 2—B	rotunda	n.	Unit 10—A
quiver	v.	Unit 2—A	round on sb		Unit 12—B
			round-up	n.	Unit 4—B
R			rub shoulders with		Unit 8—A
			ruminate on		Unit 13—A
racquet	n.	Unit 6—B	rung	n.	Unit 11—B
radical	adj.	Unit 11—A			
rafter	n.	Unit 5—A	**S**		
raider	n.	Unit 7—B			
railings	n.	Unit 10—A	sacrifice	v.	Unit 10—B
raise hell		Unit 12—A	sallow	adj.	Unit 5—B
ransack	v.	Unit 5—A	salvage	v.	Unit 6—A
rationale	n.	Unit 11—B	sardine	n.	Unit 4—A
recapitulate	v.	Unit 11—A	satire	n.	Unit 13—A
recede from		Unit 13—A	saturate	v.	Unit 11—A
recess	n.	Unit 7—B	say sth, speak, etc.		Unit 12—B
reckless	adj.	Unit 4—A	under your breath		
redeem	v.	Unit 14—B	scat	v.	Unit 12—A
refinement	n.	Unit 9—B	scoot	v.	Unit 12—A
refuge	n.	Unit 14—B	scowl	v.	Unit 7—A
regenerat	v.	Unit 6—B	scrabble	v.	Unit 9—A
regression	n.	Unit 3—A	scrap	v.	Unit 6—A
reinvent	v.	Unit 1—A	scrape	v.	Unit 10—A
rejoicing	n.	Unit 1—B	scratch	v.	Unit 12—A
relegate	v.	Unit 11—A	screech	v.	Unit 12—B
remark	n.	Unit 13—A	screw up your courage		Unit 12—B
renunciation	n.	Unit 13—B	scripture	n.	Unit 1—A
repair to		Unit 8—A	scruple	n.	Unit 8—A

scull	v.	Unit 4—A	strum	v.	Unit 5—A
scurry	v.	Unit 12—B	stultify	v.	Unit 7—A
sear	v.	Unit 12—B	stultifying	adj.	Unit 7—A
seethe	v.	Unit 9—B	subjugate	v.	Unit 14—A
seriocomic	adj.	Unit 7—A	suffrage	n.	Unit 8—B
setter	n.	Unit 10—B	summit	n.	Unit 14—B
sever	v.	Unit 2—B	summon	v.	Unit 1—B
shaft	n.	Unit 4—B	superimpose	v.	Unit 3—A
shaggy	adj.	Unit 12—A	supersede	v.	Unit 14—A
shield	n.	Unit 11—B	supremacy	n.	Unit 8—B
shinny	v.	Unit 7—A	surge	v.	Unit 12—B
shoal	n.	Unit 4—A	surmise	v.	Unit 6—B
shrivel	v.	Unit 8—B	swap	n.	Unit 13—A
simulate	v.	Unit 9—A	swoop	v.	Unit 10—A
singe	v.	Unit 10—B	symmetrical adj.		Unit 2—A
singularly	adv.	Unit 6—B			
ski	n.	Unit 4—B	**T**		
skipper	n.	Unit 4—A			
slat	n.	Unit 4—B	taboo	n.	Unit 3—B
slit	n.	Unit 12—B	take off to discontinue		Unit 9—B
slovenly	adj.	Unit 6—A	tap	v.	Unit 1—B
smite	v.	Unit 13—B	tatty	adj.	Unit 9—B
snap	v.	Unit 5—A	teetotale	n.	Unit 9—A
snapshot	n.	Unit 7—B	terse	adj.	Unit 6—B
snarl	v.	Unit 12—B	testament	n.	Unit 1—A
snarl	n.	Unit 2—B	testimony	n.	Unit 1—B
sniff /snIf/	v.	Unit 12—A	thereby	adj.	Unit 11—B
solemnity	n.	Unit 13—A	thrash	v.	Unit 7—A
sore	adj.	Unit 12—A	thrive	v.	Unit 8—A
specification	n.	Unit 3—B	thrush	n.	Unit 13—B
specimen	n.	Unit 6—A	tingle	v.	Unit 10—A
speck	n.	Unit 4—A	tinker	v.	Unit 6—A
spectacles	n.	Unit 10—A	tinny	adj.	Unit 7—A
specter	n.	Unit 13—A	to make headway		Unit 8—B
spectrum	n.	Unit 7—B	toady	n.	Unit 8—A
splash	v.	Unit 10—A	token	n.	Unit 12—A
splinter	n.	Unit 12—A	topless	adj.	Unit 4—B
spout	n.	Unit 2—A	torment	v.	Unit 12—A
sprawl	v.	Unit 5—A	tote	v.	Unit 7—B
spry	adj.	Unit 12—A	tournament	n.	Unit 5—A
stagnant	adj.	Unit 1—A	trail away		Unit 12—B
stale	adj.	Unit 6—A	trajectory	n.	Unit 8—B
stammer	v.	Unit 2—A	tramp	v.	Unit 5—A
steadfastness	n.	Unit 1—A	trample		Unit 9—A
stereotype	n.	Unit 3—A	trance	n.	Unit 4—A
sterling	n.	Unit 10—B	transfer	n.	Unit 5—B
stilt	n.	Unit 13—A	transplant	v.	Unit 14—A
stilted	adj.	Unit 6—B	transport	v.	Unit 4—A
stranglehold	n.	Unit 9—B	trap-stick	n.	Unit 13—A
stratify	v.	Unit 3—A	traverse	v.	Unit 2—A
strayed	adj.	Unit 6—A	treatise	n.	Unit 2—B

tresses	n.	Unit 10—B	verbal	adj.	Unit 6—A
tribulation	n.	Unit 1—B	verger	n.	Unit 5—B
trifle	n.	Unit 5—B	verily	adv.	Unit 14—B
trip	v.	Unit 12—B	vestry	n.	Unit 5—B
troll	n.	Unit 12—B	veteran	n.	Unit 4—B
tropical	adj.	Unit 14—A	viable	adj.	Unit 6—B
trot	v.	Unit 10—A	vibrate	v.	Unit 6—B
truant	n.	Unit 10—B	vicar	n.	Unit 5—B
tune	v.	Unit 8—A	violets	n.	Unit 10—A
turban	n.	Unit 12—B	visage	n.	Unit 13—A
turmoil	n.	Unit 9—A	vouchsafe	v.	Unit 4—B
tussle	n.	Unit 2—A			
twilight	adj.	Unit 1—B	**W**		
			wham	n.	Unit 5—A
U			whirl	v.	Unit 10—B
ultimate	adj.	Unit 14—B	whisk	v.	Unit 7—A
unravel	v.	Unit 2—B	whiting	n.	Unit 10—A
unrivaled	adj.	Unit 1—A	whoop	v.	Unit 5—B
unruffled	adj.	Unit 5—B	willful	adj.	Unit 2—B
unsullied	adj.	Unit 13—B	wise	n.	Unit 11—B
unwary	adj.	Unit 3—B	wisp	adj.	Unit 5—B
up to sth		Unit 12—B	wrench	v.	Unit 12—B
utilitarian	adj.	Unit 11—A	wriggle	v.	Unit 2—B
			writhe	v.	Unit 14—B
V					
valiant	adj.	Unit 2—B	**Y**		
vandalize	v.	Unit 4—B	year in, year out		Unit 12—A
velvet	n.	Unit 10—A	yearning	n.	Unit 14—B
venomous	adj.	Unit 2—B	yield	v.	Unit 13—B
venture	v.	Unit 5—A